*Falling Piece*

Go outside of you.
Look at yourself walking down the street.
Make yourself tumble on a stone and fall.
Watch it.
Watch other people looking.
Observe carefully how you fall.
How long it takes and in what rhythm you fall.
Observe as seeing a slow motion film.

1964 spring

# search light

consciousness      at      the      millennium

# search light

consciousness at the millennium

edited by lawrence rinder

the ccac institute

# a rt ists

cover: **Jörg Herold**, *Körper im Körper*, 1989 (details)

page 1: **Yoko Ono**, *Falling Piece*, 1964

page 2: **Gary Hill**, *Searchlight*, 1986–94 (detail)

page 3: **Diana Thater**, *Perspective is an energy*, 1995 (detail)

page 4: **The Museum of Jurassic Technology**, *The Voice of the American Gray Fox*, 1984 (detail)

# cont e nts

This book is published in connection with the exhibition *Searchlight: Consciousness at the Millennium*, opening September 1999 at the California College of Arts and Crafts, San Francisco.
It is supported by the National Endowment for the Arts, a Federal agency; Mrs. Paul L. Wattis; The James Irvine Foundation; and Grants for the Arts/The San Francisco Hotel Tax Fund.

**Publication managers**

Chris Bliss and Genoa Shepley

**Editors**

Nancy Crowley and Brian Wallis

**Designers**

*Appetite Engineers:*
Martin Venezky and Geoff Kaplan

First published in the United States of America in paperback in 1999 by Thames & Hudson Inc., 500 Fifth Avenue, New York, New York 10110

Library of Congress Catalog Card Number 99–70859

ISBN 0–500–28136–X

Printed and bound in Italy by Artegrafica

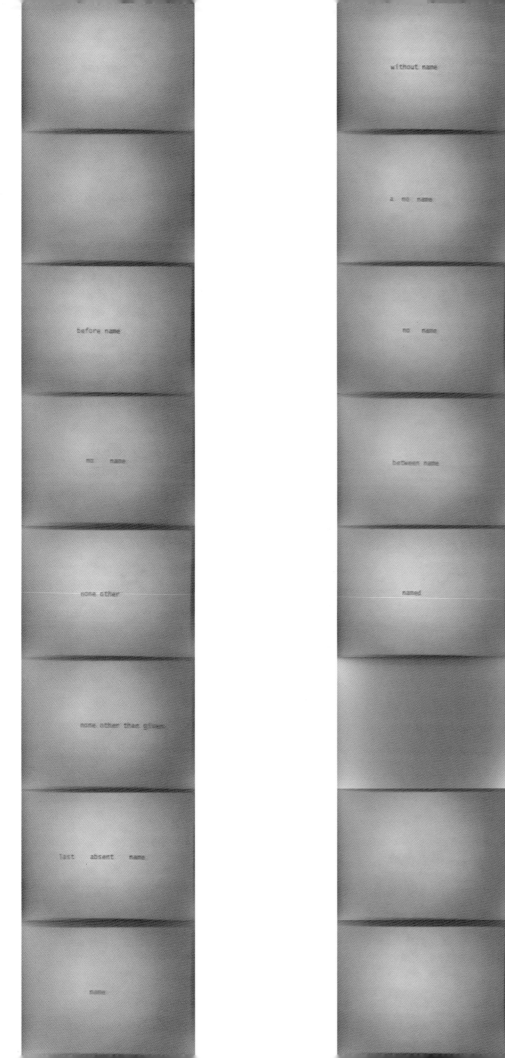

**Theresa Hak Kyung Cha**, *Exilée*, 1980

(details)

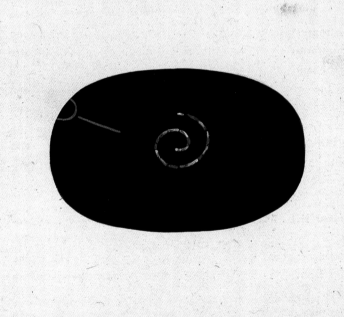

# forewo r d

This exhibition and publication represent the fulfillment of a number of goals developed by the faculty, staff, and administration of the California College of Arts and Crafts (CCAC). Several years ago, we began a process of creating a new structure that would enable the College to present the foremost contemporary art, architecture, and design from around the world. We did so with the understanding that no art school today can afford to remain quietly isolated from the currents of ideas and innovative practices encircling the globe. We envisioned a program of exhibitions, lectures, symposia, and artist residencies—all linked with the curriculum—that would act as a catalyst for experimentation and creativity.

**Thus, in 1998 CCAC formed the Institute for exhibitions and public programs.** Under the leadership of Lawrence Rinder, the Institute has brought numerous artists, architects, and designers from around the world to participate in the life of the College, both by exhibiting their work and by giving public presentations. The Institute's audience extends well beyond the College to include practicing artists, architects, and designers, as well as the general public. It is unusual to have such an ambitious schedule of exhibitions and public programs in the context of an art college, let alone in an educational institution of any kind. Nevertheless, as Rinder succinctly puts it, "greatness inspires greatness." We can think of no better place to represent the most accomplished products of our culture than within the walls of a school such as ours.

*Searchlight: Consciousness at the Millennium* has been in development since the founding of the Institute and represents its highest aspirations. Conceived by Rinder, the exhibition was developed through a dialogue with numerous members of the CCAC faculty as well as with many leading contemporary artists, philosophers, art historians, psychologists, cognitive scientists, and spiritual practitioners. A colloquium held at CCAC in the summer of 1998 brought together an extraordinary group of artists and scholars to discuss the manifold issues pertaining to the theme of the exhibition. The participants in that colloquium included Eliot Anderson, Kim Anno, Mark Bartlett, Josef Chytry, Susanne Cockrell, Don Day, Miriam Dym, David Hannah, Shirish Jain, Barry Katz, Yim Lim, Alva Noë, Tim Perkis, Hilary Rand, Yvonne Rand, Julia Rowe, Susan Schwartzenberg, Mitchell Schwarzer, Elizabeth Sher, William Sterling, Lucille Tenazas, Mark Thompson, Ignacio Valero, Martin Van Buren, Gail Wight, and Richard Wollheim. It is noteworthy that the Institute not only serves as an originator of exceptional exhibitions and public programs, but that it also plays an important role as a catalyst for interdisciplinary discussion and cross-fertilization of ideas.

opposite: **Anonymous**, Untitled tantric drawing, ca. 1995

The issues that are raised by this exhibition cut to the heart of contemporary art practice. They are issues that may appear timeless yet which, in another sense, could not be more timely. As Lawrence Rinder and George Lakoff discuss in their essay in this volume, one might almost say that a new aesthetic has evolved in the last half of the twentieth century, one that takes for its subject the *viewer's* experience of consciousness. Recognizing such watershed events is, perhaps, the most significant function of an exhibition program. As such, we are particularly proud to present this momentous exhibition at CCAC.

It is important that the exhibition take place within a context of numerous public lectures, conversations, and performances. I am grateful to Marina McDougall, CCAC Institute assistant director for programs, for her inspired organization of these programs. In addition, CCAC faculty have organized a number of special courses to explore the many facets of art and experience addressed by the exhibition. Thanks in particular to Julia Rowe, chair of the Core Program, and Martin Van Buren, dean of Humanities, for their active participation in this effort. Among the other CCAC faculty and staff who have participated in the discussions leading to the development of the exhibition are Mark Bartlett, Josef Chytry, Steven Goldstine, Mitchell Schwarzer, Elizabeth Sher, Ignacio Valero, and Gail Wight.

The exhibition has required the support of numerous staff members of the College. Kirstin Bach, program coordinator of the Institute, has proved to be a tireless, enthusiastic, and invaluable colleague. Chris Pérez, a work-study student in the Institute, has also provided crucial assistance. The Advancement Department, led by Margaret Shurgot and including Susan Avila (now director of development at the San Francisco Museum of Modern Art) and Courtney Fink, organized the fundraising drive that enabled CCAC to mount this exhibition. A publicity campaign unprecedented in scale for the College was organized by Chris Bliss, who, with the assistance of Genoa Shepley, coordinated the organization of this publication. Hassan Afrookhteh, Julie Milburn, and Consuelo Lorenzo deserve recognition for their contributions to the smooth and successful adaptation of CCAC's new building to the complex needs of this project.

The presentation of the numerous large-scale installations that are included in this exhibition required the construction of a temporary facility, itself as large as many small museums. The task of designing this facility was taken up with great skill and enthusiasm by John Randolph, Maeryta Medrano, and Chuck Howarth of Gyroscope. Their fresh and creative approach resulted in a structure that is efficient, visually compelling, and, finally, a work of art in its own right. I wish to extend thanks also to CCAC intern Jesse Salveson for his help with the preliminary model.

This catalogue is the product of the combined efforts of numerous individuals. Lawrence Rinder, as editor, gathered an extraordinary group of classic essays on the subject of consciousness and commissioned a number of excellent new texts. The reprinted works include essays by David J. Chalmers, Francis Crick and Christof Koch, William James, Steve Kolpan, Thomas Nagel, John R. Searle, Paul M. Churchland and Patricia Smith Churchland; and a conversation among the Dalai Lama, Jeremy W. Hayward, Francisco J. Varela, Geshe Palden Drakpa, Thubten Jinpa, Robert B. Livingston, Eleanor Rosch, and B. Alan Wallace. We are grateful to these authors and/or their publishers for allowing us to include their works here. I am honored that we are able to present a number of exceptional new reflections on the theme of art and consciousness. Authors of these commissioned texts are Mark Bartlett, Franck André Jamme, D. L. Pughe, and Yvonne Rand. Lawrence Rinder and George Lakoff's essay is an especially important contribution, signalling the great potential of an interdisciplinary vision. Brian Wallis has done a masterful job of editing this essay, and Nancy Crowley has provided superb copyediting and proofreading throughout the book. The design of a catalogue such as this is a subtle and difficult task, so we were pleased to enlist the services of the renowned designer—and CCAC faculty member—Martin Venezky. His collaborator, Geoff Kaplan, and assistant, Sara Cambridge, also provided exceptional insight and inspiration. Beth Weber accomplished the complicated task of coordinating the photography for this book. We are delighted that Thames & Hudson has had the faith and prescience to be the copublisher of this book.

My thanks to the chairman of the CCAC Board of Trustees, Judy Timken, to the Trustees as well as to the chair of the Institute Council, Carla Emil, and the Councilors for their support throughout this project. We could not have accomplished this extraordinary achievement without their leadership and vision.

We are grateful to the lenders to the exhibition: University of California, Berkeley Art Museum; Lafcadio Cortesi; Hauser & Wirth, Zurich; Franck André Jamme; Eli Leon; Byron R. Meyer; Museum of Contemporary Art, Chicago; Museum of Contemporary Art, San Diego; The Museum of Jurassic Technology, Culver City; and Eileen and Peter Norton, Santa Monica.

Various individuals and institutions have supported our research efforts during the course of this project, and I would like to express our gratitude to Brooke Alexander, Brooke Alexander Gallery, New York; Lynn Sharpless, Angles Gallery, Santa Monica; Ed Gilbert, Gallery Paule Anglim, San Francisco; Jacquelynn Baas, Barney Bailey, Lisa Calden, Stephanie Cannizzo, and Constance Lewallen, University of California, Berkeley Art Museum, Berkeley; Andrew Wheatley, Cabinet, London; John Cheim, Cheim & Reid Gallery, New York; Gerd Harry Lybke, Galerie EIGEN+ART, Berlin; Jerry Gorovoy; Colin Griffiths; Jon Hendricks; Steven Leiber; Eli Leon; Annette H. Mantero, Lisson Gallery, London; Lisa Spellman, 303 Gallery, New York; Wendy Williams; David Wilson; Donald Young, Donald Young Gallery, Chicago; and Angela Choon, David Zwirner, New York.

**Lorne M. Buchman, President**
**CCAC**

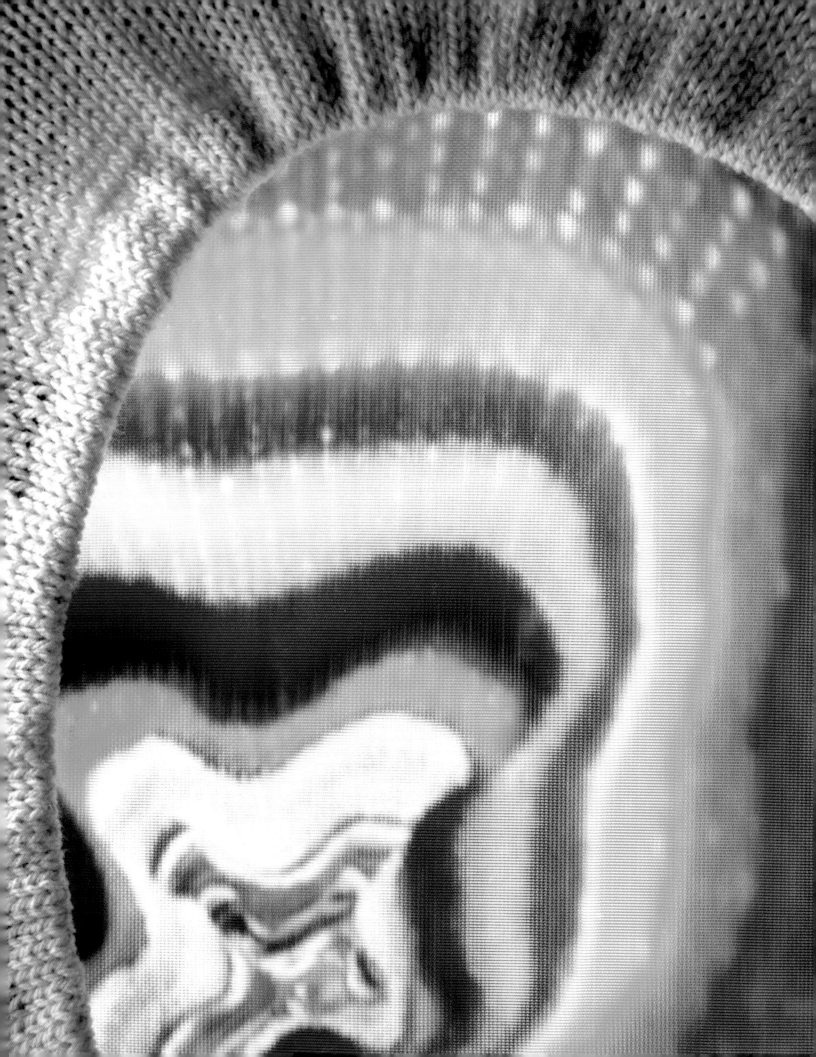

# introduction

Lawrence Rinder

The relationship between art and consciousness has been at the heart of my work as a curator. I believe that art possesses a unique capacity to embody consciousness, and thereby to heighten the viewer's awareness of his or her own consciousness. Approaching art from this perspective has allowed me to explore a diverse range of work and to notice the compelling relationships that connect traditionally discrete categories of art. The works I am drawn to are those that direct our attention to our attention, reminding us of the feeling of seeing, perceiving, and knowing.

**This exhibition is a concerted exploration of the theme of consciousness in art, bringing together a wide variety of contemporary works that engender a visceral sensation of conscious experience.** *Searchlight* combines works of art that are not usually seen together: social commentary with abstraction, the intensely personal with the anonymous and egoless, the secular with the spiritual. The exhibition does not aim to subsume their differences under the rubric of a new hegemonic theory, but rather to illuminate the often subtle and sometimes surprising ways in which these works share the remarkable ability to lead us to a fuller experience of consciousness.

Our consciousness need not be any more mysterious than our physical body; it is often defined as awareness or experience, but we might say simply that it is the sensation of being alive. It is the substance of our perceptions, our memories, and our feelings. Human consciousness has been studied exhaustively for centuries by the schools of tantra and Buddhism, among others; however, Western science has only recently turned its attention to this subject. The explosion of interest in consciousness in the fields of cognitive science, psychology, neurophysiology, and philosophy should help to dispel the ethereal aura that surrounds this subject and give us a more useful vocabulary and set of conceptual tools with which to describe its characteristics and effects.

Consciousness has been, arguably, the primary subject of Western art since the modernist revolutions of the nineteenth century shifted artists' goals from the direct representation of seen reality to the expression of felt experience. In the past few decades, however, this exploration has become much more focused, and, fueled in part by exciting new scientific discoveries, artists have developed a broad array of approaches to express the various characteristics and sensations of conscious experience. As an increasing number of scientists and philosophers have despaired of the ability of their own descriptive languages to capture the profoundly complex nature of consciousness, there is a compelling reason to pay close attention to artistic explorations of this theme. Art, unlike science, possesses an openness to subjective experience that makes it an indispensable companion to more rational and analytical investigations.

opposite: **Pascale Wiedemann,** *Heimlich,* 1996 (detail)

pages 16–17: **Lutz Bacher,** *A Normal Life,* 1995–96 (detail)

Consciousness, like other aspects of our biology, is an evolving phenomenon. Furthermore, the shape and tone of our consciousness is malleable and, in part, determined by the conditions of the culture in which we live. If certain aspects of consciousness are fundamental, others change with the times. *Searchlight* reflects on consciousness at the turn of the millennium. The opportunity here, however, is not simply to create a kind of consciousness time capsule but, much more importantly, to exploit the particular kind of reflective awareness that a millennium inspires. Rather than simply asking, "What is the consciousness of our age?" this exhibition proposes that we seize upon our millennial imagination and use it as a tool to develop heightened mindfulness for the future.

I am grateful to the contributors to this catalogue, who brought to the subject of consciousness and art profound insights from their own diverse fields. Most importantly, I am indebted to my coauthor, George Lakoff, whose exhaustive knowledge of contemporary debates on consciousness proved invaluable in articulating a systematic analysis of contemporary art from the perspective of recent scientific theory. In an exceptionally close reading of Stan Douglas's installation, *Overture,* Mark Bartlett reveals the idiosyncratic formal structures that contribute to the psychological intensity of this work. Franck André Jamme, a poet and scholar of Indian art, has written an evocative poem, "Ascension," inspired by a tantric drawing. Steve Kolpan discusses Gary Hill's mind-bending video *Why Do Things Get in a Muddle? (Come on Petunia)* in terms of Gregory Bateson's notion of the "metalogue." D. L. Pughe explores the philosophical resonances of Bill Viola's installation, *Pneuma.* Yvonne Rand, a Buddhist priest, offers her insights on perception as they pertain to a single painting by Agnes Martin. In addition, with the inspired assistance of Marina McDougall, CCAC Institute assistant director for programs, and with advice from David J. Chalmers and George Lakoff, I have selected an eclectic array of articles about consciousness from the fields of philosophy, cognitive science, and religion that represent some of the most compelling writing available on the subject.

This exhibition would not have been possible without the concerted efforts and good will of numerous individuals. I am especially grateful to the artists and their galleries, to the lenders, and to my extraordinary colleagues at CCAC for helping to bring this idea to life.

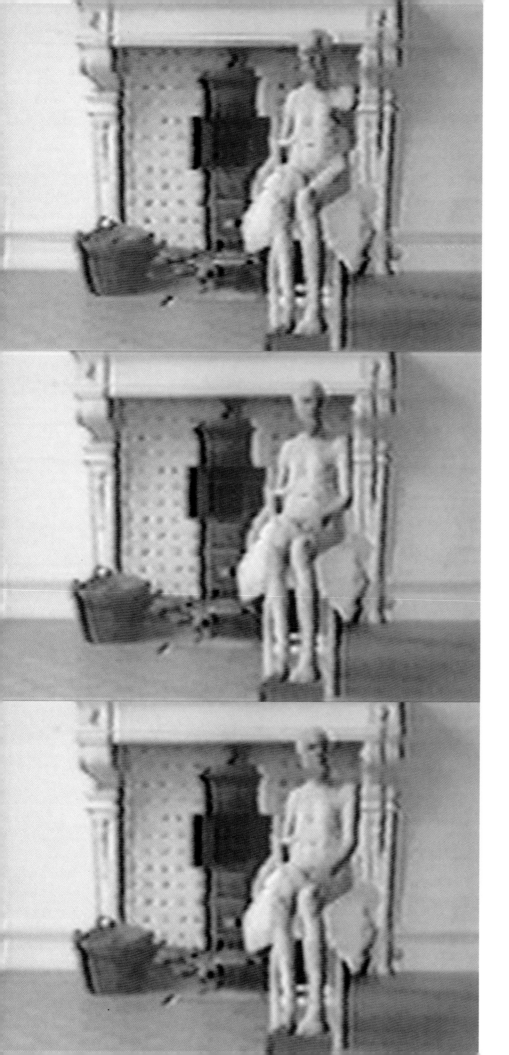

**Imogen Stidworthy,** *To,* 1996–97 (detail)

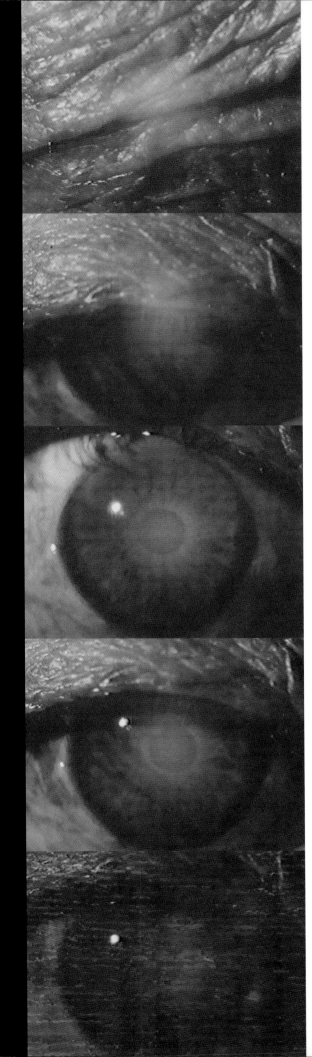

**Samuel Beckett**, *Film*, 1963–65 (detail)

# consciousness art : attending to the quality of experience

Lawrence Rinder

George Lakoff

Until quite recently consciousness was not considered a legitimate topic of scientific investigation. **Cognitive science—the interdisciplinary study of the mind—has mostly focused on unconscious mental life. Cognitive scientists have discovered that most thought is *unconscious*, that we have unconscious conceptual systems, that virtually all of language and vision work by unconscious mechanisms, and that even *memories* can be unconscious. Most of the great discoveries about the mind over the past two decades have been about the cognitive unconscious.**

**But over the past few years *consciousness* has burst onto the scene as one of the most hotly debated topics in cognitive science, neurobiology, psychology, and philosophy.** Given that different parts of the brain characterize color, shape, location, and motion, what brain mechanisms account for the unity of consciousness, for the fact that we perceive the world as a unified whole? What explains the subjective quality of an experience, say, the greenness of grass or the feel of velvet? How can we be aware at all, much less be aware of ourselves? Why are some memories conscious and others unconscious (or "implicit")? What are the limits of consciousness; what parts of what is normally unconscious can be made conscious? Answering such questions through a general theory of the divide between the conscious and the unconscious has become the Holy Grail of cognitive science.

Consciousness, particularly that aspect related to vision, has also recently emerged as an important topic in art history and criticism. Much of the work of leading scholars such as Martin Jay and Jonathan Crary has focused on the "constructed" aspects of visual consciousness; that is, ways in which our perceptions are structured by cultural phenomenon such as language. As Jay points out, however, while science itself is subject to revision, there is new evidence indicating that "...certain fairly fundamental characteristics [of vision] seem to exist, which no amount of cultural mediation can radically alter."[1]

Consider the revelation that mental imagery is processed by exactly the same part of the brain that is devoted to vision. Even congenitally blind people have mental imagery, since their visual cortexes are, in most cases, intact. The visual images we have in dreaming arise in the visual cortex as well, although nothing is "seen." Moreover, most of the information in what we "see" never passes through the retina. Instead, it is constructed by the brain on the basis of very fragmentary visual information together with other knowledge.

Or take the startling finding that color does not exist in the world. Objects in the world have reflectance properties; that is, they reflect some wavelengths of light but not others. But color requires four factors: the reflectances of objects, surrounding lighting conditions, color cones in the retina, and neural circuitry connected to those cones. Two of those factors—the color cones and the neural circuitry—are inside our bodies, not in the external world. Given reflectances and lighting conditions, the color cones and the neural circuitry together *create* colors and color categories—blue, yellow, green, red, and so on. The colors we "see" are not out there at all: There is no green in grass, no red in blood, no blue in the sky. Color arises from an interaction between us and the world. Moreover, color is contextual; the appearance of a color may depend on adjacent colors. The neurons involved in color perception take their input not just from one central point in the visual field but from a broad area surrounding a central point.

Being aware of such unconscious aspects of imagery and color is crucial to any deep understanding of how artists create conscious visions. It is also clear that metaphorical association—a key component of consciousness—plays a central role in art making. In painting after painting, Good is associated with Light and Evil is portrayed as Dark, the Powerful are depicted as Above the Powerless, Emotional Turbulence is conveyed by Storm and Emotional Calm by Fair Weather.

Metaphor involves the capacity to conceptualize and reason about the abstract in terms of concrete sensory or motor experiences. We conceptualize time in terms of motion in space ("The time for action has arrived"; "Let's look ahead to the future") because the "passage" of time is correlated with motion in our everyday experience since birth. We understand affection as warmth ("He's a warm person, but she's been cold to me") because from birth, when we are held affectionately by our parents, there is a correlation between warmth and affection. Our systems of metaphoric thought arise out of such everyday correlations. Great leaps of metaphoric imagination in both art and philosophical theory ultimately stem from such commonplace "conflations" in our experience.[2] Metaphor is necessary for any kind of abstract, philosophical, scientific, or mathematical thought.

Understanding how consciousness functions in art depends on a recognition of these unconscious underpinnings of consciousness.

## Consciousness Art

What we are calling "Consciousness Art" not only reveals the sensations and mechanisms of consciousness itself but also allows us to experience firsthand conscious sensation. Rather than simply depicting ideas about consciousness, the art in this exhibition embodies particular aspects of consciousness and makes them available, viscerally, to the viewer. The notion of consciousness helps us to see a common thread among works of art that might otherwise seem utterly disparate: Bill Viola's ephemeral video projection; Cristabel Davé's intricately patterned bark cloth paintings; Robert Barry's simple phrase, written on the gallery wall; Louise Bourgeois's sculptural "cell" incorporating enormous steel doors, arrows, a chair, and a mirror; and Rosie Lee Tompkins's quilt made from thrift-store fabrics. What unites these diverse works is not a historical movement, a cultural tradition, or a formal idea, but an approach to art that attends to or animates consciousness itself. Consciousness Art is not didactic but, rather, direct and experiential. It emphasizes "mindfulness"—an experience of profound self-awareness—over representing an exterior world or describing the technical workings of the mind.

In naming Consciousness Art, we are not creating a new category, canon, or style of art. We are describing a general tendency within art that already exists. Although virtually all works of art make use of the mechanisms of consciousness, we would argue that consciousness is central to contemporary art practice, that it is the focus of a critical mass of art made over the past three decades, not only in traditional art media but also in new and innovative forms.

Our purpose in pointing to and naming the category of Consciousness Art is to create a new awareness and understanding of such art. Understanding how each of these diverse artworks focuses on some aspect of consciousness can allow us to perceive the works in a new way, more deeply and with a richer experience.

## The Structure of Consciousness Art

Consciousness has a structure, and Consciousness Art must make use of that structure. **Most scholars agree that consciousness has at least nine main aspects: awareness, attention, qualia, unity, memory, a first-person perspective, self-awareness, conceptual framing and metaphor, and empathy. We will define these terms as follows:**

**Awareness.** Most of our everyday thought processes, sensations, and responses are unconscious—simply below the level of awareness. We are not, and could not be, aware of how we control every muscle we move, of every inference we make, or of every detail of every act we plan and carry out. We can increase our awareness a bit, but conscious awareness is only the tip of a mental iceberg.

**Attention.** We usually understand attention metaphorically as a "spotlight," or as the act of mental "focusing."[3] We may or may not be aware of that to which we give our attention. For example, we can attend to the subliminal flash of a Coke bottle on the screen of a movie theater, too fast for us to even be aware that we have seen it. We see it unconsciously, yet we are attending to it.

**Qualia.** A key element of consciousness is qualia, the irreducible character of an experience or sensation, like the redness of red, the taste of persimmon, the timbre of a cello, and so on.

**Unity.** Human consciousness is unified. We see the world as a consistent whole, not as fragmented pieces. Perceptual input to the brain *is* fragmented, however. And perceptual and conceptual processing in the brain is done separately, in different brain centers, then "brought together" to form a unified whole.

**Memory.** Consciousness requires memory; it is sometimes accompanied by distant memory, but it is dependent upon the memory of the immediately preceding conscious experience.

**First-person perspective.** A hallmark of consciousness is a perspective on a situation from the viewpoint of someone experiencing it.

**Self-awareness.** Perhaps the most striking aspect of consciousness is the ability to perceive and experience yourself experiencing the world. Self-awareness is not just the capacity to look at yourself but, beyond that, to experience yourself experiencing.

**Conceptual framing and metaphor.** Our conceptualization of experience is largely automatic and below the level of consciousness. For example, a conversation with another person can be framed as an argument, a business meeting, a public performance, a friendly discussion, or a flirtation, or more than one of these simultaneously. We can slip into such framings in ways that we are barely aware of, but each conceptual frame structures how we behave and how we understand the interaction. Similarly, we can unconsciously and automatically conceptualize metaphorically—life as a journey, time as a resource, or difficulties as obstacles—and think and act accordingly. How we conceptualize a situation and whether we are aware of the conceptualization structures our consciousness.

**Empathy.** Empathy is the capacity to internalize the experience of others; it is the consciousness of another being from the perspective of that being. Empathy is also defined as the projection of a subjective state onto an object, such as the projection of consciousness onto a machine.

These general aspects of consciousness, though themselves subject to considerable debate and discussion, provide the rudimentary framework for an understanding of Consciousness Art. To be considered Consciousness Art, a work should engage one or more of these aspects of consciousness. For example, the work might make viewers more aware of certain elements of their everyday experience, or qualia, such as sound (John Cage's "found" sound pieces); color and light (James Turrell's isolated squares of open sky); form (Marcel Duchamp's readymades—a bottle rack, a bicycle wheel on a stool, an upside-down urinal); or volume (Richard Serra's mentally and physically engaging *Torqued Ellipses*). A work of Consciousness Art may also attempt to create new qualia that have never before been encountered: new sound experiences (D. J. Spooky's ambient mixes) or new spatial experiences (Ernesto Neto's sensual fabric chambers).

Consciousness Art may also direct one's attention to one's own first-person experience (Paul Cotton's participatory sculpture *The Key to the Cipher*); reframe one's identity (Adrian Piper's challenges to racial categorization), experience of a place (Jochen Gerz's Nürnberg

top: **Suzanne Lacy,** *The Crystal Quilt,* 1987
bottom: **Ernesto Neto,** *Navedenga,* 1998
opposite: **Rosie Lee Tompkins,** Untitled
(quilted by Willia Ette Graham), 1986

Holocaust Memorial), or sense of community (Suzanne Lacy's participatory performances); provide a new unifying vision of previously disparate experiences (Maya Lin's Vietnam War Memorial); or lead one to notice the fragmentary perceptions that make up normally unified experiences (Diana Thater's deconstruction of color television).

In addition, individual works of art may employ metaphors for one or more aspects of consciousness. In contemporary art, these are some of the most common metaphors involving consciousness: Attention Is a Spotlight (constantly changing attention is conceived as a moving spotlight that illuminates objects in its path); Consciousness Is a Room (the conscious subject is a person in a room, and the ideas of which he or she is aware are objects in that room); Thought Is Language (thoughts are conceptualized as words or sentences, active thinking as speaking or writing, and passive thinking as reading or listening); Awareness Is Being Awake (lack of awareness is depicted as being asleep or otherwise unconscious); and, perhaps most importantly, the Mind Is a Body (thinking is construed as physical functioning, as acting or being acted upon as a body—"I *reached* that conclusion"; "Do you *see* what I mean?" "Let's *toss* some ideas around"; or "You don't expect me to *swallow* that!").

As we shall see, a focus on each particular aspect of consciousness defines a possible genre of Consciousness Art.

### A Brief History of Consciousness Art

Attention to consciousness itself began to be foregrounded in art during the first half of the nineteenth century. With the advent of the first significant theories of color and the initial studies of physiology, perception itself became an issue. Art historian Jonathan Crary points to Goethe's *Color Theory*, 1810 as the catalyst for several decades of intense research into the physiology of the eye and a corresponding realization of the importance of the body in the experience of vision. J. M. W. Turner was the artistic exemplar of this new understanding of embodied consciousness. "Seemingly out of nowhere," writes Crary, "[Turner's] painting of the late 1830s and 1840s signals the irrevocable loss of a fixed source of light, the dissolution of a cone of light rays, and the collapse of the distance separating an observer from the sight of optical experience."[4]

Eugène Delacroix, *Scène des massacres de Scio* (The Massacre at Chios), 1824

Crary also cites an important shift in models of perception—the move from the eighteenth-century camera obscura (used as a metaphor for vision by Descartes and many others) to the mid-nineteenth-century stereoscope, a new device utilizing paired photographs shot from slightly different perspectives to achieve a sense of three-dimensionality. In contrast to the fixed, monocular image of the camera obscura, the stereoscope depended on multiplicity and disjunction for its effect, while implicitly engaging the synthesizing function of the viewer's consciousness. Echoes of the fragmentary, disruptive nature of stereograph images began to appear in such paintings of the period as Eugène Delacroix's *Scène des massacres de Scio* (The Massacre at Chios), 1824; Gustave Courbet's *Les Paysans de Flagey revenant de la Faire* (Peasants of Flagey Returning from the Fair), 1850–55; and Edouard Manet's *Déjeuner sur l'herbe* (Picnic on the Grass), 1863.

30

Among the crucial scientific discoveries of the mid-nineteenth century was the realization that different aspects of consciousness—perception and personality—are localized in different parts of the brain and, therefore, that the unity of consciousness and perception is created by the mind. The impressionists read scientific studies of perception, especially of color perception, and sought to create paintings informed by these principles.

Some of these artists created a new form of art in which the active work of the mind in producing the unity of perception became the central issue of the work. Claude Monet, Paul Cézanne, and Vincent van Gogh were among the first artists in the Western tradition to create and master painting techniques that crucially made use of, and depended on, the cognitive mechanisms of creating unified perception.

From the perspective of Consciousness Art, we can see the impressionists arrayed along a spectrum, from those who were most engaged with issues of consciousness (Monet and Cézanne) to those who were least concerned with such concepts (Pierre Auguste Renoir and Edgar Degas). Although Renoir and Degas used theories of color perception to fracture the picture surface into innumerable facets of pure color, such technical innovation was applied simply to produce a more accurate representation of the world, an image that would capture the evanescence of light and form through the passage of time. In the work of Monet and

Cézanne, however, these perceptual theories were not simply artistic tools but the focus of their enterprise. In every work they remind the viewer that perception is active, that what we "see" is not what is on the canvas. And, by extension, what we see as the world is not in the world itself.

In the late work of Cézanne, in particular, this synthesizing function of the mind emerges quite forcefully as the focus of his paintings, not only in terms of color but also with regard to volume, texture, and spatial relations. What Cézanne addresses in these works is how the mechanisms that underlie human consciousness create our vision of the world from diverse, fragmented elements. Cézanne literally recreates the experience of three-dimensional vision on a flat canvas. This is the substance of Cézanne's elusive "sensibility," which has entranced generations of viewers, made all the more remarkable because the ostensible subject matter of the work is often so completely ordinary—trees, rocks, a valley with a mountain in the background.

left to right: **Claude Monet,** *Autumn Effect at Argenteuil,* 1873
**Paul Cézanne,** *La Montagne Sainte-Victoire,* 1904–06
**Vincent van Gogh,** *Olive Trees,* 1889

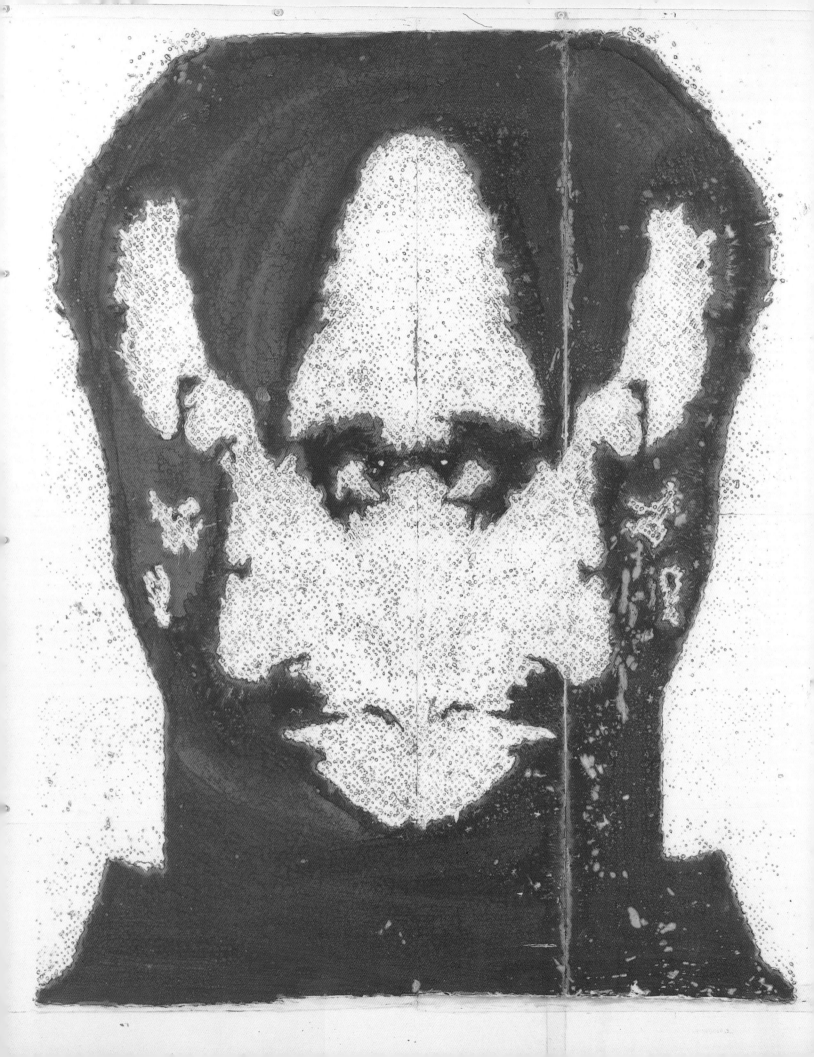

Vincent van Gogh also celebrated active perception, adding to the impressionists' vivid colors the element of linearity. Many of van Gogh's paintings and drawings are built up from patterns of lines in paint or ink that elicit the sensations of attention and flow. His sometimes rhythmic, sometimes undulating lines are renderings of the dynamic vectors of attention. Simultaneously, his turgid handling of paint evokes visual metaphors: a cypress tree becomes a blazing fire, the whorling motions of a starry sky become the roiling waves and eddies of the sea.

Consciousness was not the explicit subject matter of the paintings of van Gogh and Cézanne; their paintings clearly depict olive groves, mountains, and so on. Their work is not about consciousness but *of consciousness.* By contrast, we might consider the work of the symbolists Odilon Redon and Paul Gauguin. Redon sought to represent internal psychological and spiritual states through a combination of symbolic imagery and a vaporous, emotionally suggestive style of representation. Gauguin also used symbolism to allude to the inner reaches of the mind and spirit, even employing the exotic imagery of the South Seas to jog his European viewers out of their complacent mental habits. Redon's and Gauguin's art was meant to evoke or even to represent a certain state of consciousness, yet it is not what we mean by Consciousness Art. Their works are so veiled in layers of allegory and otherworldly illustration that they lose their visceral connection to the viewer's experience in the here and now, a crucial characteristic of Consciousness Art.

Similarly, one might think that all surrealist painting is Consciousness Art, since the surrealists deliberately set out to paint what is not and could not be real. Their works call attention to the fact that what the viewer perceives is not of this world but is a product of the imagination. But Consciousness Art is not about fantasy; it is about the mechanism of consciousness. Fantasy may or may not be about that mechanism. This distinction is what separates illustrational surrealists like Salvador Dalí from experiential surrealists like René Magritte. A Dalí painting is a representational portrayal of an impossible world; it is like a window through which you can see, clearly and unmistakably, a fantastical vision. With Dalí, the viewer's perception is never called into question; only the world is.

**René Magritte,** *La Reproduction interdite* (Reproduction Prohibited), 1937

opposite: **David Hannah,** *heidegger.3,* 1997

In the works of Magritte, however, the automatic, normally unconscious apparatus of consciousness is always at issue. Take, for example, Magritte's painting *La Reproduction interdite* (Reproduction Prohibited), 1937, which depicts a man looking in a mirror. In the mirror, the man's reflection appears to him not as he would normally see himself but as we see him, from behind. This image both violates and accords with our expectations about mirrors: the man's reflection is there, but the image is not reversed. It takes a moment to notice what's wrong, and no matter how many times we encounter the painting, it can still make us do a double-take. The painting makes us aware of our normal expectations as our accumulated experience has shaped them. The work begins to meet those expectations and then stops, again and again. The focus of the painting is not the man in the mirror but us.

In the works of the abstract expressionists, even when there is no overt subject matter, there are often allusions to consciousness. When one looks at a work by Barnett Newman, Ad Reinhardt, or Richard Diebenkorn, for instance, the experience is as much one of noticing one's own noticing as it is of noticing the painting itself. In Newman's work, such noticing has to do with color and scale—their dominance of the viewer's visual field. Newman's works are often huge—some are as much as twenty feet long—and each is mostly monochromatic. Yet the colors Newman used were typically not colors found in nature—no sky blue, no leaf green—but vibrant, chromatic reds and blues. The experience of perceiving a huge field of color in a Newman painting is, therefore, unlike any perception of color in nature, or even portrayals of nature. Similarly, in Reinhardt's virtually monochrome paintings of the 1950s and early 1960s, the viewer's sense of vision is stimulated in such a way that he or she becomes aware of what might be called the "feeling of seeing."

This attention to elements of consciousness can be contrasted with the approach of other abstract expressionists, such as William Baziotes, Willem de Kooning, Robert

**Richard Serra,** *Double Torqued Ellipse,*
1997

Motherwell, and Adolph Gottlieb. These more imagistic artists are not Consciousness Artists, despite the extent to which their works may have resulted from self-analysis or self-reflection. The abstract paintings of these artists attempt to depict a state of mind or to symbolize visually a psychological condition rather than to provide a vehicle for the viewer's own experience.

Minimalism, which emerged in the 1960s as a response to the self-absorption of much abstract expressionist work, moved forcefully in the direction of Consciousness Art. Many of the most impressive minimalist works are large, geometric sculptures, sometimes located in galleries but also sited in public or outdoor spaces. In the case of huge outdoor "earthworks," the sculptors achieved sufficient scale to engage the viewer's body as an integral element in the perception of the work. Artists such as Walter de Maria, Robert Irwin, Richard Serra, and Robert Smithson all created works that bring to the fore the relationship between the viewer's physical, bodily presence—and, sometimes, movement—and his or her cognitive perceptions. More than the product of a simple, concrete form applied to a nonfunctional object, these minimalist works link inner and outer experience, making the viewer constantly aware of his or her changing perceptions.

Minimalism echoes the philosophical approach of phenomenology, especially as outlined by writers such as Maurice Merleau-Ponty. Describing what the body brings to a mental experience, Merleau-Ponty wrote in *The Phenomenology of Perception:*

> **There is, therefore, another subject beneath me,**
> **for whom a world exists before I am here,**
> **and who marks out my place in it.**
> **This captive or natural spirit is my body,**
> **not that momentary body which is the instrument of my personal choices**
> **and which fastens upon this or that world,**
> **but the systems of anonymous "functions"**
> **which draw every particular focus into a general project.[5]**

Merleau-Ponty's "general project" can be understood as "consciousness," the basic sensation of awareness.

One possible misunderstanding of Consciousness Art is that its ultimate realization is in art that resides only in the mind, which is what conceptual art aimed for and sometimes realized. By contrast, Consciousness Art always includes a dimension of *mindfulness*. Some conceptual art engages mindfulness, and some does not.

The works of Lawrence Weiner and Robert Barry are forms of Consciousness Art. Weiner carefully crafts language to go on walls or posters, in galleries or out—language that evokes a clear and concise image in the mind of the viewer. Weiner's art is in the experience of creating an image from language. Robert Barry also uses language, written on a page or on a gallery wall. His art is not about image-creation, but is about the exploration of the mind itself via language.

Consider this work by Barry:

**ALL THE THINGS I KNOW**
**BUT OF WHICH I AM NOT**
**AT THE MOMENT THINKING—**
**1:36 PM; JUNE 15, 1969**

Thinking of something one knows but is not thinking of inevitably conjures the thought of that thing. By the time the thought occurs, however, *the moment* has passed; it has already changed, and one's state of mind has changed with it.

Joseph Kosuth, on the other hand, is a conceptual artist whose work is not Consciousness Art. In one particularly well-known example of Kosuth's work, *Chair,* 1965, the artist juxtaposes on a museum wall an actual chair, a photograph of a chair, and an enlarged Photostat of a dictionary definition of the word "chair." This work succinctly illustrates the distinctions among three different types of meaning: the material object, a pictorial representation of that object, and the linguistic rendering of it. But Kosuth's work takes us no further. The distinctions are merely depicted. Nothing in his work brings those distinctions alive in our experience. The mere depiction of something related to consciousness is not Consciousness Art.

**Contemporary Forms of Consciousness Art: The Exhibition**

We are now in a position to see the artworks in this exhibition as aspects of a single phenomenon—as forms of Consciousness Art. **In each artwork, we can recognize one or more aspects of consciousness, and in many cases we can identify key metaphors for consciousness that provide structure for the work.**

**Awareness** Awareness—the fundamental, immediate sensation of perception and cognition—is a necessary precondition for conscious attention, qualia, the comprehension of conceptual structures, and so on. Any successful work of Consciousness Art will lead viewers to an awareness of their own awareness. Nevertheless, we can see in certain works a greater focus on awareness itself, largely through the stripping away of imagery, form, or other visual elements. The radically simplified works of Agnes Martin, Ad Reinhardt, and Robert Irwin exemplify this approach.

Agnes Martin, whose work is generally considered by art historians as a kind of hinge between abstract expressionism and minimalism, perhaps more appropriately adheres to the traditions of Buddhist meditative practices. Her works, which have varied remarkably little in the course of a half-century career, consist of a sequence of horizontal lines—sometimes articulated as a grid—drawn or painted on a square canvas. Martin has written that the subject of her paintings "...is not what is seen. It is what is known forever in the mind."[6] To "see" her work, as opposed to simply "looking at" it, is to experience the paintings as tools for expanding conscious awareness. Rather than merely representing some past vision, idea, or feeling of the artist, Martin's canvases alert the viewer to the possibilities of perception in the here and now.

Similarly, Ad Reinhardt created deceptively simple paintings that lead the viewer into a sudden awareness of the sensation of seeing. The tonal contrasts in *Abstract Painting, no. 3* are so subtle that they summon overtones of pure color that can be sensed but not demarcated. Hints of color—blues and violets—seem to float over the dark surface of the picture like an impalpable haze. Reinhardt effectively dissociates our sensation of color from the physical medium of paint, evoking a transcendent, otherworldly vision.

Robert Irwin's ethereal disc sculptures celebrate perception as the bedrock of conscious awareness. As critic Lawrence Wechsler describes:

**Irwin has become increasingly convinced that perception precedes conception, that every thought or idea arises within the context of an indefinite field of perceptual presence, which it thereupon rushes to delimit.[7]**

Irwin's discs create a luminous atmosphere of light and space that expands indefinitely beyond the material parameters of the disc itself to include the surrounding space, extending into the very eye and mind of the viewer.

Another work that elicits the viewer's sensation of awareness, but in a much different way, is Douglas Gordon's *30 Seconds Text*. This installation consists of a darkened room in which a single light bulb suddenly illuminates a panel of text. The text, which takes approximately thirty seconds to read, describes a 1905 experiment conducted in France by a Doctor Baurieux on the decapitated head of a criminal named Languille. Baurieux recorded that the man's head remained conscious for approximately thirty seconds after it was severed from his body. The light in the installation goes out after exactly thirty seconds, creating for the viewer a disturbingly visceral sensation of the experience the text has just described. Gordon simply and effectively employs the metaphor of Consciousness as Light to connect the viewer to the sensation of disembodied awareness.

**Attention** The aspect of consciousness known as attention is evoked in works by Gary Hill, Bill Viola, Stan Douglas, Lutz Bacher, and Stuart Sherman. Hill's *Searchlight* consists of a large, darkened room in which the artist has positioned what looks like a telescope slowly swiveling on a tripod. The "telescope" actually contains at its tip a tiny video monitor that casts an image, moving along a wall as the telescope turns. The image slowly changes from an indistinct wash of light when the telescope is directed along the wall, to a tiny, focused image of waves crashing on a seashore when the telescope and the wall are, momentarily, perpendicular. Hidden speakers in the wall produce low-volume sounds of waves. Hill's work captures the sensation of one's attention moving from undifferentiated awareness into sharp focus. The work is also a careful arrangement of potent metaphors, including Consciousness as a Room, Attention as a Spotlight (or telescope), and Consciousness as the Sea. As such, the work creates a kind of closed circuit in which consciousness seems to be reflecting upon itself. The sea is the sea of consciousness, which comes into focus only momentarily. Attending to and focusing on the sea within the room is itself a form of consciousness—the direction of attention to whatever is in the room. As a result, the work

page 36: **Robert Irwin**, Untitled, 1969

makes us, metaphorically, conscious of our consciousness. Engendering a sense of self-reflection, the piece suggests a state of deep meditation, echoed in the repetitive, self-enfolding action of the crashing waves.

Bill Viola's *Pneuma* similarly expresses the delicate relationship between awareness and attention. The artist has described the installation as follows:

**"Pneuma" is an ancient Greek word**
**that has no equivalent in contemporary terms.**
**Commonly translated as soul or spirit, it refers as well to breath,**
**and was conceived as an underlying essence or life force**
**which ran through all things of nature**
**and animated or illuminated them with Mind.**
**In the installation, images alternately emerge and submerge**
**into the shimmering visual noise, the ground of all images,**
**and often hover at the threshold of recognition and ambiguity.**
**Indistinct, shifting, and shadowy,**
**the projections become more like memories or internal sensations**
**rather than recorded images of actual places and events**
**as the viewer becomes surrounded**
**and submerged in their essence.**[8]

*Pneuma* cannot be so much "understood" as intuited: it is more structured than random, abstract images, but less structured than a discursive narrative or descriptive scene. While Hill's *Searchlight* enacts various conditions of consciousness, from undifferentiated awareness to focused attention, *Pneuma* strikes a middle ground between these states and stays there. It allows the viewers themselves to become attuned to their own experiences of fluctuating awareness and attention in relation to the indistinct visual and audio information. *Pneuma* also expresses the notion, which the eighteenth-century German philosopher Gottfried Wilhelm von Leibniz called "panpsychism," that consciousness extends beyond the human—or even the animal—mind into all aspects of reality, organic and inorganic. Panpsychism, considered a long-dead relative of metaphysics, has recently re-emerged in the writings of the philosopher David J. Chalmers. Relating consciousness to information, Chalmers writes:

**Physics requires information states**
**but cares only about their relations, not their intrinsic nature;**
**phenomenology requires information states**
**but cares only about the intrinsic nature.**
**[Panpsychism] postulates a single basic set of information unifying the two.**
**We might say that internal aspects of these states are phenomenal,**
**and the external aspects are physical. Or as a slogan:**

**Experience is information from the inside;**
**physics is information from the outside.**[9]

opposite: **Ad Reinhardt**, *Abstract Painting, no. 3*, 1960–63

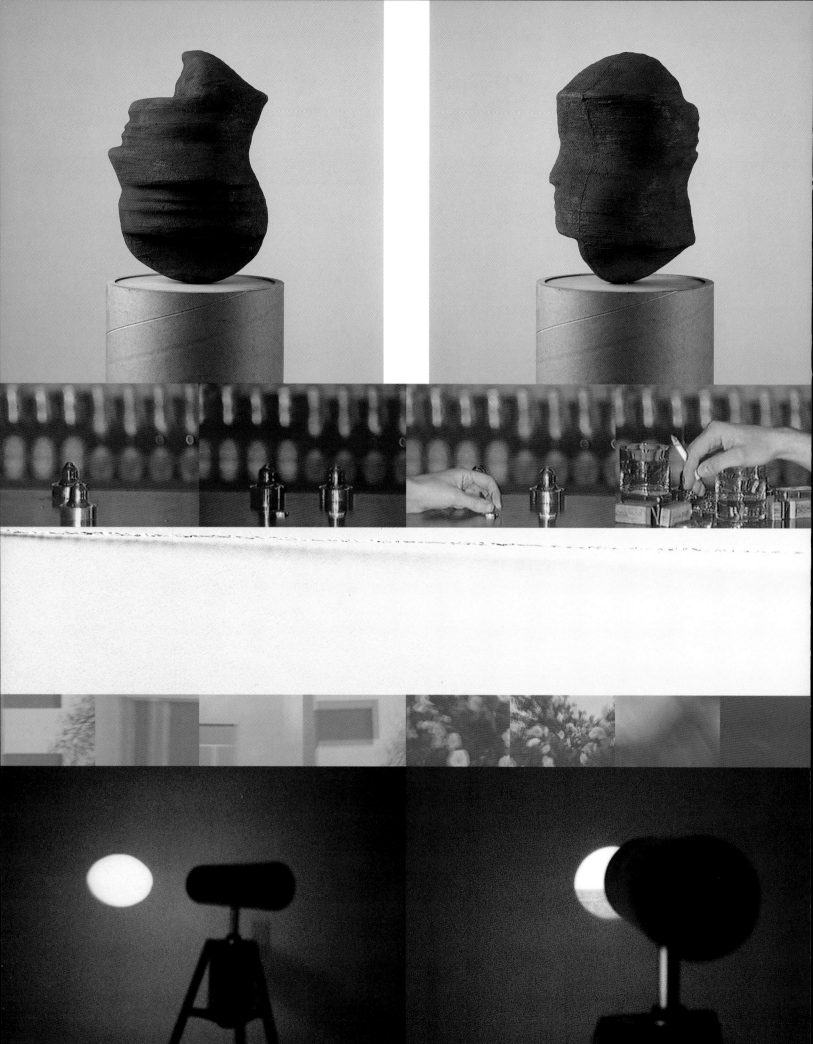

Stan Douglas's installation, *Overture,* consists of a late nineteenth-century black-and-white film shot from the front of a train as it winds its way on tracks curving along the side of a mountain. The train periodically enters tunnels, during which time the film—and the room— goes dark. The accompanying soundtrack is a recitation taken from the "Overture" section of Marcel Proust's *Remembrance of Things Past.* It is in this section of the novel that the bedridden narrator, inspired by the familiar taste of a Madeleine cookie, begins to recall, in extraordinary detail, the events and sensations of his life. The film imagery incorporated into this work makes implicit use of a number of metaphors for consciousness. There is Consciousness as Light, Unconsciousness as Darkness, and Thought as Motion. The conscious awareness of one's own thought is seen metaphorically as a train in motion going in and out of tunnels, going from states of awareness to lack of awareness. As described by

Mark Bartlett in this catalogue, Douglas's work involves complex manipulations of Proust's original text, which add to the evocative, dreamlike experience of the work.

Compare Douglas's evocation of Proust to Lutz Bacher's video projection, *A Normal Life.* In this work, which resembles an amateur home video, Bacher presents a family gathering on the occasion of a birthday. The artist juxtaposes sections in which the camera is held by one of the family members, actively mediating the precarious family dynamic, with sections in which the camera rests on the backyard table as family members, apparently unaffected by the camera's presence, carry on various conversations. In these latter sections, the camera captures vague reflections of the family members in a large window. Voices, both male and female, overlay and interweave to create an impression of a composite consciousness, one woven from the aggregate memories, experiences, and points of view of this family constellation. While Douglas's work evokes a sensation of being conscious as being "deep" in one's own mind, Bacher's video proposes a kind of horizontal consciousness in which awareness and attention are unmoored from any individual and bounce back and forth among members of a social group, shifting the first-person perspective from person to person in an "infinite eluding of meaning."[10]

Stuart Sherman's single-channel video *Berlin (West)/Andere Richtungen* playfully leads the viewer on a kind of Easter-egg-hunt of attention. As he wanders around Berlin, Sherman narrates his own acts of attending to various ordinary phenomena. For example, at one point he notices that he is standing with one foot slightly ahead of the other. Halfway

44

through the video, Sherman is replaced by another performer whom we follow through a series of similarly banal encounters with his own focused attention; however, the voice-over has shifted to German. By changing languages, Sherman effectively—at least for non-German speakers—unmoors language from the act of noticing, something that is normally exceedingly difficult to do.

**Qualia**                When we are attending to a particular sensation, we experience what are known as *qualia*, the irreducible qualities of perceptions (e.g., the redness of red). Qualia play an important role in many of the works in this exhibition. In certain pieces, however, we can see that qualia are the focus of the works. Ad Reinhardt, for example, presents us with what appears to be a black painting, but which slowly reveals itself as

a subtly differentiated grid of nine hues of dark blue. Reinhardt's work is stripped of naturalism and symbolism, relying solely on our ability to isolate the sensation of color from the universe of perceptions.

Rosie Lee Tompkins's textile is as powerfully evocative of color qualia as is Reinhardt's painting; in addition, Tompkins offers a remarkably nuanced experience of material and texture with her composition, which consists of velvet and velveteen. Tompkins, however, does envision a complex symbolic order for the colors she uses and is less interested in her works' material qualities than she is in their spiritual potency. The viewers' attention to qualia as discovered in Tompkins's extraordinary pieces and their appreciation of the artist's spiritual aims need not be mutually exclusive.

By distilling particular qualia from the general field of perceptions, works such as Reinhardt's and Tompkins's heighten our awareness of qualia. Each piece opens us to a flood of qualia, and a flood of accompanying emotions.

**Unity**                One of the key aspects of consciousness is that we experience it as a unity, rather than as the fragmented collection of perceptions and memories from which it is composed. The mind has numerous mechanisms for eliciting the sensation of unity, perhaps foremost among them the perceptual phenomenon known as "gestalt formation." A gestalt is an overall form perceived at its most minimal level of organization. The mind automatically tends to organize information, and does so in basic geometries:

above: **Martin Creed**, *chrome and brass,*
*Work No. 42,* 1990 (details)

pages 42–43; top to bottom:
**Markus Raetz**, *Kopf II,* 1992
**Martin Creed**, *chrome and brass, Work*
*No. 42,* 1990 (details)
**Diana Thater**, *Perspective is an energy,*
1995 (details)
**Gary Hill**, *Searchlight,* 1986–94

circles, squares, lines, and so on. There are also more complex gestalts—such as the arrangement of individual features into a "face"—that play an important role in the unified functioning of consciousness.

Markus Raetz's sculpture *Kopf II* relies on the mind's propensity to organize perceptual information into gestalts. It alerts us to this very propensity, however, by balancing right on the edge of coherence and incoherence. In this sculpture, Raetz has formed a cast-iron bust that from one angle appears to be right-side-up and from another upside-down. The mercurial imagery succinctly and humorously reminds us how easily our perceptions can shift from one gestalt to the next. Thus, Raetz actively engages the viewer in a process of self-reflection about the organizing mechanisms of the mind.

David Hannah's painting, *heidegger.3,* similarly exploits the neural mechanisms of the brain that recognize the physiognomic patterns of a face. Hannah's large-scale work presents a doubled image of the face of philosopher Martin Heidegger; however, the image is doubled in a Rorschach-like mirror image and has lost much of its clarity in the process of reproduction and enlargement. Despite the degree of distortion, we can clearly make out the patterns of eyes, nose, and mouth. The work forces us to recognize the process of reconstructing an image from available clues, and thus our role in perception, in keeping with Heidegger's own philosophy.

Martin Creed's deceptively simple video, *chrome and brass, Work No. 42,* is an exercise in gestalt formation masquerading as a "barstool opera." The camera is focused on the narrow space defined by two adjacent salt and pepper shakers, identical in form, on a bar counter. We observe a man and a woman (at least as defined by gender-specific indicators such as styles of wristwatches, etc.) sit down next to each other, order beer and sandwiches, smoke cigarettes, and leave. The soundtrack throughout the piece consists of well-known operatic duets. Creed has orchestrated the work so that all of the objects on the right side of the screen echo the golden color of the pepper shaker, while all those on the left reflect the silver color of the chrome salt shaker. Each object has a twin of the opposite color on the opposite side. Thus, the screen is divided into two zones of sensation. Everything on one side is almost the same as everything on the other side: there is only one dimension of difference: chrome versus brass, Becks versus Lamot Pils beer, a hairy wrist versus a smooth one, and so on. The work makes the gestalt of isomorphic reflection visual while unmasking the speciousness of "difference."

Color television works by combining three colors, which the brain sees as one. Diana Thater's art reminds us that the unified image we see on a color television set is created by our brains. She achieves this by separating out the colors in such a way that we cannot quite combine them into a unified image. Consider Thater's multimedia work, *Perspective is an energy*. On a single table, four video monitors display four images simultaneously. The images are of hand-held tours through parts of four different gardens—two seventeenth-century gardens, an eighteenth-century Romantic garden, and a twentieth-century modern garden. Each image is color separated and then reassembled with its red, green, and blue each slightly larger or smaller than the others so that the images look as if they are being drawn into a hole in the center of the screen. The instability of the unrealized image attunes the viewer's attention to typically unconscious unification processes.

**Memory** The unifying function of consciousness depends to some degree on our ability to remember. Memory provides the continuity that is crucial to engendering perceptions of unified experience. Cristabel Davé's paintings on bark cloth (pounded mulberry bark) were made with a technique uniquely suited to conveying memory's role in the unifying, yet elastic, mechanisms of consciousness. Davé, like many artists from the Maisin tribe of Papua New Guinea, paints most of her works in four sections. The bark cloth is folded into quarters so that only the first section is visible. Davé then paints a design, "from the imagination" (as many Maisin describe their nonconventional approach), onto the first section.[11] The cloth is then turned over to expose the second section onto which Davé paints her memory of the design she made on the first section. This process is repeated two more times until the whole cloth is covered. When the piece is fully painted and unfolded, what is revealed is an image from the imagination seen through the veil of memory and time. Davé's work suggests that memory functions as a kind of conscious glue, uniting over time, through the sensation of familiarity, images that might otherwise be disparate experiences. As indicated by Davé's works included in this exhibition, in Maisin art there can be enormous variation in the degree of replication from section to section. Such variation attests not only to the artist's state of mind during the process of creation but also to the underlying flexibility of the art form—absolute conformity from section to section is not required; rather, it serves as a foil against which eccentricities may occur.

Theresa Hak Kyung Cha's film and video installation, *Exilée,* uses repetition, fades, and real and metaphorical afterimages to allude to the fundamental role that memory plays in our consciousness. *Exilée* is complex, interweaving historical, linguistic, spiritual, and personal dimensions of memory into a single resonant work. Cha alludes to Japan's efforts, during its colonial administration of Korea, to expunge the nation's memory of its language and customs; simultaneously, she embeds her own personal experience of exile and memory into this larger historical and cognitive framework to evoke a sensation of how voluntary and involuntary memories (e.g., afterimages) inflect our moment-to-moment consciousness.

**First-Person Perspective** Consciousness is not only unified; it is singular. It is experienced as a unique possession of individual human beings. Your consciousness is your own, and you sense it as such. Mysterious as it is—neither philosophy nor cognitive science has made much headway in explaining first-person experience—this phenomenon must be recognized as an essential property of consciousness.

In her single-channel video, *2 into 1,* Gillian Wearing presents alternating shots of a mother and her twin boys, who speak about their feelings for each other. Wearing undermines our stable sense of first-person consciousness by making the boys' words, lip-synced, appear to come from their mother's mouth, and the mother's, lip-synced, from the boys' mouths. The result is humorous but also profoundly unsettling. This work separates first-person experience from other aspects of consciousness, making us acutely aware of how much we ignore other people's experiences of us.

Adrian Piper, *Cornered*, 1988

page 48: **Louise Bourgeois**, *Culprit Number Two* (preliminary version), 1998

page 49: **Kristin Oppenheim**, *Hey Joe*, 1996

**Self-Awareness**          Self-awareness is a normal part of everyday consciousness. One can be aware or not aware of what one is saying, thinking, or doing. Self-awareness, as a faculty that one can cultivate, is a goal of psychotherapy as well as of Buddhism. The dark side of self-awareness is a form of paranoiac self-searching, an inward quest for our shortcomings in the face of what we perceive as the accusations of others.

Louise Bourgeois's large-scale sculpture, *Culprit Number Two*, creates a powerful image of this profoundly isolating form of self-awareness. Her work consists of a circle of tall, metal doors—some of which have been struck by arrows—surrounding a single, small chair. The chair faces a small, round mirror. In this work, self-awareness is expressed in terms of its opposition to the outside world: enclosed within a fortress-like cell, attacked from without, the self turns back on itself in a state of withdrawn contemplation.

Another negative form of self-awareness results when one knows and disapproves of oneself. The protagonist in Samuel Beckett's *Film*, played by Buster Keaton, is all too self-aware. The camera follows Keaton through the streets and into his apartment. At every turn, Keaton is confronted by the stares of others: passers-by on the street, his own cat and little dog, a mirror, a poster on the wall of his room, and, finally, the camera (and film viewer) itself. He shrinks from these confrontations in terror as if incapable of bearing the weight of another's observation of him, as if others can see in him what he sees in himself.

**Conceptual Framing and Metaphor**     Conceptual framing is an aspect of consciousness that determines the form of numerous works of art. Indeed, a conceptual frame can be understood as an integral aspect of a work itself, as much as the material it is made of: if you misconstrue the conceptual frame, you risk missing the point of the work altogether. Many works in this exhibition draw attention to the power of conceptual framing as an aspect of conscious experience. Among the most remarkable in this respect are pieces by Kristin Oppenheim, Imogen Stidworthy, Adrian Piper, and Jörg Herold.

Kristin Oppenheim's installation, *Hey Joe*, consists of two beams of light that pass back and forth in an empty room. "The viewer is hit by the lights," writes Oppenheim, "which might initially feel like circus lights, but gradually become more like prison-yard search lights."[12] The work is accompanied by a soundtrack in which the artist recites the lyrics of the song, "Hey Joe (where you goin' with that gun in your hand?)," popularized by Jimi Hendrix. "The voice," says Oppenheim, "which appears and disappears, is mysterious and drowsy, as if in a stupor and slightly possessed."[13] Oppenheim's soundtrack leads us into a haunting experience of this simple environment. In this way, the artist helps us to experience the degree to which our engagement with a conceptual frame, in this case a psycho-emotional narrative, colors our experience of an event.

In Imogen Stidworthy's two-screen video installation, *To*, the viewer is confronted with multiple conceptual frames and must either reconcile them into a consistent experience or embrace their contradictions. *To* contrasts two images: a naked, elderly man sitting in a chair in an empty room as he recounts a series of autobiographical anecdotes as well as the story of the film *The Roman Spring of Mrs. Stone* (based on the novel by Tennessee Williams), and a woman who appears periodically to type a flurry of words on a typewriter. Is she typing the words that he is speaking? Are his words fictional? Why does her typing seem so erratic and the clatter of the keys so aggressive while the man's speech flows smoothly and his nakedness suggests the ultimate vulnerability? By juxtaposing these two potentially related but distinct scenes, Stidworthy raises the viewer's awareness of framing in everyday life—the constant attempt to integrate disparate frames into an overall coherent narrative, and the ways in which the jagged edges of these competing conceptual frames create cognitive dissonance.

In Adrian Piper's multimedia work, *Cornered,* the artist directly addresses the viewer, appearing on a television monitor pushed into a corner of a room behind an overturned table. On the wall adjacent to the table hang two birth certificates for the artist's father: one that categorizes him as white and the other that describes him as octoroon, or one-eighth black. Drawing attention to her own racially ambiguous appearance, Piper questions the viewer's conceptual framework of racial categorizations.

Jörg Herold's film installation, *Körper im Körper,* evokes the nineteenth-century German legend of Kaspar Hauser to give form to the ambiguous relationship between language and consciousness. Kaspar Hauser was a young man who suddenly appeared one morning in the town square of Nürnberg, standing mutely and holding a simple note requesting that he be given care and shelter. Hauser, who had been raised as a kind of feral child without any exposure to the world or to education, was adopted by various townspeople and taught to speak, read, and write. As his consciousness began to be organized by language, however, Hauser became increasingly despondent and expressed regret that he had been robbed of his previous innocence.

In Herold's installation, evocative film shots of buildings, windows, walking figures, and other simple images are juxtaposed with a soundtrack in which a voice haltingly speaks the German word for each thing pictured. The shadowy atmosphere of the images simultaneously suggests an emerging into the light of consciousness and an apocalyptic darkening of the world. The piece was made as an allegory, after the fall of the Berlin Wall but before a full integration of the East German state into West Germany. As an East German, Herold uses this work to express his apprehension of an impending loss of innocence—like Kaspar Hauser's—on the eve of integration into the capitalist world.

**Empathy**                    Another aspect of consciousness touched on in this exhibition is empathy. One form of empathy is the projection of consciousness onto another—another sentient being or even an inanimate object, such as a computer. Deep Blue, the computer that beat Gary Kasparov at chess, has filled many people with anxiety over what they have taken to be its "conscious" powers. Cybernetics theorist Valentino Braitenberg's observation that a machine needn't be complex to elicit such a perception is borne out by Paul Kaiser and Shelley Eshkar's simple computer animation, *If by Chance,* and by Pascale Wiedemann's anthropomorphized video knitting, *Heimlich.*

Kaiser and Eshkar's work presents simple, geometric forms that move in random sequences. Kaiser and Eshkar have set out to create the minimal conditions for projected volition and narrative structure. Wiedemann's *Heimlich* is baroque in comparison, an alternately endearing and annoying work, combining a lengthy, multicolored knit tube that encases a video monitor at one end and rises, stem-like, to the ceiling at the other. The video displays a pulsating view of the knit tube from within, suggesting that the video image is, in fact, the organic interior of this gigantic stocking. A soundtrack of high-pitched babbling accompanies the work. As ludicrous as it may appear, *Heimlich* makes one think it is alive and conscious.

*The Voice of the American Gray Fox,* a diorama-like display developed for The Museum of Jurassic Technology in Culver City, California, similarly "fools" the viewer into projecting consciousness onto an inanimate object. This work consists of a glass case in which a stuffed fox glares out at the viewer, its lips drawn back in an aggressive sneer. The sound of growling can be heard. Looking into an apparatus attached to the case, the viewer can see a hologram of a man sitting in a chair and realize that it is actually this man—one of Hollywood's most accomplished animal-sound imitators—who is making these growling sounds. The realization that the growling sounds are made by a man does not, however, dissipate the mystery of the piece. On the contrary, the man's mimicry is so realistic that we find ourselves simply shifting from projecting fox consciousness onto the stuffed fox to projecting fox consciousness onto the tiny, growling hologram of a man.

In addition to the works in this exhibition that embody the nine main aspects of consciousness, there are a number of works that evade such categorization but that nevertheless function primarily to evoke visceral experiences of consciousness.

Among these are works that derive from non-Western cultures, including a selection of tantric paintings from India. Tantra is an ancient form of spiritual self-cultivation that has developed manifestations in both the Hindu and Buddhist faiths. Practitioners of tantra employ a number of methods to attune their minds to specific aspects of consciousness. One method is the representation of, and meditation upon, abstract designs, known as *yantras*, which have been refined over the centuries to elicit particular states of consciousness.

While some of these tantric images bear uncanny resemblances to works of Western abstraction, their purpose is quite different. They are part of a cultural technology for developing various aspects of consciousness that has evolved over thousands of years. A number of Western artists who have studied the tantric tradition create works that *are* related—works such as Agnes Martin's paintings or the multimedia works of La Monte Young and Marian Zazeela. For several decades, Young and Zazeela have created sound-and-light environments that function as aids to meditation. *Music and Light Box* is their first work of this kind, consisting of a small box that, when placed in a darkened room, emits a combination of magenta and green light and a distinctive midrange sound. The vibrations of the sound waves create a dual sensation: they can be felt as well as heard. In addition, the experience of the sound varies as one moves through the room, growing stronger or almost disappearing at different locations. While *Music and Light Box* functions on the one hand as an experiential environment for tuning one's awareness to the qualia of light and sound, it is, on the other hand, like a yantra, intended to evoke states of mind, particularly the sensation of "time standing still."[14]

Primarily in the Buddhist tradition—but also significantly among Western thinkers from Lewis Carroll to James Joyce to Gregory Bateson—the riddle or *koan* has been used as a path toward heightened consciousness. The koan is, ultimately, not rationally comprehensible in itself, but each attempt to make sense of it develops one or another of one's capacities for consciousness. Contemporary artists such as Rodney Graham and Gary Hill create experiential koans—works that embody visual, temporal, spatial, and symbolic paradoxes to evoke the sometimes contradictory multiplicities of consciousness.

Rodney Graham's film installation, *Vexation Island*, consists of a film loop—produced with Hollywood-like color and detail—of a buccaneer marooned on a desert island, alone except for his trusty parrot. We see the buccaneer lying beneath a slender palm tree on a sandy beach as if asleep, unconscious, or, perhaps, dead. After a time the man awakes, stands up, and is suddenly walloped on the head by a coconut. He collapses, and the film loops again, ad infinitum. In this work there are two common metaphors for consciousness: Consciousness as Being Awake and Consciousness as an Ocean. The pirate is on the edge of consciousness in both metaphors—on the edge of the ocean and just waking up. The falling coconut is an external force that constantly keeps him from achieving full consciousness.

*Vexation Island* also suggests, by negative example, what might be considered a tenth fundamental aspect of consciousness: its forward motion; that is, our consciousness seems to be future-oriented and cumulative. An experience of conscious repetition (as in the phenomenon of déjà vu) can be profoundly disconcerting. Graham's film playfully invites us to reflect on the paradox of a consciousness that loops and, in effect, stands still, thereby allowing us to appreciate our own sensation of consciousness' forward motion.

Gary Hill's single-channel video *Why Do Things Get in a Muddle? (Come on Petunia)* portrays a conversation between the philosopher Gregory Bateson and his daughter, Cathy (who doubles as Alice in Wonderland). As Steve Kolpan states in his essay in this catalogue, the work is structured as a "metalogue," to borrow one of Bateson's own neologisms. A metalogue is "a conversation about some problematic subject. The conversation should be such that not only do the participants discuss the problem, but the structure of the conversation as a whole is also relevant to the same subject."[15]

In this work, the problem is a question of time, entropy, and perception: Cathy/Alice asks her father, "Why do things get in a muddle?" In the course of answering this seemingly innocent question, the character of Bateson—and we, the viewers—are only led into deeper and deeper muddles. Hill plays extraordinary tricks with our perception as Bateson and his daughter lapse into backwards speech that is, nevertheless, heard as forward speech because the artist has reversed the direction of the tape. Their words are understandable but sound strange, as if spoken by machines. The narrative proceeds in a forward direction although the actors performed it in reverse.

At the end of the tape, Cathy/Alice asks Bateson, "Where does the light go when you blow the candle out?" This question forces us, as a koan would, to notice the framings and metaphors that underlie our consciousness. We understand Existence metaphorically as Presence, and Ceasing to Exist as Going Away. In this metaphor, the light goes away. To notice the metaphor is to notice how we think, to notice the conceptual buttressing of our conscious reason. The question, a koan-like question—as children's questions often are— leads us to reflect on the metaphors of our own everyday thought processes.

## Moral and Political Implications of Consciousness Art

One of the most interesting findings in the field of neurobiology concerns what may be the basis for empathy. **There is an area of the brain's prefrontal cortex (F5) where "mirror neurons" are located. These are neurons that both control movements and recognize the corresponding movements in others. For example, it has been shown that a mirror neuron in the prefrontal cortex of monkeys will fire either when the monkey, say, presses a bar or sees another monkey pressing a bar. Although such experiments have only been done on monkeys, humans have an equivalent anatomical structure, presumably with mirror neurons that carry out the same functions. Such neural structures are thought to be required for empathy, the capacity to feel in oneself what someone else is experiencing.[16]**

Empathy is at the heart of Consciousness Art. To see why, consider the role of the awakening of consciousness in the Buddhist goal of cultivating compassion. A truly compassionate, or empathetic, person, in order to feel what another feels, must be aware of what he or she brings to the interaction; that is, he or she must be conscious of his or her own body to feel what it is like to be in another body. Correspondingly, he or she must be conscious of his or her own values, his or her own interests, and his or her own world view to be sure that he or she is not imposing it in a compassionate interaction. An awareness of consciousness in all of its aspects is thus a prerequisite for compassion. Consciousness Art, through exploring, developing, and stimulating all the aspects of consciousness, contributes to the cultivation of compassion.

Some forms of politics are built directly on empathy and compassion: the progressive politics of working to end poverty, hunger, and oppression, for example. There is also a politics in which empathy and compassion are anathema, the conservative politics that sees the politics of compassion as misguided "do-gooding" that just hurts the people it is trying to help.

The political lines drawn by compassion have only recently been described in detail in George Lakoff's *Moral Politics*, which examines the largely unconscious conceptual systems behind conservative and progressive thought. To simplify the argument of the book, progressive and conservative politics are based on conflicting moral systems that grow out of opposing family models. Conservative politics are produced by a strict-father morality, one that stresses discipline, strict rights and wrongs, punishment, and tough love. To survive in the world, according to this view, children must be taught right from wrong and be imbued

page 56: **Rodney Graham**, *Vexation Island*, 1997 (detail)

page 57: *Vexation Island* (production still)

with self-discipline, which, through the pursuit of self-interest, should result in self-reliance. Empathy and compassion in this view are generally seen as counterproductive: helping those in need may undermine the discipline needed for self-reliance, and, therefore, "do-gooders" just make things worse.

Progressive politics, on the other hand, are born from nurturant-parent morality, in which empathy and compassion are central. The aim of the nurturant family is not only to care for the children but also to raise them to be nurturers, too. Nurturance requires empathy (to know what another needs), self-nurturance (in order to be able to care for others), responsibility, self-fulfillment, protectiveness, fairness, and open communication. The first requirement is empathy, which, in turn, requires self-awareness. Consciousness and compassion are thus *the* central progressive values. This does not mean that they do not exist in conservative morality, but only that they rank well below the values of discipline and respect for moral authority.

Militant-progressive politics combines both systems: it has nurturant goals and strict-father means. Its goals are to help the helpless, protect the oppressed, and create unity. But its means are judgmental, coercive, punishing, and divisive. Much of the art commonly recognized as "political" today comes out of militant-progressive politics. From the militant-progressive point of view, Consciousness Art is apolitical, especially when it has no overt political content. From this perspective, to be apolitical is to be immoral, to lack political consciousness, to do nothing to help, and, thus, implicitly to support the status quo.

Militantly progressive practitioners of political art tend to be blind to the nurturant politics of Consciousness Art. Conservatives tend to be blind to the fact that Consciousness Art is art at all, because the awakening of consciousness and the development of empathy and compassion are not primary conservative values, either moral or aesthetic. Thus, neither militant progressives nor conservatives have noticed the moral and political dimensions of Consciousness Art.

It is important that Consciousness Artists themselves, as well as the general public, become aware of the moral and political dimensions of Consciousness Art. The fact that, for the most part, these dimensions are implicit, not explicit, lends a subtle richness to the art. Consciousness is not merely a condition accompanying our existence; it is at the center of our lives. The aspects of consciousness, from attention to empathy, span a broad range of human concerns, and in many parts of the world are taken to be at the center of human concerns. Consciousness Art—art that is primarily concerned with the aspects of consciousness and conveys those aspects viscerally—is a vitally important part of our culture.

Our society urgently needs to develop the capacities on which Consciousness Art is centered: empathy, attentiveness, self-awareness, an awareness of how we and others frame the world, and an appreciation of the qualitative aspects of life.

Lawrence Rinder is the director of the CCAC Institute for exhibitions and public programs. Among the exhibitions he has organized are *Louise Bourgeois: Drawings* and *In a Different Light* at the Berkeley Art Museum; and *Theresa Hak Kyung Cha: Other Things Seen, Other Things Heard* at the Whitney Museum of American Art.

George Lakoff is professor of linguistics and cognitive science at the University of California, Berkeley. He is the author of numerous books including *Metaphors We Live By* (coauthored with Mark Johnson); *Women, Fire, and Dangerous Things: What Categories Reveal About the Mind; Moral Politics;* and, most recently, *Philosophy in the Flesh* (coauthored with Mark Johnson).

60

1    Martin Jay, *Downcast Eyes: The Denigration of Vision in Twentieth-Century French Thought* (Berkeley: University of California Press, 1993), 5.

2    See George Lakoff and Mark Johnson, *Philosophy in the Flesh* (New York: Basic Books, 1998).

3    Diego Fernandez-Duque and Mark L. Johnson, "Attention Metaphors: How Metaphors Guide the Cognitive Psychology of Attention" (University of Oregon, 1998–99).

4    Jonathan Crary, *Techniques of the Observer: On Vision and Modernity in the Nineteenth Century* (Cambridge, Massachusetts: MIT Press, 1990), 138.

5    Maurice Merleau-Ponty, *The Phenomenology of Perception,* trans. Colin Smith (London: Routledge and Kegan Paul, 1962), 254.

6    Agnes Martin, *Writings/Schriften* (Ostfildern: Cantz-Verlag, 1991), 15.

7    Lawrence Wechsler, *Seeing Is Forgetting the Name of the Thing One Sees: A Life of Contemporary Artist Robert Irwin* (Berkeley: University of California Press, 1982), 180.

8    David A. Ross, *Bill Viola* (New York: The Whitney Museum of American Art, 1997), 111.

9    David J. Chalmers, *The Conscious Mind: In Search of a Fundamental Theory* (New York: Oxford University Press, 1996), 305.

10    Lutz Bacher, conversation with the author (Rinder), 28 January 1999.

11    Natalie Rarama et al., conversation with the author (Rinder), 10 August 1997.

12    Kristin Oppenheim, untitled project description (New York: 303 Gallery, 12 November 1998).

13    Ibid.

14    La Monte Young and Marian Zazeela, "Music and Light Box" (unpublished project description, 1988), 3.

15    Gregory Bateson, quoted in Steve Kolpan, "Bateson Through the Looking Glass," *Video/Arts* (Winter 1986): 21.

16    See G. Rizzolatti et al., Behav. Brain Res. 2 (1981), 147–163; G. Rizzolatti et al., Exp. Brain Res. 71 (1988), 491–507; G. Rizzolatti et al., Cogn. Brain Res. 3 (1996), 131–141; G. Rizzolatti et al., Exp. Brain Res. 111 (1996), 246–252.

opposite: **Jörg Herold**, *Körper im Körper,* 1989 (details)

this page and pages 64, 66: **Gary Hill,**
*Why Do Things Get in a Muddle?*
*(Come on Petunia),* 1984 (details)

# bateson through the looking glass

Steve Kolpan

In 1948, Gregory Bateson wrote "Metalogue: Why Do Things Get in a Muddle?" This short piece was not published until 1972 in his now-famous book, *Steps to an Ecology of Mind.* Bateson's book became, along with Stewart Brand's *Whole Earth Catalog* and *Co-Evolution Quarterly* and the works of Herbert Marcuse, Norman O. Brown, and John Lilly, a voice of mindset change floating on a wave from California to the rest of the world. (Bateson taught at University of California, Santa Cruz, and was appointed to the Board of Regents of the University of California by then-governor Jerry Brown in 1976.) Bateson, who died in 1980 at the age of 80, had become something of an intel-lectual/pop culture guru, a position that, unfortunately, tended to obscure the important ground-breaking work he had done in the areas of communication theory, anthropology, mental illness, cybernetics, alcoholism, and cetacean communication; and the development of an epistemology relevant to a burgeoning and open culture/counterculture. *Steps to an Ecology of Mind* is Gregory Bateson's gift and testament to a new way of thinking clearly and holistically about the human condition—a condition that cannot exist separately from the fascinating process of evolution, which affects all living things and all of the processes created by living things.

**A metalogue is, according to Bateson, "a conversation about some problematic subject.** The conversation should be such that not only do the participants discuss the problem, but the structure of the conversation as a whole is also relevant to the same subject." In other words, the metastructure of the conversation is illustrating the problem at hand. The very first piece in *Steps to an Ecology of Mind* is "Metalogue: Why Do Things Get in a Muddle?" The context for this metalogue is a conversation between Bateson and his daughter, Cathy (Mary Catherine Bateson, who authored a biography of her mother, Margaret Mead). Cathy asks her "daddy" why things get so "muddled up," and

> why there are so many ways
> to be in a state of **muddleness,**
> but only very few ways to be
> **"tidy."**

Of course, the metastructure of the conversation is such that it is an ongoing series of muddles between father and daughter, which attempts to create clarity, resolution, and "tidiness." The question, "Why do things get in a muddle?" quickly becomes an analogy for the concept of entropy—in nature things tend toward the undifferentiated, the unpredictable, the

random: a muddle. Bateson's adult logic is shown to be in sharp contrast to the intuition of his precocious child, who keeps the metalogue flowing on the abstract level while Daddy is trying to lock concepts into a preordained set of ideas and values. Staying true to the metastructure of the essay, the question itself is never resolved—the ultimate muddle.

### Enter video artist Gary Hill.

Over the past years, Gary Hill's work has been characterized by astute, richly layered ideas and a deceptive technique, almost a legerdemain, that mimics high technology while subverting it. These strongly embraced qualities can be seen in such videotapes as *Videograms* (1981), *Happenstance* (1983), and *Primarily Speaking* (1983). For the occasion of Hill's video, *Why Do Things Get in a Muddle? (Come on Petunia)*, the artist has departed from the authorship of the text, and has decided to let Gregory Bateson and, just as importantly, Charles Dodgson (a.k.a. Lewis Carroll) speak for him. It is quite difficult to describe Hill's tape to the uninitiated. However, a short synopsis is in order.

Hill and two performers, Katherine Anastasia and Charles Stein, have created a metatape within a metalogue. In *Why Do Things Get in a Muddle? (Come on Petunia)*, Anastasia assumes the role of the daughter, but for this tape her name is changed from Cathy (Bateson) to Alice (of *Through the Looking Glass* by Lewis Carroll). She is dressed exactly like the Alice we remember from the original illustrations by John Tenniel in both *Alice's Adventures in Wonderland* and *Through the Looking Glass*—apron and all. Stein assumes the role of Bateson/Daddy—a scholarly, pensive, near-pedantic type, who smokes a pipe and reads at his desk. He is at home in the world of ideas (and so, it appears, is his daughter), but he is about to be taken on a journey, along with the tape's audience, to a place where nonsense and the logic of a child (and Alice, in particular) rule, a place where front is back, left is right, one is many, and up is down—sometimes. Daddy never leaves his own frame of reference, but he sees the world as his daughter sees it—through the looking glass.

Specifically, both Anastasia and Stein slip into talking and moving backward, mostly in real time. The tape is then played backward to create forward speech and motion. The effect is mesmerizing. The language sounds like pidgin Swedish in English. The movement gives the impression that the motion of the tape is slowed down. We are in real time, but in dream time as well. The tape was edited back to front, the last sequences first, all backward, and then a reverse copy was made. This tape slowly becomes a meditation on the blown mind, on both the technical and conceptual/contextual levels.

The tape begins with a hazy, slow-motion pan of some Alice artifacts, including a wooden representation of Tweedledee and Tweedledum. We hear the voice of Hill speaking backward/forward, saying, "I know what you're thinking about, but it ain't so, no how. Contrariwise, if it was so, it might be; and if it were so it would be; but as it isn't it ain't. That's logic." Here we are introduced to an inversion/perversion of Bertrand Russell's "Theory of Logical Types." An example of this theory is that one cannot say, "This sentence is false," because it becomes a degenerate tautological statement. Carroll/Dodgson, himself

a mathematician, dealt with the same issues and problems as Russell, but treated them differently. He used nonsense to point out the co(s)mic problem of finding truth in the absolute—another name for science.

At this juncture in the tape, the performers are speaking forwards, with a bit of backwards thrown in for confusion and alienation. In fact, Stein is reading (on camera) from a copy of *Steps to an Ecology of Mind*, in the deadest possible deadpan. Anastasia, by contrast, although reading her lines from cards off camera, revels in the performance aspect of the activity she has undertaken. She is a thirty-year-old woman acting the part of a little girl, and somehow she pulls it off. Perhaps it is the strong contrast with Stein, who, when reading from Bateson early in the tape, offers a prime example of what literary critic Denis Donoghue in his book on cultural theory, *Ferocious Alphabets,* calls

## graphireading.

The words are just that—words, devoid of personality, words without a speaker. Anastasia, on the other hand, comes across as a strong example of what Donoghue has called

## epireading,

where all literature must have a voice and a speaker behind it. Anastasia is interpreting Cathy Bateson through Alice through Anastasia. Stein is reading Bateson without the voice of Stein or Bateson. Perhaps the key here is that Carroll's work is considered literature, while Bateson's work is considered information. Literature is more prone to voicing. Information is devoid of the personal voice. (I tend to look at the metalogues as works of art rather than information.) I must say that Stein's reading or graphic reading is a constant reminder of Bateson's (and Stein's?) rootedness in what appears to be a static perception of reality. Later in the tape, Stein loosens up as his Bateson/Daddy character becomes exasperated with Alice's questions. Anastasia maintains the Alice persona throughout the tape, never lapsing into a character without a voice.

Little by little, the backwards action begins to take over the tape. When Alice talks about keeping her shelf tidy, she is talking backward/forward (remember: talking backward played back backward = forward). When she says the word "shelf," the tape enters into a self-referencing mode for several sequences, demonstrating what Hill has termed an "acoustic palindrome." Alice says, "Here on the end of this shelf/flesh/shelf/flesh," as her hand opens and closes. This happens later in the tape when Daddy's physical/psychical position is totally disoriented by the use of a camera-rotation device, made especially for this tape, so that left, right, up and down, backward and forward become part of one process.

The central issue of the metalogue is trying to ascertain how titles in a movie ("Come on Petunia") are put together "by the movie people" in order to be read by the audience. Alice points out that "Come on Petunia" could be rearranged to read "Once Upon a Time." Here Hill takes an interesting liberty with the Bateson text. Originally Bateson and Cathy are

**Gary Hill**, Phonetic cue cards for the production of *Why Do Things Get in a Muddle? (Come on Petunia)*, 1984 discussing a movie title, *Donald*. Obviously the use of "Come on Petunia/Once Upon a Time" lends itself more to the Alice fantasy than the Batesonian "Donald/Old Dan."

Alice has no problem with the interchange of "Come on Petunia" for "Once Upon a Time," but Bateson corrects this "misconception." He cannot accept that things can be "tidy" in their muddleness. He refers to things that "only happen in the movies," and could not occur in nature. Here a conversation ensues about making backward motion in film appear to be forward. When Alice asks why the camera in the movies has to be upside-down (soon after Hill's camera operates upside-down), Daddy says that he won't deal with that question. He says this is another question entirely, not the original question about mixedness and muddleness.

It is quite telling that Bateson has chosen to include this aspect of the metalogue. Bateson is perhaps best known for the development of the Double Bind Theory of Schizophrenia. Here his own child, Cathy/Alice, asks him to explain something that she doesn't understand (the camera position). He deflects the question, but not before his child responds by saying,

**"Daddy, you've got to answer the question another day. Don't forget! You won't forget, will you, Daddy? Because I might not remember. Please, Daddy."**

Daddy responds, "Okay, but another day. Now, where were we?" Interestingly enough, in 1949 Bateson, as part of the research team at the Langley-Porter Clinic in California, made a film illustrating that the minor patterns of familial interchange are the major sources of mental illness (rather than childhood traumata, which was the prevailing wisdom). I am sure that Bateson has intentionally kept his pleading/deflecting sequence in the metalogue to illustrate this concept. This is not to say that this pattern created serious illness, but rather to demonstrate the ease with which any conversation can lapse into a schizoid scenario.

I should touch on the *Through the Looking Glass* symbology briefly. First, the set constructed for this tape makes Alice a very large figure, surrounded by minuscule furniture and everyday objects. Daddy, on the other hand, is in perfect proportion to his familiar environment. When Alice looks at Daddy she is often focusing on a mirror image of him. When she makes a declarative statement, such as when she talks about how the place for her paint box should be considered "tidy," she says "only one place," and we perceive one finger go up, one digit, the number one. However, at the same time we see a mirror image of her finger, thus producing the image of two fingers and the introduction of more than one place for her paints (or anything else).

The concept of "tidy" is one of the first ideas introduced by Carroll when Alice falls through the looking glass into a room with a warm fireplace (just like Hill's set) and a chessboard (just like Hill's set). Because of the asymmetric positions of the king and queen on a chessboard, the pieces are mirror images of each other when the board is first set up to play. The moves on Hill's chessboard are some of the moves from *Through the Looking Glass.* Also, Carroll/Dodgson makes quite a few allusions to corkscrews—a helix. In the *Muddle* tape, Hill has replaced this helix with another one—the gyroscope. The gyroscope will always move in the same way, no matter what the earth's rotation might be, so it is not affected by earthly considerations. A lot of care has been exercised by Gary Hill to make this set both commonplace and magical.

The Victorian critic and historian G. K. Chesterton wrote an essay called "A Defense of Nonsense" in 1901, the year Bateson was born. Chesterton states that

## "nonsense is a way of looking at existence that is akin to religious humility and wonder."

How times have changed. It is to Hill's credit that he has brought back this sense of wonder and inspiration to a medium that often relies on science-fair technology to create effect.

The introduction of *Through the Looking Glass* to the Bateson text is not so capricious as it might appear. Bateson grew up in England. His father was a well-known biologist, William Bateson, who coined the term "genetics." *Through the Looking Glass* was published in 1896, only five years before Gregory Bateson's birth. There is no doubt that Bateson encountered the work of Lewis Carroll as a child, and he makes mention of Carroll in his later life as an influence on his perception. Specifically, he refers to Carroll's sense of play and nonsense in discussing Carroll's stand against evolution as exemplified in *Through the Looking Glass.*

In an interview that Stewart Brand conducted with Bateson for *Harper*'s, Bateson cited Carroll's concept of the "Bread and Butterfly" in *Through the Looking Glass* as an early allusion to the "double bind." The "Bread and Butterfly" has wings of bread and butter and a head made of a lump of sugar. Alice says, "What does it live on?" The answer is, "Weak tea with cream in it." Alice immediately realizes that its head will dissolve in its food, but if it gets no food, it will also die (so says the gnat). So the "Bread and Butterfly" dies because either it can't get food or because its head dissolves in its source of nourishment. This is the double bind in classic form. In Hill's tape (and Bateson's metalogue), the logic of Daddy can either kill the intuition of the child or not answer her question. The double bind again.

Finally, *Why Do Things Get in a Muddle? (Come on Petunia)* asks two questions—one from Bateson, one from Carroll. Before going to bed, Alice asks Daddy, "Why do grownups have wars, instead of fighting the way children do?" Daddy refuses to answer the question, and leaves yet another question unanswered. The question from *Through the Looking Glass* forms the last words in the tape. While Daddy is playing the accordion, one of the very few instruments that has the same intonation when played backward or forward, Alice asks, "Where does the light go when you blow the candle out?" This question is also answered, both by Bateson and the audience—there is no reply at all.

If we look at these two questions as "anti-statements," the first being an antiwar state-ment, the second being an antimatter statement, an interesting proposition is raised. If we see Hill's tape as a mirror, a looking glass, Alice's question about grownups fighting wars destroys the metaphor of logic so prevalent in "adult" thinking. Is it logical to bring our-selves to the brink of extinction? Alice knows the answer to that one, and so do we.

The second question is more of a *koan*. Again employing the mirror that Hill's work holds up to us, we are able to think of light as matter, and the lack of it as antimatter. Parti-cles and antiparticles have been shown in the laboratory to be the mirror image of forms of the same structure. Thus, light and antilight would explode on contact, which would be the case with any meeting of matter and antimatter. Our nuclear obsession can theoreti-cally go beyond fusion and fission, in which only a small amount of mass is converted into energy. We may be leading ourselves down the road to the ultimate nuclear power on the other side of the looking glass. Will Alice be there? Will anti-Alice be there?

Steve Kolpan is an author and professor of wine studies and gastronomy at the Culinary Institute of America, Hyde Park, New York. His books include *Exploring Wine* and, forthcoming, *Wines of Niebaum-Coppola: A Sense of Place*.

71

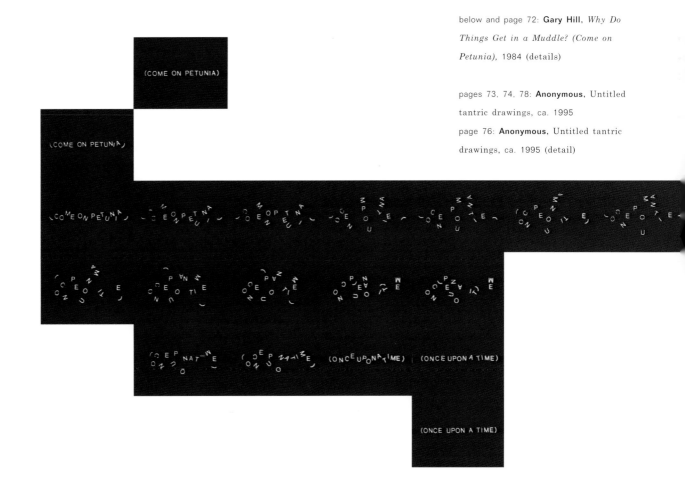

below and page 72: **Gary Hill**, *Why Do Things Get in a Muddle? (Come on Petunia)*, 1984 (details)

pages 73, 74, 78: **Anonymous**, Untitled tantric drawings, ca. 1995
page 76: **Anonymous**, Untitled tantric drawings, ca. 1995 (detail)

# ascension

Franck André Jamme

L'appliquée répète sans cesse ses pensées et ses gestes. Pose ses pieds, ses pierres, avec exactitude. L'un après l'autre, l'une après l'autre, à un cil près.

**LA PIERRE NOIRE DU CHAOS DU MONDE**
**LA PIERRE ROUGE DE L'ENERGIE DU MONDE**
**LA PIERRE BLANCHE DE L'ESSENCE DU MONDE**

Tout retourné, bien sûr, pour l'œil:

**LA PIERRE BLANCHE DE L'ESSENCE DU MONDE**
**LA PIERRE ROUGE DE L'ENERGIE DU MONDE**
**LA PIERRE NOIRE DU CHAOS DU MONDE**

Et elle bâtit ainsi les marches mêmes qu'elle monte. Avec sobriété et majesté. Uniquement vêtue de son long manteau de confusion, de force et d'infini. Si long, si rassemblant. Terre, vie, ciel.

Même si chaque fois, quand elle s'élève, quand elle monte encore, on peut apercevoir les lignes pures de ses chevilles. Pures et changeant de monde, chaque fois. Jusqu'au sommet. Délire, présence, lumière.

Alors, arrivée là-haut, elle se penche. Elle lance maintenant des mots qui ont l'air sans conséquence. Même si l'ascension a été rude, à construire et à habiter. Juste l'air:

"Il suffit de monter, vous savez, ce n'est pas si difficile. Mais sans jamais oublier la marche que l'on quitte. Et sans tension non plus trop appuyée vers la prochaine. D'une façon presque distraite, presque insouciante. Sans y penser. Pas de poids, pas de possession."

# ascension

Franck André Jamme

(trans. Carolyn West with E. Alex Pierce)

The careful one repeats unceasingly her thoughts and gestures. Sets her feet, her stones with exactitude. One step after the other, one stone after the other, fit to an eyelash width.

**BLACK STONE OF THE WORLD'S CHAOS
RED STONE OF THE WORLD'S ENERGY
WHITE STONE OF THE WORLD'S ESSENCE**

All is upside-down, of course, in the eye:

**WHITE STONE OF THE WORLD'S ESSENCE
RED STONE OF THE WORLD'S ENERGY
BLACK STONE OF THE WORLD'S CHAOS**

And like this she builds the very steps she climbs. Soberly and majestically. Clothed only in her long coat of confusion, power, and infinity. So long and so gathered. Earth, life, sky.

Even if each time, when she climbs, when she rises up again, one might glimpse the pure lines of her ankles. Pure and the world changes, each time. Far as the summit. Delirium, presence, light.

Then, arriving at the height, she bends. Now she cries out words that appear without consequence. The same as if the ascension had been harsh, to construct and live in. Just the appearance:

"It's enough to rise up, you know, it isn't difficult. Yet not forgetting the steps you've left behind. And without tension, no longer so intent upon the next one. In a way, almost absent-minded, almost carefree. Without thought. No weight, no possession."

Franck André Jamme's recent books are *Un diamant sans étonnement* and *Question*. He was a consulting curator, focusing on contemporary Indian art, for the groundbreaking 1989 exhibition *Magicians of the Earth* at the Centre Georges Pompidou in Paris.

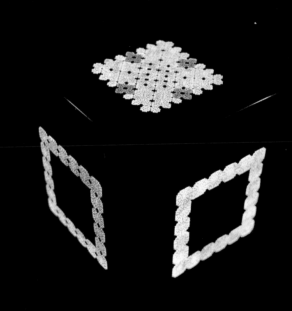

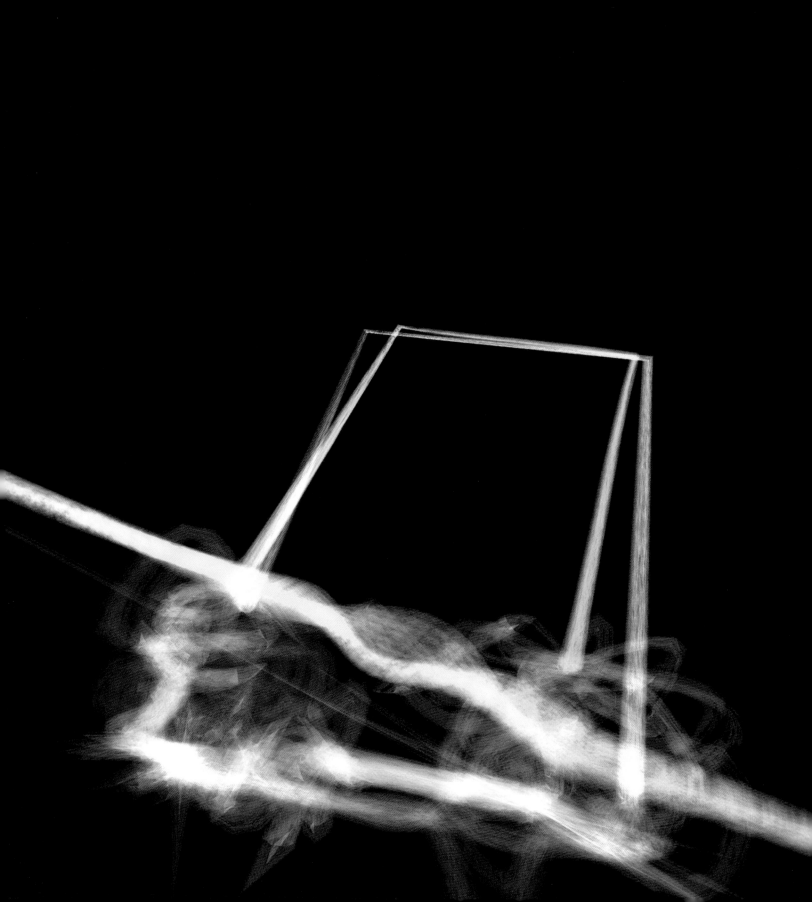

Pascale Wiedemann, *Heimlich,* 1996

opposite: **Paul Kaiser and Shelley Eshkar,**
*If by Chance,* 1999 (detail)
page 79: **Rosie Lee Tompkins,** Untitled
(quilted by Willia Ette Graham), 1986
(detail)
page 80: **Cristabel Davé,** Untitled, ca. 1995
(detail)
page 81: **La Monte Young and Marian
Zazeela,** *Music and Light Box,* 1967–68
page 85: **Douglas Gordon,** *30 Seconds Text,*
1996

## 30 seconds text.

In 1905 an experiment was performed in France where a doctor tried to communicate with a condemned man's severed head immediately after the guillotine execution.

"Immediately after the decapitation, the condemned man's eyelids and lips contracted for 5 or 6 seconds...I waited a few seconds and the contractions ceased, the face relaxed, the eyelids closed half-way over the eyeballs so that only the whites of the eyes were visible, exactly like dying or newly deceased people.

At that moment I shouted "Languille" in a loud voice, and I saw that his eyes opened slowly and without twitching, the movements were distinct and clear, the look was not dull and empty, the eyes which were fully alive were indisputably looking at me. After a few seconds, the eyelids closed again, slowly and steadily.

I addressed him again. Once more, the eyelids were raised slowly, without contractions, and two undoubtedly alive eyes looked at me attentively with an expression even more piercing than the first time. Then the eyes shut once again. I made a third attempt. No reaction. The whole episode lasted between twenty-five and thirty seconds."

...on average, it should take between twenty-five and thirty seconds to read the above text.

*Notes on the experiment between Dr. Baurieux and the criminal Languille (Montpellier, 1905) taken from the Archives d'Anthropologie Criminelle.*

# bill viola, *pneuma,* 1994

D. L. Pughe

> (La porte basse c'est une bague ... où la gaze
> Passe. ... Tout meurt, tout rit dans la gorge qui jase ...
> L'oiseau boit sur ta bouche et tu ne peux le voir ...
> Viens plus bas, parle bas ... Le noir n'est pas si noir ...)

> (The low door is a ring ... where gauze filters. ...
> All dies away, laughs, in the babbling throat ...
> The bird sips from your mouth, you cannot see it ...
> Come lower, speak low ... The dark is not so dark ...)

—Paul Valéry, "La Jeune Parque"

**There is a deep, blurry realm of consciousness where images slowly form,
begin to resemble something you know, then sink back into your unconscious.** In *Pneuma*, 1994. Bill Viola pulls you in and up, then back and forth, out,
away, and gone. His swirling abstract images shift and change, grow lighter and darker,
move softly and slowly enough that they don't invite any fear. You know they are something, but it is comforting to feel your way along through a dark that is not so very
dark. The area just beyond what is "imaginable" is, after all, what Immanuel Kant called
"the sublime." Blurry, cloud-like processions give way to glowing auras, the mirage of a
tower shimmers into view. becomes a lethargic, gray-flecked tornado that gracefully
blows into chaff. But nothing is really quite what it seems. A lumbering procession of
cascading comets can sharpen for an instant. revealing daisies blowing on a field.
Common things appear blurred in order to escape the banal images in which they are
usually trapped.

Viola's vision echoes the way Friedrich Nietzsche pulled apart many satisfied notions of
perspective over a century ago. All modes of viewing the world became possible, destroy-
ing the idea of one masterful or truthful vantage point on the world. Each of us, at any
instant, experiences only a fragmentary point of view, one among multitudes, and
Nietzsche encouraged us to develop "more eyes" with which to observe the world.[1] While
such open-ended observation may be disorienting, Nietzsche claimed it was nothing new:

> **"Are we not plunging continually?
> Backward, sideward, forward, in all directions?
> Is there still any up or down? Are we not straying
> as through an infinite nothing?"[2]**

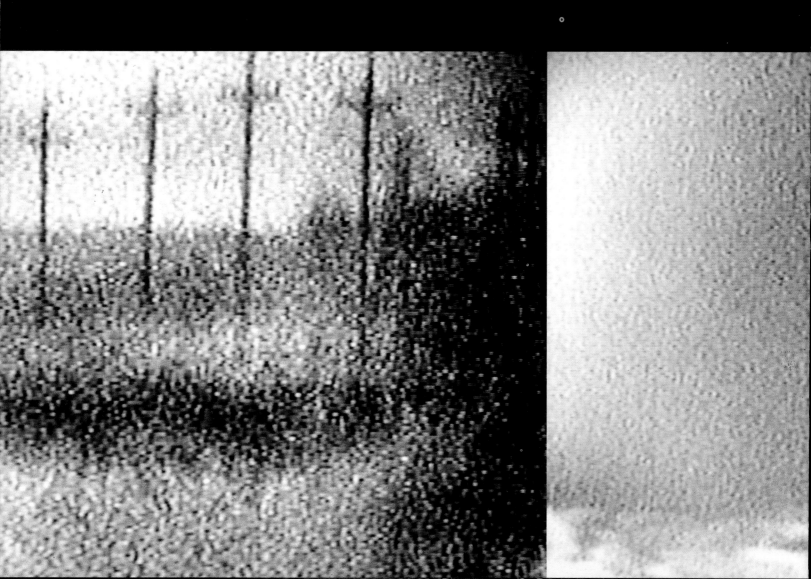

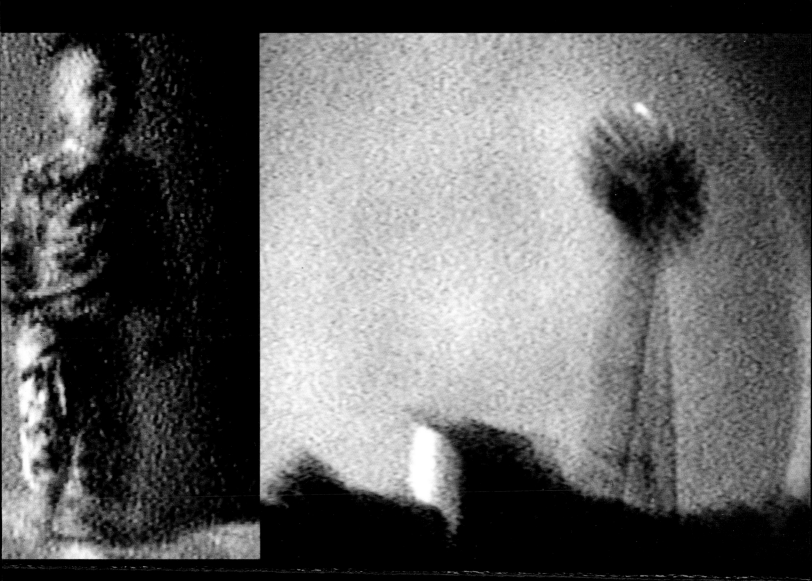

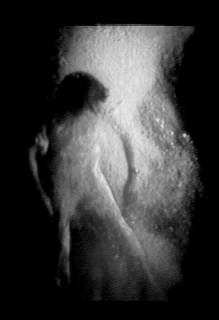
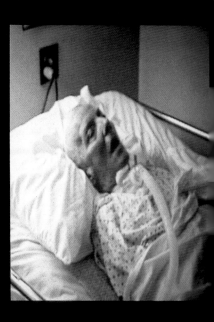

clockwise: **Bill Viola**, *Nantes Triptych*, 1992

*The Reflecting Pool*, 1977–79

*The Sleepers*, 1992

Nietzsche's "perspectivism" also meant that well-worn perspective devices—Gothic flattened two-dimensionality, Renaissance three-dimensional vanishing points, undulating haptic Baroque physicality, and Non-Euclidean hyperbolic space—could now somehow be employed all at once.

Viola enjoys exploring these possibilities, playing mostly with our ideas of depth—blurriness is sometimes associated with speed, but more often with evocations of distance. Leonardo da Vinci had set the standard with his method for "atmospheric perspective" in which objects in the landscape were "less carefully finished as they are farther away."[3] In Viola's landscapes, a series of "unfinished" overlapping hills pulls occasionally into sharper focus—but by a step *backward* instead of forward, revealing the contours of a nude torso. Dark branches on a gray autumn sky are, in fact, hairs lightly touching a cheek.

**The extreme close-up of intimate vision
has the same grainy, unfinished quality as that of distance, and perhaps,
for Viola, is the way we most often see the people we love:
their features melting into an essential idea we hold of them.**

Impressionism, in its revolutionary heyday, was also an explosive perspective device. Impressionists were the first to be accused of pulling da Vinci's background technique into the foreground: messy, unfinished spatters were allowed to stand for a final whole. Viola's vision suggests the same pointillism of the gray and edgeless elegance of Seurat's drawings or Monet's winter paintings, which appear to have been done through a veil of heavy snow. What Viola makes us consider is the inherent beauty in seeing the world this way, unimproved by spectacles, or color, or sharply defined meaning.

Aqueous perspective had preoccupied Viola in earlier works, beginning with *The Reflecting Pool*, 1977–79; again in his faces at the bottom of liquid-filled barrels in *The Sleepers* in 1992; and with the suspended, floating figure in *Nantes Triptych* of 1992. He enjoys the distortions we experience underwater. He is also constantly drawn to what he calls "gestures of thought," and in *Pneuma* he dives into the perspective within the "stream of consciousness" itself. William James had noted that this "stream" has a "halo of relations," a fringe surrounding one "big, blooming buzzing Confusion."[4] Dancing on this threshold, swimming in and out of horizons of awareness, is apparently Viola's favorite approach. Grainy smudges of dust collect, swirl and swarm, shiver like a column of smoke, and occasionally cascade like a meteor shower. And in the shift from one slowly focused image to another, a blank intermission of calm occurs, a resting place with filtered light fluctuating on the dark screen behind shut eyes.

As flecks and shapes and movement return, they begin the way that memories rise, haunt us for a moment, then slip away. A boy twists on a mattress in laughter. A child steps into the street, only to evaporate in silence. A wandering hand carrying a lantern glows for a moment, then flickers and fades from view. It is the stuff of dreams, but also the images that buzz and bloom as we think, speak, remember. It is "the free water of consciousness": "come lower, speak low," images form, ripen into drops, fall into a rippling stream.

D. L. Pughe is currently exploring the metaphors used in abstraction in both science and art, and has recently completed a book, *The Space Between Us: Empathy and Understanding*.

1      Friedrich Nietzsche, *The Genealogy of Morals*, trans. Walter Kaufmann and R. J. Hollingdale (New York: Random House, Vintage Books, 1969), 119.

2      Friedrich Nietzsche, *The Gay Science*, trans. Walter Kaufmann and R. J. Hollingdale (New York: Random House, Vintage Books, 1974), 181.

3      William Dunning, *Changing Images of Pictorial Space* (Syracuse: Syracuse University Press, 1991), 44.

4      William James, *Writings 1879–1899* (New York: The Library of America, 1992), 165.

# proust / douglas / edis o n :
# "...something  dark    inde e d ... "

Mark Bartlett

But sometimes...it is necessary to make holes, to introduce voids and white spaces, to rarify the image, by suppressing many things that have been added to make us believe that we are seeing everything. It is necessary to make a division or make emptiness in order to find the whole again.[1]

Do you realize how simple a desire is? Sleeping is a desire. Walking is a desire. Listening to music, or making music, or writing, are desires. A spring, a winter are desire. Old age also is a desire. Even death. Desire never needs interpreting, it is it which experiments.[2]

Consciousness, awareness, is a great capacity, but it is not made for solutions or for interpretations. It is when consciousness has abandoned solutions and interpretations that it conquers its light, its gestures, its sounds, and its decisive transformation.[3]

Remembrance is not structured like a cathedral or a garment; it is built like a web.[4]

Gilles Deleuze

**Stan Douglas's film loop installation,** *Overture,* **1986, begins with what** is **Deleuze called a type of division or emptiness that actually articulates a** s **whole.** Paradoxically, this is a whole full of voids and white spaces suppressing many things. *Overture*'s "beginning" is itself such a paradox. It is a double opening formed by a s caesura, in which the viewer is placed always between two elements of the film—between ns scenes from Edison's early train films,[5] and the reordered fragments from the "Overture" to o: Proust's monumental work, *Remembrance of Things Past.*

Our experience of *Overture* "begins" randomly somewhere within the work's endless loop as it cycles through seven-minute periods. We enter the room at a chance moment that determines our experience of the installation, thereby tying the initial conditions upon which we base our interpretation to that place in the loop. We might enter the room at the moment when the film compresses silence and darkness, a Cagean silence that is a vigorous sound,[6] and the darkness that Proust envisioned inhabiting the times of both sleep and waking. In this way, splicing sight and sound, we enter the piece through its caesura and bodily enact, or produce, its text in the triple dimensions of site/citation/sight, which the title sets collectively in motion. Or again, *Overture* could open for us the image of the Canadian Rockies viewed from the vantage of an invisible train conductor, or from the "eye" of the invisible locomotive engine itself. This moment could be silent or accompanied by an amateur, male voice reading passages from the Proust "Overture." Both this text, and the black-and-white, silent films suggest another form of opening; our experience is situated historically at the opening of the twentieth century—textually, sometime between

pages 93, 94, 98, 103: **Stan Douglas,** *Overture,* 1986 (details)

1908, when Proust begins to write *Remembrance,* and 1914, when its first volume is published in France; visually, sometime between 1899 and 1901, when the films were originally shot by the Edison Film Company.

So what was deceptively simple at first experience quickly becomes a complex structure, organized by slight divisions of difference that slowly become apparent to the careful observer, and function to *seduce* the viewer to further investigation. The allusion to platonic eros here is elemental yet divergent. For while the film provokes us to question, it refuses platonic answers, keeping the questions always in suspense, or keeping the circuit of knowledge moving in a restless pursuit of itself. The object of knowledge, produced through desire, is kept in circulation, and therefore, paradoxically, never becomes objectified, never assumes its apparent form or content. "Desire never needs interpreting, it is it which experiments." Nor is Douglas interested in maintaining the old notion of beauty leading to truth. The degenerated and overexposed film quality and the amateur voice resist norms of beauty, shading instead toward indiscernibility. But this indiscernibility has a shape that causes questions to emerge in a series of pairs from the doubling of the opening. Are the train-tunnel sequences all the same?/How has the text been edited? What is the time of the film footage?/What is the time of the text? What is the place of the film?/What is the place of the text? Where is the camera located?/Where is the writer located? Is it a train view?/Or is it a train conductor view? So while the allusions to the allegories of eros and the cave are unavoidable, the textual/cinematic cave is one of a very different order. Both platonic allusions are operative components of the text of references that *Overture* draws into its kaleidoscopic web.[7]

Neither cathedral nor garment, the installation is constructed like a web, with a highly specified infrastructure. The filmic text is a montage of three train-tunnel landscape sequences of equal duration, which repeat without variation. The film's structure consists of train-tunnel landscapes 1-2-3, 1'-2'-3', where the ['] signifies the same visual content but a different voice-over text. Train-tunnel landscape 1 is continuous, while tunnel-train landscapes 2-3 (and 2'-3') are each composites of two different films, structured so that the tunnel the train leaves is on a different track in a different film from the one it enters. This is perceptible, but only with careful viewing. The voice-over fused with landscape 1 is a continuous passage from the Proust "Overture," the first line from paragraph four. However, this voice-over does not repeat. Nor are the voice-overs for landscapes 2-3, 1'-2'-3' continuous. These discontinuous texts are complex amalgamations of sentences and sentence fragments that appear to be semantically coherent, and to a great extent are, in fact, coherent. The conflation of text and the movement-image operate in tandem to make them seem continuous even when they are not.

The central philosophical question we are prompted to ask is: what type of overture is *Overture? Overture* appears in the form of concentric circles made discontinuous through the tightly structured splice of tape and text, in the edits that shift almost imperceptibly from image to image and from signification to signification, and in the definitional slippage at the etymological origin of the title: in the cut between *opertura* and *apertura,* between overture and aperture. The work not only takes the form of montage in multiple senses, but is *about being montage,* articulating multiple significations/perceptions. Douglas's intent is to present

both a model of consciousness and a performative context in which consciousness is articulated and *literally* constructed in a determinate way. The geometry of the circle operates in
*Overture* like a grid that is opposed by nongrid elements; it is cross-cut by other fields of
force, other vectors of signification. In their critique of the x-y coordinate system, or grid,
Deleuze and Guatarri comment:

97

> **Opposed to the punctual system (the grid) are linear, or rather multilinear, systems.**
> **Free the line, free the diagonal: every musician or painter has this intention.**
> **One elaborates a punctual system or a didactic representation,**
> **but with the aim of making it snap, of sending a tremor through it.**
> **A punctual system is most interesting when there is a musician, painter, writer,**
> **philosopher to oppose it, who even fabricates it in order to oppose it,**
> **like a springboard to jump from. History is made only by those who oppose history**
> **(not by those who insert themselves into it, or even reshape it).**[8]

*Overture* is a montage of conceptual components in that it oscillates between the two discursive domains of overture and aperture (orifice, aurality, visuality, prelude, etc.) and in the
way that it oscillates between the discursive and the highly specific form of this discursive's
phenomenal embodiment (degenerated film image, train perspective, slight camera pan,
"unprofessional" sounding voice-over, voice always beginning in midspeech, etc.). Douglas
has carefully conflated the visual and the aural, treating them as a single combinatorial information unit that is serially interrupted by units of another, similarly constructed conflation of
darkness and silence. But the work also operates as montage by assuming a musical form
on the one hand—an overture is an orchestral piece written usually as a single movement in
sonata form, with an exposition, a development, and a recapitulation (train-tunnel sequences
1-2-3/1'-2'-3')—and, on the other hand, by appropriating it as the literary device used by
Proust as the "opening" of *Swann's Way*—signaling a third conflation, that of literature and
music. The result is that *Overture* assumes the form of multilinear montage in which

> **...everything happens at once: the line breaks free of the point as origin;**
> **the diagonal breaks free of the vertical and the horizontal as coordinates;**
> **and the transversal breaks free of the diagonal**
> **as a localizable connection between two points.**
> **In short, a block-line passes amid sounds and propels itself**
> **by its own nonlocalizable middle.**[9]

The film is multilinear montage in another sense as well; it operates through the process of
condensation that Freud described in *Interpretation of Dreams*. Dreams are overdeter-
mined, meaning that multiple strands of signification are compressed into seemingly insignificant details, like linguistic or imagistic puns, or such slight variations as the substitution of
an 'a' for an 'o.' Hence, we must activate the double reading of both aperture and overture,
opening and closing signification like sleeping and waking, like entering and leaving the train
tunnels, like watching the train passages and hearing the Proust passages simultaneously.
*Overture* should be interpreted as enacting a dream-state articulated by the double sense
of "passage" here iterated, and as creating an occasion for the viewer not only to passively

witness someone else's dream but, if he or she allows, actually to become immersed in and come literally to dream Douglas's *Overture*, and therefore to introject and remember something of the collective social history of the twentieth century of which we are late subjects.

This brings us to another conflation; to the consideration of a late-twentieth-century form of subjectivity that can only be named Proust/Douglas/Edison. It is with this triple nomination—each with its own internal circuits of signification running on parallel tracks that open the distance in which other combinatorial meanings can circulate—that the viewer identifies, and introjects, as a complex unit. I dream the dream of Proust/Douglas/Edison and it *circulates as my consciousness* within the frame of the consciousness he/they construct. The claim of Proust/Douglas/Edison is that this is a *literal* process, a material process, not a representational process. *Overture* has nothing to do with an "out there." It has to do only with the self-referential circuits it constructs and connects through the vectors of dream, desire, and interpretation.

Proust himself corroborates this:

> **A book is the product of a different self from the one we manifest in our habits,**
>
> **in society, in our vices. If we mean to try to understand this self**
>
> **it is only in our inmost depths, by endeavoring to reconstruct it there,**
>
> **that the quest can be achieved.**[10]

Proust's view is that *Remembrance* is the location of a literal reconstruction of self, and it is with this reconstruction that Douglas engages. He reconstructs Proust's text-self, just as he reconstructs Edison's image-self, and thereby inserts himself in the caesura between them. The back-slashes of Proust/Douglas/Edison signify the edit, the cut, the splice that make film and subjectivity much more than mere analogs of one another. *Overture* must be taken to be a textual/cinematic model of the moment of consciousness becoming conscious. We are not here operating in the realm of metaphor or representation, but in the realm of literality. Proust/Douglas/Edison is a literal, material location of consciousness within the discursive formation of *Overture*'s double and doubling structure.

**But let's look for a moment deeper into the complex textual aspects of** *Overture*. The first transcription from Douglas's film is faithful to Proust's text in that it does not amalgamate different sentences and/or sentence fragments; however, it is the only text that doesn't.

Landscape I—train-tunnel/text "passage" 1

1    I would fall asleep again, and thereafter would reawaken for short snatches only, just long enough to hear the regular creaking of the wainscot, or to open my eyes to stare at the shifting kaleidoscope of the darkness, to savour, in a momentary glimmer of consciousness, the sleep which lay heavy upon the furniture, the room, the whole of which I formed but an insignificant part and whose insensibility I should very soon return to share. [p. 4][11]

Within the structure of Douglas's work, the text can only "begin" *in media res*. Its content, however, mirrors the dark/light, sound/silence, on/off structure of *Overture*. Proust describes a state between waking and sleeping, between hearing ("the creaking of the wainscot") and seeing ("the shifting kaleidoscope of the darkness"), between subjectivity and objectivity ("sleep which lay heavy upon the furniture"), between place and nonplace ("whose insensibility I should very soon return to share"). Proust's text is a model of memory at the moment of waking in the same way that Douglas's *Overture* is a model of consciousness becoming conscious. Multilinear montage is both an aesthetic form and the form that consciousness itself takes.

The synthetic aesthetic register in which Douglas's work must be situated is expressed in another way by Deleuze in *Cinema I:*

> **First, while the movement-image and its sensory-motor signs were
> in a relationship only with an indirect image of time (dependent on montage),
> the pure optical and sound image, its opsigns and sonsigns,
> are directly connected to a time-image which has subordinated movement.
> It is this reversal which means that time is no longer the measure of movement
> but movement is the perspective of time: it constitutes a whole cinema of time,
> with a new conception and new forms of montage.
> In the second place, at the same time as the eye takes up a clairvoyant function,
> the sound as well as visual elements of the image enter into internal relations
> which means that the whole image has to be "read," no less than seen,
> readable as well as visible. For the eye of the seer as of the soothsayer,
> it is the "literalness" of the perceptible world which constitutes it
> like a good book.**[12]

Here, Deleuze brings together much of the previous discussion. Movement is subordinated to the time-image and its perspective that gives movement its particular experiential sensation (the movement of the train with all its phenomenal specificity). For Proust/Douglas/Edison, if time is no longer a scale of measurement, then pure duration as an abstract magnitude has been re-embodied in a physical dimension and reshaped by coordinates such as the rhythms of sleeping and waking of Proust/Douglas's text or Douglas/Edison's train-tunnel oscillations. Each is doubly inscribed in the figure of the "turn of the century," and in the figure of the toy/adult train familiar to every child/adult. The train of *Overture* is a condensation of both the child train of imagination's becoming and the adult train of industrialization—but this train is fitted with a cinematic prosthesis that constructs consciousness as an oscillation between the camera operator/train conductor and the train. It is this structure of movement that gives time its perspectives—which must be understood in terms of Nietzsche's noninertial and multiplicitous perspectivism.[13] The dominance of an adult time sensibility is challenged by Proust's description of the world of an eight-year-old boy, forming one temporal perspective, while the historical dimension of the turn of the century forms another. Douglas's appropriation of both the Edison film and the Proust text in 1986 forms yet another temporal perspective, opening what Hegel described as the past in the depths of the present.

Because the time-image is a form of cognition comprised of internal relations with its own layered complexities, the "literalness" of the "perceptible world" is inextricably textual/visual; Douglas's film as a "whole image" must be "readable as well as visible" if the different temporalities are to become knowable. Hence, it is the literalness of the perceptible world that makes the work readable like a good book, in the same way that Proust reconstructs the self in the literality of writing a book. It is the temporal reflexivity of those processes, of reading as much as seeing, of collapsing seer and soothsayer, that constitutes a new form of montage.

Landscape II—train-tunnel/text "passage" 2

2    ...[when] I had put out my candle, my eyes would close so quickly that I had not even time to say
     to myself: "I'm Falling asleep." And half an hour later the thought that it was time to go to sleep
     would awaken me; I would make as if to put away the book, which I imagined was still in my
     hands, and to blow out the light. ...[p. 3]

2a   My body, still too heavy with sleep to move, would endeavor to construe from the pattern of its
     tiredness the position of its various limbs, in order to deduce therefrom the direction of the wall,
     the location of the furniture, to piece together and give a name to the house in which it lay. [p. 6]

Douglas's installation constitutes a new form of multilinear montage in its use of circularity as a closed but unbounded system, without beginning or end. Formally, it is an edge in the sense of circumference, just as visually the aperture of the camera frames an edge that constricts what can be seen of the narrow cliff edge skirted by the train tracks. It is the edge of "the thought...[of going] to sleep [that] would awaken" and of the movement "from the pattern of . . . tiredness" to the pattern of limbs and the room and the whole house. It frames the edge of the deconstructive/hermeneutic "always already."

Landscape III—train-tunnel/text "passage" 3

3    ...at the same time my sight would return and I would be astonished to find myself in a state of
     darkness, pleasant and restful enough for my eyes, but even more, perhaps, for my mind, to which
     it appeared incomprehensible, without a cause, ... [p. 3]

Proust has it differently; what the comma after "cause" elides is the phrase "...something dark indeed..." This darkness, for the mind, is indeed something dark, although for the body, for the eyes, it had been something pleasant and restful. Consciousness, "literally perceptible," is pleasant; consciousness for the mind is something uncaused, incomprehensible, and dark. Before sight returned, the world was visible; the moment sight returns, the world is dark. Douglas takes us directly to the filmic moment in which darkness is dispelled and time is revealed; not any time, but the symbolic liminal edge of the deep night, when all things dark are revealed.

3a   I would strike a match to look at my watch. Nearly midnight. [p. 4]

3b   Certainly I was now well awake. ... [p. 9]

3c   ...my brain, lingering in cogitation over when things had happened and what they had looked like...
     [p. 6]

3d   ...showed me in perspective the deserted countryside through which a traveler is hurrying towards
     the nearby station... [p. 3]

Douglas edits Proust's text as film is edited; Landscape III is comprised of the associative text-frames of five disjunctive jumpcuts that narratively cohere but conceptually disintegrate—the certainty of being awake is undermined by the lingering cogitation; as the brain, in response to "when things had happened and what they had looked like," depicts the traveler, the amodern subject, hurrying from no apparent cause to an entirely undesignated "nearby station." It is a dark image of alienation. *Overture* demonstrates an aesthetic of darkness that keeps all movement shifting.

Landscape IV—train-tunnel/text "passage" 1'

1'   Nearly midnight. The hour when an invalid, who has been obliged to set out on a journey and to sleep in a strange hotel, awakened by a sudden spasm, sees with glad relief a streak of daylight showing under his door. Thank God, it is morning! [p. 4]

1'a   ...he can ring, and someone will come to look after him. The thought of being assuaged gives him strength to endure his pain. He is certain he heard footsteps; they come nearer, and then die away. The ray of light beneath his door is extinguished. It is midnight; someone has just turned down the gas. ... [p. 4]

The literary repetition, "Nearly midnight," links the sleeper/dreamer to the traveler/invalid, shifting from various subjectivities until, in yet another version of the overture form at work, Douglas continues to open us deeper into uncertainty.

Landscape V—train-tunnel/text "passage" 2'

2'   ...and when I awoke in the middle of the night ... [p. 5]

2'a   ...I could not even be sure at first who I was. ... [p. 5]

2'b   For it always happened that when I awoke like this, and my mind struggled in an unsuccessful attempt to discover where I was, everything revolved around me through the darkness; things, places, years. [p. 6]

2'c   These shifting and confused gusts of memory never lasted for more than a few seconds; it often happened that, in my brief spell of uncertainty as to where I was, I did not distinguish the various suppositions of which it was composed any more than, when we watch a horse running, we isolate the successive positions of its body as they appear upon a bioscope. [p. 7]

The "uncertainty as to where I was" is framed by a series of unconnected gusts of ephemeral memory, themselves resisting decomposition within the human sensorium, within perceptual consciousness. Cognitive consciousness, represented by the bioscope, and by the train, is a mechanical form of consciousness that during the twentieth century has become increasingly dominant, and increasingly introjected; and, therefore, more and more closely resembling a consciousness that can only be modeled on variations of human/machine syntheses. The limits of what can be known, of what can be experienced, are very sharply drawn.

Landscape VI—train-tunnel/text "passage" 3'

3'   I lost all sense of the place in which I had gone to sleep. ... [p. 5]

3'a   This impression would persist for some moments after I awoke; it did not offend my reason, but lay

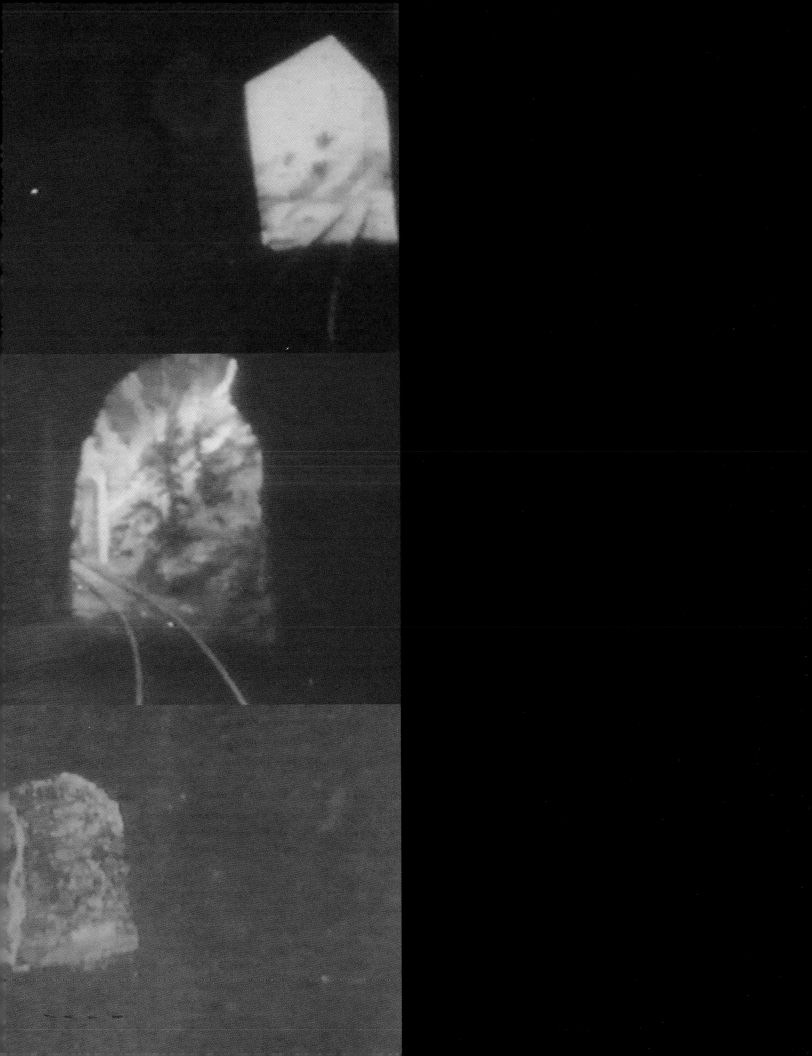

like scales upon my eyes and prevented me [them] from registering the fact that the candle was no longer burning. [p. 3]

3'b  I lay stretched out in bed, my eyes staring upwards, my ears straining, my nostrils flaring, my heart beating... [p. 8]

3'c  ...[finally] the ignorance of the waking moment had, in a flash, if not presented me with a distinct picture, at least persuaded me of the possible presence... [p. 9]

3'd  ...[of a room] in the uncertain light. ... [p. 9]

It is necessary to remember that halfway through, the film returns to its Douglas/Edison visual origin, to its structural visual center, the filmic equivalent of a circle's center, which regulates its sameness—a sameness then decentered by the complex differences of Proust/Douglas's text. The triple subject Proust/Douglas/Edison is embedded in this repetition as the figure of return. That this cinematic subjectivity enters/reenters through the holes and voids and whiteness of the elisions and suppressed texts of difference, implies

> **Finally, the fixity of the camera does not represent the only alternative to movement.**
> **Even when it is mobile, the camera is no longer content sometimes to**
> **follow the characters' movement, sometimes itself to undertake movements**
> **of which they are merely the object, but in every case**
> **it subordinates description of a space to the functions of thought.**
> **This is not the simple distinction between the subjective and the objective,**
> **the real and the imaginary, it is on the contrary their indiscernibility which will**
> **endow the camera with a rich array of functions,**
> **and initiate a new conception of the frame and reframings.**
> **Hitchcock's premonition will come true: a camera-consciousness which would no longer**
> **be defined by the movements it is able to follow or make,**
> **but by the mental connections it is able to enter into.**
> **And it becomes questioning, responding, objecting, provoking,**
> **theorematizing, hypothesizing, experimenting,**
> **in accordance with the open list of logical conjunctions**
> **("or," "therefore," "if,"**
> **"because," "actually,"**
> **"although").[14]**

These mental connections, however, always appear "in the uncertain light." "Consciousness, awareness, is a great capacity, but it is not made for solutions or for interpretations." It is always also the movement of turn/return, of enter/reenter, which nests within our wakefulness, like our diurnal sleep, "...something dark indeed..."

Mark Bartlett is a cultural theorist and associate professor of humanities and sciences and graduate studies at the California College of Arts and Crafts, Oakland and San Francisco, California.

1    Gilles Deleuze, *Cinema I: The Movement Image,* trans. Hugh Tomlinson and Barbara Habberjam (Minnesota: University of Minnesota Press, 1986) excerpted in *The Deleuze Reader,* ed. Constantin V. Boundas (New York: Columbia University Press, 1993), 183.

The work of the French philosopher Gilles Deleuze has been profoundly and widely influential in all cultural circles. Deleuze and his collaborator, Felix Guattari, produced a body of thought rich in new terminology and ideas (body without organs, assemblage, deterritorization, nomad aesthetics, rhizomatics, schizoanalysis, time image, etc.) that many have found both generative and finely tooled enough to make sense of our particularly complex world.

2    Gilles Deleuze with Claire Parnet, *Dialogues,* trans. Hugh Tomlinson and Barbara Habberjam (New York: Columbia University Press, 1987) excerpted in *The Deleuze Reader,* ed. Constantin V. Boundas (New York: Columbia University Press, 1993), 136.

3    Gilles Deleuze, *Superpositions* (Paris: Les Editions de Minuit, 1979) excerpted in *The Deleuze Reader,* ed. Constantin V. Boundas (New York: Columbia University Press, 1993), 22.

4    Deleuze, *Proust et les Signes* (Paris: Presses Université de France, 1975) excerpted in *The Deleuze Reader,* ed. Constantin V. Boundas (New York: Columbia University Press, 1993), 134.

5    Thomas Edison played a very important role in the development of film. Late in the nineteenth century, he adopted French physiologist Étienne Jules Marey's photographic gun and developed the 35mm format with four perforations per frame, which has become the contemporary standard. A decade-long evolution from a one-at-a-time individual viewing experience to the collective viewing experience as we know it today ensued. The train was one of the main subjects of these early films.

6    Primarily a composer and writer, John Cage has had enormous influence on twentieth-century art in every media. Along with Marcel Duchamp, one of his most enduring aesthetic contributions was the use of indeterminism, or chance operations, as a method by which his music compositions and creative texts were composed. His use of silence is characteristic. In many of his works, he integrates periods of silence of various lengths, some relatively long. Cage's point is that music is everywhere, and the silences bring to one's attention the music of the everyday.

7    The discussion of this paragraph refers to the "Allegory of the Cave" in Plato's *Republic.* In the allegory, Plato describes people chained to chairs and facing a wall of a cave on which shadows play. These individuals have never experienced any other world, and so take the shadows as objective knowledge. Behind and above them, however, are lamps before which objects parade and events take place, thereby casting the shadows. Above these objects is the "real world" illuminated by the sun. Plato asserts that those who live only through their senses are like those chained to chairs who live in a world of illusion. For a philosopher, "true" knowledge is based only on an understanding of those things that cause the shadows. In Plato's theory of knowledge, truths are immaterial, universal, and immutable ideas or concepts known only through reason. The sun in the allegory symbolizes the divine source of ideal truth. It is the philosopher's task to lead the cave dwellers from the cave into the sun. The philosopher first seduces acolytes with beauty, which entices them to the higher and more virtuous quest for truth. Beauty, whether the beauty of the shadows or the beauty of people, stimulates desire, or eros. In Douglas's work the visual segments of the film in which the train is in the tunnel are analogous to the cave. The "real world" of the landscape is analogous to the play of shadows. The audiences of films are analogous to those chained to their chairs, and the train conductor and cameraman, with the implied machinery of the train and camera, are analogous to philosophers. Proust's text addresses in part the conflict between knowledge that derives from the body and that which derives from the mind.

8    Deleuze and Guattari, *A Thousand Plateaus: Capitalism and Schizophrenia,* trans. Brian Massumi (Minneapolis: University of Minnesota Press, 1987) excerpted in *The Deleuze Reader,* ed. Constantin V. Boundas (New York: Columbia University Press, 1993), 48.

9    Ibid., 51.

10    Marcel Proust, *Against Sainte-Beuve,* quoted in "Marcel Proust," D. J. Enright, *In Search of Lost Time,* trans. C. K. Scott Moncrieff and Terence Kilmartin, revised by D. J. Enright, vol. 1 (New York: The Modern Library, 1992), viii.

11    Marcel Proust, "Overture" to *Swann's Way,* trans. C. K. Scott Moncrieff and Terence Kilmartin (New York: Vintage Books, 1989). All Landscape quotations are taken from, and all accompanying page numbers refer to, this source.

12    Gilles Deleuze, *Cinema I: The Movement Image,* trans. Hugh Tomlinson and Barbara Habberjam (Minnesota: University of Minnesota Press, 1986) excerpted in *The Deleuze Reader,* ed. Constantin V. Boundas (New York: Columbia University Press, 1993), 184.

13    "Perspectivism" in Nietzsche's work is an interpretive method that inverts the meaning of well-defined terms for the purpose of "revaluing" the values of Eurocentric culture. The Renaissance form of perspective reduces multiple points of view to a singular position. Nietzsche's perspectivism means exactly the opposite of this. For Nietzsche, every perspective is unique to each spectator in each context. There can be no singular, universal position that represents absolute and unequivocal truth.

14    Gilles Deleuze, *Cinema I: The Movement Image,* trans. Hugh Tomlinson and Barbara Habberjam (Minnesota: University of Minnesota Press, 1986) excerpted in *The Deleuze Reader,* ed. Constantin V. Boundas (New York: Columbia University Press, 1993), 184.

ALL THE THINGS I KNOW
BUT OF WHICH I AM NOT
AT THE MOMENT THINKING—
1:36 PM; JUNE 15, 1969

Robert Barry

## Some Tones of White and Gray

gray

white

ashen

pearl-gray, pearly

cinereous (= ash-gray)

canescent (= becoming white)

silver

dove-colored

slaty

nacreous (= mother-of-pearl)

creamy

calcareous (= full of lime)

bleached

the color of mercury

a mackerel sky

leaden

pewter

milky

opalescent

opaline

# on seeing *untitled #3:* white and bands of graphite

Yvonne Rand

Art often stimulates or jolts me into *seeing* what I ordinarily would only look at. **The painting by Agnes Martin that is the subject of this essay is a case in point. The painting moves me to consider once again the differences between** *looking at* **and** *seeing.* **But what is** *looking at?* **What is** *seeing?* **Is** *looking at* a process of *not seeing,* of looking while my mind is somewhere else, of not being present in the process of seeing?

A friend told me about her recent trip to Storm King Art Center in upstate New York. She reported not liking the sculpture there. She did not understand it. She thought most of it was ugly. She felt enormous resistance to being there. And yet, afterwards, she began to notice stacks of chairs. She began to see I-beams in roof structures. She began to see many things she had walked by, which she had looked at previously but had not seen in this sense of being present, fully attentive, with no distractions. Truly seeing. For my friend, the ordinary world of chairs and buildings and cars came alive as a direct result of going to Storm King, resistance and all.

**One late afternoon in September I drove to San Francisco to see an untitled Agnes Martin painting in a private collection.** The painting is smaller than other works by Martin I have seen. And it is, as the title describes, a series of horizontal bands of white paint and graphite. The owner of the painting greeted me and showed me some of the art in his collection. After a brief visit he left me in a comfortable chair in front of the Martin painting. I sat there, alone, for close to an hour.

As I allowed my mind to quiet and to be worked on by the painting, the luminous, shimmering surfaces of the canvas gradually differentiated. The painting became an object of meditation in the sense that I intended to be fully with the surface of the canvas before me, open to whatever reflection and perception might arise in the moment. I experienced

Objectivity, our seal of veracity, resides only in the concrete and measurable, it would seem. But everything is not concrete and measurable; far from it. Concrete facts and tangible data are only ingredients of truth, scattered in disorder until the subjective mind is allowed to bring them into cohesion. Truth, it has been demonstrated over and over, is what we make it, and the value of it to ourselves does not rest in a final absoluteness which is in any case impossible of attainment, but in the use we make of it.

— **Edith Simon** *

*Edith Simon, *Luther Alive: Martin Luther and the Making of the Reformation* (Garden City, New York: Doubleday and Company, Inc., 1968), 30–31.

increasing calmness. I began to register the colors and surfaces of the painting. They kept changing and they began to glow. Light appeared to hover just off the surface of the canvas itself. I could see each band in its particularity, distinct and unlike any other. The longer I gazed at the painting, the more I could see the distinctive individual quality of each horizontal band. The bands looked alive, even and consistent, freely drawn, and strikingly unmechanical. As the natural light began to dim, the colors in the painting began to shine and individuate. I saw hints of pink and green. Was the sense of shifting color in my mind? Was it in the painting itself? As my eyes came in contact with the painting and the entire process of perception occurred, was there some activity or change or distortion in the arising of perception itself? I know, intellectually, that the new colors I was seeing were in my perception rather than in the painting. But I was seeing green and pink!

As I left the house I looked up into the early evening sky.

## The sky was filled with layers of fog and clouds; small patches of blue showed and the last light of day lingered. The grayness was incandescent and the color and light mottled, layered, varied, changing.

The beauty of the evening sky elicited joy, and I knew that my seeing of that evening sky was a seeing directly made possible by my time seeing the Martin painting. In the months since that September afternoon, moments recur of clear, expanded, vivid awareness of pearly white, modulated light on and through clouds. A whole range of light and color and surface in the natural world, especially the sky, feels more accessible to me. Instead of viewing a gray and overcast day as one flat grayness, inevitably monotone, I now perceive distinct, separate, and discrete layers of fog and clouds and the light and color they reflect.

The risk in looking at work with apparently repetitious elements is tending to a quick reaction, to a generalization, even before one is fully present with the work. Agnes Martin challenges our habitual ways of experiencing the world, be they in ordinary daily experiences, with one's breath, or in looking at a work of art. One can so easily think, "I have seen this before. Oh, I live in a repeatable universe." Are we afraid, perhaps, that we live in a repeatable universe and that we may become bored?

For a number of years I have been studying and practicing in the stream of what Buddhism calls *mind training*. Within Buddhist meditation there is a persistent focus on cultivating one's capacity to be present with things as they are, to cultivate one's ability to see each thing and each being and each moment as though for the first time, to know exactly and in particular the characteristics of various states of consciousness. The *home base* in this tradition is awareness of particular sensations of the physical body and of the breath in all of its various and vast characteristics. With consciousness and substantial and consistent practice in the Buddhist mind-training tradition one may cultivate increasingly more and more refined awareness, both inner and outer. And a question like, "Oh, do I live in a repeatable universe?" typically becomes the focus of curiosity and inquiry

and investigation. Agnes Martin herself comes from her own experience within the philosophical and psychological inner science of Buddhism. So I am not surprised to find that I am so drawn to her work in the ways I am describing here.

As American culture and life become more and more filled with almost continuous distractions (e.g., canned music in elevators and in stores, music playing through headsets of portable devices, music when we are put on hold on the telephone), our tolerance for experience that requires a slowed-down pace, a capacity to be present, diminishes. Our frantic, noisy, alienated culture challenges and erodes the capacity for stillness and quiet. Agnes Martin's paintings require the viewer to be still, to be present, to allow the mind to soften if any shifts into expanded and heightened consciousness are to occur.

Since that September afternoon I experience, often, brief moments that resonate with the consciousness that arose on viewing Martin's untitled painting of bands of white and graphite. Thus, as I sit at my desk and write with a pencil, I *see* the gravelly quality of the dark gray graphite on the paper; while I am walking in the garden, my eye falls on small pieces of white plastic electrical plugs and abalone shell that lie, side by side, in a bowl of water, glimmering, pearly, iridescent; I look up into the sky filled with storm clouds and I see white, gray, and near-black, modulated and varied and more beautiful than I have ever seen before. I have confidence in my ability to see gray and white fully now.

Some years ago I saw an exhibit of Agnes Martin's paintings in New York. But seeing them in the midst of a jostling throng, standing for only a few minutes before each painting, being pushed along by the crowd of people, moving too quickly from one painting to the next, I had only a foretaste of the impact of spending an entire hour with one painting, uncrowded, undisturbed. On the occasion when I was able to sit in front of one painting for an hour, her work dropped in to my physical body and consciousness profoundly, and the reverberations still ring on and on.

The process of *looking at* goes on all the time. True *seeing* is rare. What is the difference between the two? Do I really know, experientially, the difference between *looking at* a person as I pass her on the street and actually *seeing* her? Do I see more fully when I forget the name of the thing seen? Real seeing means making contact, without any prejudice or expectation or limitation; it means connecting free of judgment or reaction. I propose that real seeing is not conditioned or habitual but is fresh and unbiased.

These days my days and dawns and dusks are filled with more moments of joy, calm, and beauty. Since that overcast September afternoon when I sat with Agnes Martin's own experience of seeing, manifested in the shimmering bands of white and graphite on her canvas, I see much more than I can remember being capable of seeing before. Martin's work is so simple. And yet it is not easy. As life speeds up and complicates our experience beyond any earlier imagining, we should treasure any occasion to be still, to let the mind rest, to allow seeing to take place. As someone who looks at paintings and who hopes, actually, to see them, I participate gladly and gratefully with the artist and her creation of what is new and unknown.

opposite: **Agnes Martin**, *Untitled #3*, 1993 (detail)

Agnes Martin works at the edge of experience,
persistently asking

**what is true?**
**what is so?**
**what is possible?**

So might anyone who wishes to see with vivacity,
clarity,
and humility.

114

opposite: **Theresa Hak Kyung Cha,** *Exilée,*
1980 (detail)

page 116: **Robert Irwin,** Untitled, 1969
(detail)

Yvonne Rand is a
Zen Buddhist priest and a
meditation teacher.
She lives and practices at
Redwood Creek Temple in
Muir Beach, California.

# the principles of psycho logy

William James

## Chapter IX'
## The Stream of Thought.

Editor's note:
This excerpt from
chapter nine of
*The Principles of
Psychology* includes
only the first three
of James's "Five
Characters in
Thought."
All page and chapter
references in this
excerpt pertain to
the Dover Publica-
tions, Inc., edition
of this work.

We now begin
our study of the mind
from within. **Most books start with sensations, as the simplest mental facts, and proceed synthet-
ically, constructing each higher stage from those below
it. But this is abandoning the empirical method of investigation. No one ever had a simple sensation by itself.
Consciousness, from our natal day, is of a teeming multiplicity of objects and relations, and what we call simple sensations are results of discriminative attention,
pushed often to a very high degree. It is astonishing
what havoc is wrought in psychology by admitting at the
outset apparently innocent suppositions, that nevertheless contain a flaw. The bad consequences develop
themselves later on, and are irremediable, being woven
through the whole texture of the work. The notion that
sensations, being the simplest things, are the first things
to take up in psychology is one of these suppositions.
The only thing which psychology has a right to postulate
at the outset is the fact of thinking itself, and that must
first be taken up and analyzed. If sensations then prove
to be amongst the elements of the thinking,
we shall be no worse off as respects them
than if we had taken them
for granted
at the start.** *The first fact
for us, then, as psychologists,
is that thinking of some sort goes on.*
I use the word thinking...for every form of consciousness indiscrimi-
nately. If we could say in English 'it thinks,' as we say 'it rains' or 'it
blows,' we should be stating the fact most simply and with the mini-
mum of assumption. As we cannot, we must simply say that *thought
goes on.*

### Five Characters in Thought.

How does it go on? We notice immediately five
important characters in the process, of which it shall be the duty of
the present chapter to treat in a general way:

1    Every thought tends to be part of a personal consciousness.
2    Within each personal consciousness thought is always changing.
3    Within each personal consciousness thought is sensibly
     continuous.
4    It always appears to deal with objects independent of itself.
5    It is interested in some parts of these objects to the exclusion of
     others, and welcomes or rejects—*chooses* from among them, in
     a word—all the while.

In considering these five points successively,
we shall have to plunge *in medias res* as regards our vocabulary,
and use psychological terms which can
only be adequately defined in later chapters of the book. But every one knows
what the terms mean in a rough way; and
it is only in a rough way that we are now
to take them. This chapter is like a
painter's first charcoal sketch upon his
canvas, in which no niceties appear.

### 1 Thought
tends to
Personal Form.

When I say *every
thought is part of a personal consciousness,* 'personal consciousness' is
one of the terms in question. Its meaning
we know so long as no one asks us to
define it, but to give an accurate account
of it is the most difficult of philosophic
tasks. This task we must confront in the
next chapter; here a preliminary word will
suffice.

In this room—this lecture-room, say—
there are a multitude of thoughts, yours
and mine, some of which cohere mutually, and some not. They are as little each-
for-itself and reciprocally independent as
they are all-belonging-together. They are
neither: no one of them is separate, but
each belongs with certain others and
with none beside. My thought belongs
with my other thoughts, and your thought
with your other thoughts. Whether anywhere in the room there be a mere
thought, which is nobody's thought, we
have no means of ascertaining, for we
have no experience of its like. The only
states of consciousness that we naturally
deal with are found in personal con-
sciousnesses, minds, selves, concrete
particular I's and you's.

Each of these minds keeps its own
thoughts to itself. There is no giving or
bartering between them. No thought even
comes into direct *sight* of a thought in
another personal consciousness than its
own. Absolute insulation, irreducible plu-
ralism, is the law. It seems as if the elementary psychic fact were not *thought* or
*this thought* or *that thought,* but *my
thought,* every thought being *owned.*
Neither contemporaneity, nor proximity in
space, nor similarity of quality and content

Anonymous, Untitled tantric drawing,
ca. 1995

are able to fuse thoughts together which are sundered by this barrier of belonging to different personal minds. The breaches between such thoughts are the most absolute breaches in nature. Everyone will recognize this to be true, so long as the existence of *something* corresponding to the term 'personal mind' is all that is insisted on, without any particular view of its nature being implied. On these terms the personal self rather than the thought might be treated as the immediate datum in psychology. The universal conscious fact is not 'feelings and thoughts exist,' but 'I think' and 'I feel.'[2] No psychology, at any rate, can question the *existence* of personal selves. The worst a psychology can do is so to interpret the nature of these selves as to rob them of their worth. A French writer, speaking of our ideas, says somewhere in a fit of anti-spiritualistic excitement that, misled by certain peculiaritities [sic] which they display, we 'end by personifying' the procession which they make,—such personification being regarded by him as a great philosophic blunder on our part. It could only be a blunder if the notion of personality meant something essentially different from anything to be found in the mental procession. But if that procession be itself the very 'original' of the notion of personality, to personify it cannot possibly be wrong. It is already personified. There are no marks of personality to be gathered *aliunde*, and then found lacking in the train of thought. It has them all already; so that to whatever farther analysis we may subject that form of personal selfhood under which thoughts appear, it is, and must remain, true that the thoughts which psychology studies do continually tend to appear as parts of personal selves.

I say 'tend to appear' rather than 'appear,' on account of those facts of sub-conscious personality, automatic writing, etc., of which we studied a few in the last chapter. The buried feelings and thoughts proved now to exist in hysterical anæsthetics, in recipients of post-hypnotic suggestion, etc., themselves are parts of *secondary personal selves*. These selves are for the most part very stupid and contracted, and are cut off at ordinary times from communication with the regular and normal self of the individual; but still they form conscious unities, have continuous memories, speak, write, invent distinct names for themselves, or adopt names that are suggested; and, in short, are entirely worthy of that title of secondary personalities which is now commonly given them. According to M. Janet these secondary personalities are always abnormal, and result from the splitting of what ought to be a single complete self into two parts, of which one lurks in the background whilst the other appears on the surface as the only self the man or woman has. For our present purpose it is unimportant whether this account of the origin of secondary selves is applicable to all possible cases of them or not, for it certainly is true of a large number of them. Now although the *size* of a secondary self thus formed will depend on the number of thoughts that are thus split-off from the main consciousness, the *form* of it tends to personality, and the later thoughts pertaining to it remember the earlier ones and adopt them as their own. M. Janet caught the actual moment of inspissation (so to speak) of one of these secondary personalities in his anæsthetic somnambulist Lucie. He found that when this young woman's attention was absorbed in conversation with a third party, her anæsthetic hand would write simple answers to questions whispered to her by himself. "Do you hear?" he asked. *"No,"* was the unconsciously written reply. "But to answer you must hear." *"Yes, quite so."* "Then how do you manage?" *"I don't know."* "There must be some one who hears me." *"Yes."* "Who?" *"Someone other than Lucie."* "Ah! another person. Shall we give her a name?" *"No."* "Yes, it will be more convenient." *"Well, Adrienne, then."* "Once baptized, the subconscious personage," M. Janet continues, "grows more definitely outlined and displays better her psychological characters. In particular she shows us that she is conscious of the feelings excluded from the consciousness of the primary or normal personage. She it is who tells us that I am pinching the arm or touching the little finger in which Lucie for so long has had no tactile sensations."[3]

In other cases the adoption of the name by the secondary self is more spontaneous. I have seen a number of incipient automatic writers and mediums as yet imperfectly 'developed,' who immediately and of their own accord write and speak in the name of departed spirits. These may be public characters, as Mozart, Faraday, or real persons formerly known to the subject, or altogether imaginary beings. Without prejudicing the question of real 'spirit-control' in the more developed sorts of trance-utterance, I incline to think that these (often deplorably unintelligent) rudimentary utterances are the work of an inferior fraction of the subject's own natural mind, set free from control by the rest, and working after a set pattern fixed by the prejudices of the social environment. In a spiritualistic community we get optimistic messages, whilst in an ignorant Catholic village the secondary personage calls itself by the name of a demon, and proffers blasphemies and obscenities, instead of telling us how happy it is in the summer-land.[4]

Beneath these tracts of thought, which, however rudimentary, are still organized selves with a memory, habits, and sense of their own identity, M. Janet thinks that the facts of catalepsy in hysteric patients drive us to suppose that there are thoughts quite unorganized and impersonal. A patient in cataleptic trance (which can be produced artificially in certain hypnotized subjects) is without memory on waking, and seems insensible and unconscious as long as the cataleptic condition lasts. If, however, one raises the arm of such a subject it stays in that position, and the whole body can thus be moulded like wax under the hands of the operator, retaining for a considerable time whatever attitude he communicates to it. In hysterics whose arm, for example, is anæsthetic, the same thing may happen. The anæsthetic arm may remain passively in positions which it is made to assume; or if the hand be taken and made to hold a pencil and trace a certain letter, it will continue tracing that letter indefinitely on the paper. These acts, until recently, were supposed to be accompanied by no consciousness at all: they were physiological reflexes. M. Janet considers with much more plausibility that feeling escorts them. The feeling is probably merely that of the position or movement of the limb, and it produces no more than its natural effects when it discharges into the motor centres which keep the position maintained, or the movement incessantly renewed.[5] Such thoughts as these, says M. Janet, "are known by *no one,* for disaggregated sensations reduced to a state of mental dust are not synthetized [sic] in any personality."[6] He admits, however, that these very same unutterably stupid thoughts tend to develop memory,—the cataleptic ere long moves her arm at a bare hint; so that they form no important exception to the law that all thought tends to assume the form of personal consciousness.

> 2 Thought
> is in Constant
> Change.

I do not mean necessarily that no one state of mind has any duration—even if true, that would be hard to establish. The change which I have more particularly in view is that which takes place in sensible intervals of time; and the result on which I wish to lay stress is this, that *no state once gone can recur and be identical with what it was before.* Let us begin with Mr. Shadworth Hodgson's description:

*"I go straight to the facts, without saying I go to perception, or sensation, or thought, or any special mode at all. What I find when I look at my consciousness at all is that what I cannot divest myself of, or not have in consciousness, if I have any consciousness at all, is a sequence of different feelings. I may shut my eyes and keep perfectly still, and try not to contribute anything of my own will; but whether I think or do not think, whether I perceive external things or not, I always have a succession of different feelings. Anything else that I may have also, of a more special character, comes in as parts of this succession. Not to have the succession of different feelings is not to be conscious at all. ...The chain of consciousness is a sequence of* differents."[7]

Such a description as this can awaken no possible protest from any one. We all recognize as different great classes of our conscious states. Now we are seeing, now hearing; now reasoning, now willing; now recollecting, now expecting; now loving, now hating; and in a hundred other ways we know our minds to be alternately engaged. But all these are complex states. The aim of science is always to reduce complexity to simplicity; and in psychological science we have the celebrated 'theory of *ideas*' which, admitting the great difference among each other of what may be called concrete conditions of mind, seeks to show how this is all the resultant effect of variations in the *combination* of certain simple elements of consciousness that always remain the same. These mental atoms or molecules are what Locke called 'simple ideas.' Some of Locke's successors made out that the only simple ideas were the sensations strictly so called. Which ideas the simple ones may be does not, however, now concern us. It is enough that certain philosophers have thought they could see under the dissolving-view-appearance of the mind elementary facts of *any* sort that remained unchanged amid the flow.

And the view of these philosophers has been called little into question, for our common experience seems at first sight to corroborate it entirely. Are not the sensations we get from the same object, for example, always the same? Does not the same piano-key, struck with the same force, make us hear in the same way? Does not the same grass give us the same feeling of green, the same sky the same feeling of blue, and do we not get the same olfactory sensation no matter how many times we put our nose to the same flask of cologne? It seems a piece of metaphysical sophistry to suggest that we do not; and yet a close attention to the matter shows that *there is no proof that the same bodily sensation is ever got by us twice.*

*What is got twice is the same* OBJECT. We hear the same *note* over and over again; we see the same *quality* of green, or smell the same objective perfume, or experience the same *species* of pain. The realities, concrete and abstract, physical and ideal, whose permanent existence we believe in, seem to be constantly coming up again before our thought, and lead us, in our carelessness, to suppose that our 'ideas' of them are the same ideas. When we come, some time later, to the chapter on Perception, we shall see how inveterate is our habit of not attending to sensations as subjective facts, but of simply using them as stepping-stones to pass over to the recognition of the realities whose presence they reveal. The grass out of the window now looks to me of the same green in the sun as in the shade, and yet a painter would have to paint one part of it dark brown, arother [sic] part bright yellow, to give its real sensational effect. We take no heed, as a rule, of the different way in which the same things look and sound and smell at different distances and under different circumstances. The sameness of the *things* is what we are concerned to ascertain; and any sensations that assure us of that will probably be considered in a rough way to be the same with each other. This is what makes off-hand testimony about the subjective identity of different sensations well-nigh worthless as a proof of the fact. The entire history of Sensation is a commentary on our inability to tell whether two sensations received apart are exactly alike. What appeals to our attention far more than the absolute quality or quantity of a given sensation is its *ratio* to whatever other sensations we may have at the same time. When everything is dark a somewhat less dark sensation makes us see an object white. Helmholtz calculates that the white marble painted in a picture representing an architectural view by moonlight is, when seen by daylight, from ten to twenty thousand times brighter than the real moonlit marble would be.[8]

Such a difference as this could never have been *sensibly* learned; it had to be inferred from a series of indirect considerations. There are facts which make us believe that our sensibility is altering all the time, so that the same object cannot easily give us the same sensation over again. The eye's sensibility to light is at its maximum when the eye is first exposed, and blunts itself with surprising rapidity. A long night's sleep will make it see things twice as brightly on wakening, as simple rest by closure will make it see them later in the day.[9] We feel things differently according as we are sleepy or awake, hungry or full, fresh or tired; differently at night and in the morning, differently in summer and in winter, and above all things differently in childhood, manhood, and old age. Yet we never doubt that our feelings reveal the same world, with the same sensible qualities and the same sensible things occupying it. The difference of the sensibility is shown best by the difference of our emotion about the things from one age to another, or when we are in different organic moods. What was bright and exciting becomes weary, flat, and unprofitable. The bird's song is tedious, the breeze is mournful, the sky is sad.

To these indirect presumptions that our sensations, following the mutations of our capacity for feeling, are always undergoing an essential change, must be added another presumption, based on what must happen in the brain. Every sensation corresponds to some cerebral action. For an identical sensation to recur it would have to occur the second time *in an unmodified brain.* But as this, strictly speaking, is a physiological impossibility, so is an unmodified feeling an impossibility; for to every brain-modification, however small, must correspond a change of equal amount in the feeling which the brain subserves.

All this would be true if even sensations came to us pure and single and not combined into 'things.' Even then we should have to confess that, however we might in ordinary conversation speak of getting the same sensation again, we never in strict theoretic accuracy could do so; and that whatever was true of the river of life, of the river of elementary feeling, it would certainly be true to say, like Heraclitus, that we never descend twice into the same stream.

But if the assumption of 'simple ideas of sensation' recurring in immutable shape is so easily shown to be baseless, how much more baseless is the assumption of immutability in the larger masses of our thought!

For there it is obvious and palpable that our state of mind is never precisely the same. Every thought we have of a given fact is, strictly speaking, unique, and only bears a resemblance of kind with our other thoughts of the same fact. When the identical fact recurs, we *must* think of it in a fresh manner, see it under a somewhat different angle, apprehend it in different relations from those in which it last appeared. And the thought by which we cognize it is the thought of it-in-those-relations, a thought suffused with the consciousness of all that dim context. Often we are ourselves struck at the strange differences in our successive views of the same thing. We wonder how we ever could have opined as we did last month about a certain matter. We have outgrown the possibility of that state of mind, we know not how. From one year to another we see things in new lights. What was unreal has grown real, and what was exciting is insipid. The friends we used to care the world for are shrunken to shadows; the women, once so divine, the stars, the woods, and the waters, how now so dull and common; the young girls that brought an aura of infinity, at present hardly distinguishable existences; the pictures so empty; and as for the books, what *was* there to find so mysteriously significant in Goethe, or in John Mill so full of weight? Instead of all this, more zestful than ever is the work, the work; and fuller and deeper the import of common duties and of common goods.

But what here strikes us so forcibly on the flagrant scale exists on every scale, down to the imperceptible transition from one hour's outlook to that of the next. Experience is remoulding us every moment, and our mental reaction on every given thing is really a resultant of our experience of the whole world up to that date. The analogies of brain-physiology must again be appealed to to corroborate our view.

Our earlier chapters have taught us to believe that, whilst we think, our brain changes, and that, like the aurora borealis, its whole internal equilibrium shifts with every pulse of change. The precise nature of the shifting at a given moment is a product of many factors. The accidental state of local nutrition or blood-supply may be among them. But just as one of them certainly is the influence of outward objects on the sense-organs during the moment, so is another certainly the very special susceptibility in which the organ has been left at that moment by all it has gone through in the past. Every brain-state is partly determined by the nature of this entire past succession. Alter the latter in any part, and the brain-state must be somewhat different. Each present brain-state is a record in which the eye of Omniscience might read all the foregone history of its owner. It is out of the question, then, that any total brain-state should identically recur. Something like it may recur; but to suppose *it* to recur would be equivalent to the absurd admission that all the states that had intervened between its two appearances had been pure nonentities, and that the organ after their passage was exactly as it was before. And (to consider shorter periods) just as, in the senses, an impression feels very differently according to what has preceded it; as one color succeeding another is modified by the contrast, silence sounds delicious after noise, and a note, when the scale is sung up, sounds unlike itself when the scale is sung down; as the presence of certain lines in a figure changes the apparent form of the other lines, and as in music the whole æsthetic effect comes from the manner in which one set of sounds alters our feeling of another; so, in thought, we must admit that those portions of the brain that have just been maximally excited retain a kind of soreness which is a condition of our present consciousness, a codeterminant of how and what we now shall feel.[10]

Ever some tracts are waning in tension, some waxing, whilst others actively discharge. The states of tension have as positive an influence as any in determining the total condition, and in deciding what the *psychosis* shall be. All we know of submaximal nerve-irritations, and of the summation of apparently ineffective stimuli, tends to show that *no* changes in the brain are physiologically ineffective, and that presumably none are bare of psychological result. But as the brain-tension shifts from one relative state of equilibrium to another, like the gyrations of a kaleidoscope, now rapid and now slow, is it likely that its faithful psychic concomitant is heavier-footed than itself, and that it cannot match each one of the organ's irradiations by a shifting inward iridescence of its own? But if it can do this, its inward iridescences must be infinite, for the brain-redistributions are in infinite variety. If so coarse a thing as a telephone-plate can be made to thrill for years and never reduplicate its inward condition, how much more must this be the case with the infinitely delicate brain?

I am sure that this concrete and total manner of regarding the mind's changes is the only true manner, difficult as it may be to carry it out in detail. If anything seems obscure about it, it will grow clearer as we advance. Meanwhile, if it be true, it is certainly also true that no two 'ideas' are ever exactly the same, which is the proposition we started to prove. The proposition is more important theoretically than it at first sight seems. For it makes it already impossible for us to follow obediently in the footprints of either the Lockian or the Herbartian school, schools which have had almost unlimited influence in Germany and among ourselves. No doubt it is often *convenient* to formulate the mental facts in an atomistic sort of way, and to treat the higher states of consciousness as if they were all built out of unchanging simple ideas. It is convenient often to treat curves as if they were composed of small straight lines, and electricity and nerve-force as if they were fluids. But in the one case as in the other we must never forget that we are talking symbolically, and that there is nothing in nature to answer to our words. *A permanently existing 'idea' or 'Vorstellung' which makes its appearance before the footlights of consciousness at periodical intervals, is as mythological an entity as the Jack of Spades.*

What makes it convenient to use the mythological formulas is the whole organization of speech, which, as was remarked a while ago, was not made by psychologists, but by men who were as a rule only interested in the facts their mental states revealed. They only spoke of their states as *ideas of this or of that thing*. What wonder, then, that the thought is most easily conceived under the law of the thing whose name it bears! If the thing is composed of parts, then we suppose that the thought of the thing must be composed of the thoughts of the parts. If one part of the thing have [sic] appeared in the same thing or in other things on former occasions, why then we must be having even now the very same 'idea' of that part which was there on those occasions. If the thing is simple, its thought is simple. If it is multitudinous, it must require a multitude of thoughts to think it. If a succession, only a succession of thoughts can know it. If permanent, its thought is permanent. And so on *ad libitum*. What after all is so natural as to assume that one object, called by one name, should be known by one affection of the mind? But, if language must thus influence us, the agglutinative languages, and even Greek and Latin with their declensions, would be the better guides. Names did not appear in them inalterable, but changed their shape to suit the context in which they lay. It must have been easier then than now to conceive of the same object as being thought of at different times in non-identical conscious states.

This, too, will grow clearer as we proceed. Meanwhile a necessary consequence of the belief in permanent self-identical psychic facts that absent themselves and recur periodically is the Humian doctrine that our thought is composed of separate independent parts and is not a sensibly continuous stream. That this doctrine entirely misrepresents the natural appearances is what I next shall try to show.

3    Within each
     personal consciousness,
     thought is sensibly
     continuous.

I can only define 'continuous' as that which is without breach, crack, or division. I have already said that the breach from one mind to another is perhaps the greatest breach in nature. The only breaches that can well be conceived to occur within the limits of a single mind would either be *interruptions*, time-gaps during which the consciousness went out altogether to come into existence again at a later moment; or they would be breaks in the *quality*, or content, of the thought, so abrupt that the segment that followed had no connection whatever with the one that went before. The proposition that within each personal consciousness thought feels continuous, means two things:

1    That even where there is a time-gap the consciousness after it feels as if it belonged together with the consciousness before it, as another part of the same self;
2    That the changes from one moment to another in the quality of the consciousness are never absolutely abrupt.

The case of the time-gaps, as the simplest, shall be taken first. And first of all, a word about time-gaps of which the consciousness may not be itself aware.

On page 200 we saw that such time-gaps existed, and that they might be more numerous than is usually supposed. If the consciousness is not aware of them, it cannot feel them as interruptions. In the unconsciousness produced by nitrous oxide and other anæsthetics, in that of epilepsy and fainting, the broken edges of the sentient life may meet and merge over the gap, much as the feelings of space of the opposite margins of the 'blind spot' meet and merge over that objective interruption to the sensitiveness of the eye. Such consciousness as this, whatever it be for the onlooking psychologist, is for itself unbroken. It *feels* unbroken; a waking day of it is sensibly a unit as long as that day lasts, in the sense in which the hours themselves are units, as having all their parts next each other, with no intrusive alien substance between. To expect the consciousness to feel the interruptions of its objective continuity as gaps, would be like expecting the eye to feel a gap of silence because it does not hear, or the ear to feel a gap of darkness because it does not see. So much for the gaps that are unfelt.

With the felt gaps the case is different. On waking from sleep, we usually know that we have been unconscious, and we often have an accurate judgment of how long. The judgment here is certainly an inference from sensible signs, and its ease is due to long practice in the particular field.[11] The result of it, however, is that the consciousness is, *for itself*, not what it was in the former case, but interrupted and continuous, in the mere time-sense of the words. But in the other sense of continuity, the sense of the parts being inwardly connected and belonging together because they are parts of a common whole, the consciousness remains sensibly continuous and one. What now is the common whole? The natural name for it is *myself, I*, or *me*.

When Paul and Peter wake up in the same bed, and recognize that they have been asleep, each one of them mentally reaches back and makes connection with but *one* of the two streams of thought which were broken by the sleeping hours. As the current of an electrode buried in the ground unerringly finds its way to its own similarly buried mate, across no matter how much intervening earth; so Peter's present instantly finds out Peter's past, and never by mistake knits itself on to that of Paul. Paul's thought in turn is as little liable to go astray. The past thought of Peter is appropriated by the present Peter alone. He may have a *knowledge*, and a correct one too, of what Paul's last drowsy states of mind were as he sank into sleep, but it is an entirely different sort of knowledge from that which he has of his own last states. He *remembers* his own states, whilst he only *conceives* Paul's. Remembrance is like direct feeling; its object is

William James (1842–1910) is one of the founders of modern psychology. He taught psychology and philosophy at Harvard University, and his books *Principles of Psychology, The Varieties of Religious Experience,* and *Pragmatism* have exerted a powerful influence on these and other fields of study throughout the twentieth century.

suffused with a warmth and intimacy to which no object of mere conception ever attains. This quality of warmth and intimacy and immediacy is what Peter's *present* thought also possesses for itself. So sure as this present is me, is mine, it says, so sure is anything else that comes with the same warmth and intimacy and immediacy, me and mine. What the qualities called warmth and intimacy may in themselves be will have to be matter for future consideration. But whatever past feelings appear with those qualities must be admitted to receive the greeting of the present mental state, to be owned by it, and accepted as belonging together with it in a common self. This community of self is what the time-gap cannot break in twain, and is why a present thought, although not ignorant of the time-gap, can still regard itself as continuous with certain chosen portions of the past.

Consciousness, then, does not appear to itself chopped up in bits. Such words as 'chain' or 'train' do not describe it fitly as it presents itself in the first instance. It is nothing jointed; it flows. A 'river' or a 'stream' are the metaphors by which it is most naturally described. *In talking of it hereafter, let us call it the stream of thought, of consciousness, or of subjective life.*

1  A good deal of this chapter is reprinted from an article 'On some Omissions of Introspective Psychology' which appeared in 'Mind' for January 1884.

2  B. P. Bowne: Metaphysics, p. 362.

3  L'Automatisme Psychologique, p. 318.

4  Cf. A. Constans: Relation sur une Epidémie d'hystéro-démonopathie en 1861. 2me ed. Paris, 1863. —Chiap e Franzolini: L'Epidemia d'isterodemonopatie in Verzegnis. Reggio, 1879. —See also J. Kerner's little work: Nachricht von dem Vorkommen des Besessenseins. 1836.

5  For the Physiology of this compare the chapter on the Will.

6  *Loc. cit.* p. 316.

7  The Philosophy of Reflection, I. 248, 290.

8  Populäre Wissenschaftliche Vorträge, Drittes Heft (1876), p. 72

9  Fick, in L. Hermann's Handb. d. Physiol., Bd. III. Th. I. p. 225.

10  It need of course not follow, because a total brain-state does not recur, that no *point* of the brain can ever be twice in the same condition. That would be as improbable a consequence as that in the sea a wave-crest should never come twice at the same point of space. What can hardly come twice is an identical *combination* of wave-forms all with their crests and hollows reoccupying identical places. For such a total combination as this is the analogue of the brain-state to which our actual consciousness at any moment is due.

11  The accurate registration of the 'how long' is still a little mysterious.

# what is it like to be a bat ?

Thomas Nagel

Consciousness is what makes **the mind-body problem really intractable. Perhaps that is why current discussions of the problem give it little attention or get it obviously wrong. The recent wave of reductionist euphoria has produced several analyses of mental phenomena and mental concepts designed to explain the possibility of some variety of materialism, psychophysical identification, or reduction.[1] But the problems dealt with are those common to this type of reduction and other types, and what makes the mind-body problem unique, and unlike the water-$H_2O$ problem or the Turing machine-IBM machine problem or the lightning-electrical discharge problem or the gene-DNA problem or the oak tree-hydrocarbon problem,** Every **is ignored.** reductionist has his favorite analogy from modern science. It is most unlikely that any of these unrelated examples of successful reduction will shed light on the relation of mind to brain. But philosophers share the general human weakness for explanations of what is incomprehensible in terms suited for what is familiar and well understood, though entirely different. This has led to the acceptance of implausible accounts of the mental largely because they would permit familiar kinds of reduction. I shall try to explain why the usual examples do not help us to understand the relation between mind and body—why, indeed, we have at present no conception of what an explanation of the physical nature of a mental phenomenon would be. Without consciousness the mind-body problem would be much less interesting. With consciousness it seems hopeless. The most important and characteristic feature of conscious mental phenomena is very poorly understood. Most reductionist theories do not even try to explain it. And careful examination will show that no currently available concept of reduction is applicable to it. Perhaps a new theoretical form can be devised for the purpose, but such a solution, if it exists, lies in the distant intellectual future.

Conscious experience is a widespread phenomenon. It occurs at many levels of animal life, though we cannot be sure of its presence in the simpler organisms, and it is very difficult to say in general what provides evidence of it. (Some extremists have been prepared to deny it even of mammals other than man.) No doubt it occurs in countless forms totally unimaginable to us, on other planets in other solar systems throughout the universe. But no matter how the form may vary, the fact that an organism has conscious experience *at all* means, basically, that there is something it is like to *be* that organism. There may be further implications about the form of the experience; there may even (though I doubt it) be implications about the behavior of the organism. But fundamentally an organism has conscious mental states if and only if there is something that it is like to *be* that organism—something it is like *for* the organism.

We may call this the subjective character of experience. It is not captured by any of the familiar, recently devised reductive analyses of the mental, for all of them are logically compatible with its absence. It is not analyzable in terms of any explanatory system of functional states, or intentional states, since these could be ascribed to robots or automata that behaved like people though they experienced nothing.[2] It is not analyzable in terms of the causal role of experiences in relation to typical human behavior—for similar reasons.[3] I do not deny that conscious mental states and events cause behavior, nor that they may be given functional characterizations. I deny only that this kind of thing exhausts their analysis. Any reductionist program has to be based on an analysis of what is to be reduced. If the analysis leaves something out, the problem will be falsely posed. It is useless to base the defense of materialism on any analysis of mental phenomena that fails to deal explicitly with their subjective character. For there is no reason to suppose that a reduction which seems plausible when no attempt is made to account for consciousness can be extended to include consciousness. Without some idea, therefore, of what the subjective character of experience is, we cannot know what is required of a physicalist theory.

While an account of the physical basis of mind must explain many things, this appears to be the most difficult. It is impossible to exclude the phenomenological features of experience from a reduction in the same way that one excludes the phenomenal features of an ordinary substance from a physical or chemical reduction of it—namely, by explaining them as effects on the minds of human observers.[4] If physicalism is to be defended, the phenomenological features must themselves be given a physical account. But when we examine their subjective character it seems that such a result is impossible. The reason is that every subjective phenomenon is essentially

From *Philosophical Review* 83 (1974). Copyright 1974 Cornell University. Reprinted by permission of the publisher.

opposite: **The Museum of Jurassic Technology,** *The Voice of the American Gray Fox,* 1984 (detail)

pages 128–129: **Samuel Beckett,** *Film,* 1963–65 (details) connected with a single point of view, and it seems inevitable that an objective, physical theory will abandon that point of view.

Let me first try to state the issue somewhat more fully than by referring to the relation between the subjective and the objective, or between the *pour-soi* and the *en-soi*. This is far from easy. Facts about what it is like to be an $X$ are very peculiar, so peculiar that some may be inclined to doubt their reality, or the significance of claims about them. To illustrate the connection between subjectivity and a point of view, and to make evident the importance of subjective features, it will help to explore the matter in relation to an example that brings out clearly the divergence between the two types of conception, subjective and objective.

I assume we all believe that bats have experience. After all, they are mammals, and there is no more doubt that they have experience than that mice or pigeons or whales have experience. I have chosen bats instead of wasps or flounders because if one travels too far down the phylogenetic tree, people gradually shed their faith that there is experience there at all. Bats, although more closely related to us than those other species, nevertheless present a range of activity and a sensory apparatus so different from ours that the problem I want to pose is exceptionally vivid (though it certainly could be raised with other species). Even without the benefit of philosophical reflection, anyone who has spent some time in an enclosed space with an excited bat knows what it is to encounter a fundamentally *alien* form of life.

I have said that the essence of the belief that bats have experience is that there is something that it is like to be a bat. Now we know that most bats (the microchiroptera, to be precise) perceive the external world primarily by sonar, or echolocation, detecting the reflections, from objects within range, of their own rapid, subtly modulated, high-frequency shrieks. Their brains are designed to correlate the outgoing impulses with the subsequent echoes, and the information thus acquired enables bats to make precise discriminations of distance, size, shape, motion, and texture comparable to those we make by vision. But bat sonar, though clearly a form of perception, is not similar in its operation to any sense that we possess, and there is no reason to suppose that it is subjectively like anything we can experience or imagine. This appears to create difficulties for the notion of what it is like to be a bat. We must consider whether any method will permit us to extrapolate to the inner life of the bat from our own case,[5] and if not, what alternative methods there may be for understanding the notion.

Our own experience provides the basic material for our imagination, whose range is therefore limited. It will not help to try to imagine that one has webbing on one's arms, which enables one to fly around at dusk and dawn catching insects in one's mouth; that one has very poor vision, and perceives the surrounding world by a system of reflected high-frequency sound signals; and that one spends the day hanging upside down by one's feet in an attic. In so far as I can imagine this (which is not very far), it tells me only what it would be like for *me* to behave as a bat behaves. But that is not the question. I want to know what it is like for a *bat* to be a bat. Yet if I try to imagine this, I am restricted to the resources of my own mind, and those resources are inadequate to the task. I cannot perform it either by imagining additions to my present experience, or by imagining segments gradually subtracted from it, or by imagining some combination of additions, subtractions, and modifications.

To the extent that I could look and behave like a wasp or a bat without changing my fundamental structure, my experiences would not be anything like the experiences of those animals. On the other hand, it is doubtful that any meaning can be attached to the supposition that I should possess the internal neurophysiological constitution of a bat. Even if I could by gradual degrees be transformed into a bat, nothing in my present constitution enables me to imagine what the experiences of such a future stage of myself thus metamorphosed would be like. The best evidence would come from the experiences of bats, if we only knew what they were like.

So if extrapolation from our own case is involved in the idea of what it is like to be a bat, the extrapolation must be incompletable. We cannot form more than a schematic conception of what it *is* like. For example, we may ascribe general *types* of experience on the basis of the animal's structure and behavior. Thus we describe bat sonar as a form of three-dimensional forward perception; we believe that bats feel some versions of pain, fear, hunger, and lust, and that they have other, more familiar types of perception besides sonar. But we believe that these experiences also have in each case a specific subjective character, which it is beyond our ability to conceive. And if there is conscious life elsewhere in the universe, it is likely that some of it will not be describable even in the most general experiential terms available to us.[6] (The problem is not confined to exotic cases, however, for it exists between one person and another. The subjective character of the experience of a person deaf and blind from birth is not accessible to me, for example, nor presumably is mine to him. This does not prevent us each from believing that the other's experience has such a subjective character.)

If anyone is inclined to deny that we can believe in the existence of facts like this whose exact nature we cannot possibly conceive, he should reflect that in contemplating the bats we are in much the same position that intelligent bats or Martians[7] would occupy if they tried to form a conception of what it was like to be us. The structure of their own minds might make it impossible for them to succeed, but we know they would be wrong to conclude that there is not anything precise that it is like to be us: that only certain general types of mental state could be ascribed to us (perhaps perception and appetite would be concepts common to us both; perhaps not). We know they would be wrong to draw such a skeptical conclusion because we know what it is like to be us. And we know that while it includes an enormous amount of variation and complexity, and while we do not possess the vocabulary to describe it adequately, its subjective character is highly specific, and in some respects describable in terms that can be understood only by creatures like us. The fact that we cannot expect ever to accommodate in our language a detailed description of Martian or bat phenomenology should not lead us to dismiss as meaningless the claim that bats and Martians have experiences fully comparable in richness of detail to our own. It would be fine if someone were to develop concepts and a theory that enabled us to think about those things; but such an understanding may be permanently denied to us by the limits of our nature. And to deny the reality or logical significance of what we can never describe or understand is the crudest form of cognitive dissonance.

This brings us to the edge of a topic that requires much more discussion than I can give it here: namely, the relation between facts on the one hand and conceptual schemes or systems of representation on the other. My realism about the subjective domain in all its forms implies a belief in the existence of facts beyond the reach of human concepts. Certainly it is possible for a human being to believe that there are facts which humans never *will* possess the requisite concepts to represent or comprehend. Indeed, it would be foolish to doubt this, given the finiteness of humanity's expectations. After all, there would have been transfinite numbers even if everyone had been wiped out by the Black Death before Cantor discovered them. But one might also believe that there are facts which *could* not ever be represented or comprehended by human beings, even if the species lasted forever—simply because our structure does not permit us to operate with concepts of the requisite type. This impossibility might even be observed by other beings, but it is not clear that the existence of such beings, or the possibility of their existence, is a precondition of the significance of the hypothesis that there are humanly inaccessible facts. (After all, the nature of beings with access to humanly inaccessible facts is presumably itself a humanly inaccessible fact.) Reflection on what it is like to be a bat seems to lead us, therefore, to the conclusion that there are facts that do not consist in the truth of propositions expressible in a human language. We can be compelled to recognize the existence of such facts without being able to state or comprehend them.

I shall not pursue this subject, however. Its bearing on the topic before us (namely, the mind-body problem) is that it enables us to make a general observation about the subjective character of experience. Whatever may be the status of facts about what it is like to be a human being, or a bat, or a Martian, these appear to be facts that embody a particular point of view.

I am not adverting here to the alleged privacy of experience to its possessor. The point of view in question is not one accessible only to a single individual. Rather it is a *type*. It is often possible to take up a point of view other than one's own, so the comprehension of such facts is not limited to one's own case. There is a sense in which phenomenological facts are perfectly objective: one person can know or say of another what the quality of the other's experience is. They are subjective, however, in the sense that even this objective ascription of experience is possible only for someone sufficiently similar to the object of ascription to be able to adopt his point of view—to understand the ascription in the first person as well as in the third, so to speak. The more different from oneself the other experiencer is, the less success one can expect with this enterprise. In our own case we occupy the relevant point of view, but we will have as much difficulty understanding our own experience properly if we approach it from another point of view as we would if we tried to understand the experience of another species without taking up *its* point of view.[8]

This bears directly on the mind-body problem. For if the facts of experience—facts about what it is like *for* the experiencing organism—are accessible only from one point of view, then it is a mystery how the true character of experiences could be revealed in the physical operation of that organism. The latter is a domain of objective facts *par excellence*—the kind that can be observed and understood from many points of view and by individuals with differing perceptual systems. There are no comparable imaginative obstacles to the acquisition of knowledge about bat neurophysiology by human scientists, and intelligent bats or Martians might learn more about the human brain than we ever will.

This is not by itself an argument against reduction. A Martian scientist with no understanding of visual perception could understand the rainbow, or lightning, or clouds as physical phenomena, though he would never be able to understand the human concepts of rainbow, lightning, or cloud, or the place these things occupy in our phenomenal world. The objective nature of the things picked out by these concepts could be apprehended by him because, although the concepts themselves are connected with a particular point of view and a particular visual phenomenology, the things apprehended from that point of view are not: they are observable from the point of view but external to it; hence they can be comprehended from other points of view also, either by the same organisms or by others. Lightning has an objective character that is not exhausted by its visual appearance, and this can be investigated by a Martian without vision. To be precise, it has a *more* objective character than is revealed in its visual appearance. In speaking of the move from subjective to objective characterization, I wish to remain noncommittal about the existence of an end point, the completely objective intrinsic nature of the thing, which one might or might not be able to reach. It may be more accurate to think of objectivity as a direction in which the understanding can travel. And in understanding a phenomenon like lightning, it is legitimate to go as far away as one can from a strictly human viewpoint.[9]

In the case of experience, on the other hand, the connection with a particular point of view seems much closer. It is difficult to understand what could be meant by the *objective* character of an experience, apart from the particular point of view from which its subject apprehends it. After all, what would be left of what it was like to be a bat if one removed the viewpoint of the bat? But if experience does not have, in addition to its subjective character, an objective nature that can be apprehended from many different points of view, then how can it be sup-

posed that a Martian investigating my brain might be observing physical processes which were my mental processes (as he might observe physical processes which were bolts of lightning), only from a different point of view? How, for that matter, could a human physiologist observe them from another point of view?[10]

We appear to be faced with a general difficulty about psychophysical reduction. In other areas the process of reduction is a move in the direction of greater objectivity, toward a more accurate view of the real nature of things. This is accomplished by reducing our dependence on individual or species-specific points of view toward the object of investigation. We describe it not in terms of the impressions it makes on our senses, but in terms of its more general effects and of properties detectable by means other than the human senses. The less it depends on a specifically human viewpoint, the more objective is our description. It is possible to follow this path because although the concepts and ideas we employ in thinking about the external world are initially applied from a point of view that involves our perceptual apparatus, they are used by us to refer to things beyond themselves—toward which we *have* the phenomenal point of view. Therefore we can abandon it in favor of another, and still be thinking about the same things.

Experience itself, however, does not seem to fit the pattern. The idea of moving from appearance to reality seems to make no sense here. What is the analogue in this case to pursuing a more objective understanding of the same phenomena by abandoning the initial subjective viewpoint toward them in favor of another that is more objective but concerns the same thing? Certainly it *appears* unlikely that we will get closer to the real nature of human experience by leaving behind the particularity of our human point of view and striving for a description in terms accessible to beings that could not imagine what it was like to be us. If the subjective character of experience is fully comprehensible only from one point of view, then any shift to greater objectivity—that is, less attachment to a specific viewpoint—does not take us nearer to the real nature of the phenomenon: it takes us farther away from it.

In a sense, the seeds of this objection to the reducibility of experience are already detectable in successful cases of reduction; for in discovering sound to be, in reality, a wave phenomenon in air or other media, we leave behind one viewpoint to take up another, and the auditory, human or animal viewpoint that we leave behind remains unreduced. Members of radically different species may both understand the same physical events in objective terms, and this does not require that they understand the phenomenal forms in which those events appear to the senses of members of the other species. Thus it is a condition of their referring to a common reality that their more particular viewpoints are not part of the common reality that they both apprehend. The reduction can succeed only if the species-specific viewpoint is omitted from what is to be reduced.

But while we are right to leave this point of view aside in seeking a fuller understanding of the external world, we cannot ignore it permanently, since it is the essence of the internal world, and not merely a point of view on it. Most of the neobehaviorism of recent philosophical psychology results from the effort to substitute an objective concept of mind for the real thing, in order to have nothing left over which cannot be reduced. If we acknowledge that a physical theory of mind must account for the subjective character of experience, we must admit that no presently available conception gives us a clue how this could be done. The problem is unique. If mental processes are indeed physical processes, then there is something it is like, intrinsically,[11] to undergo certain physical processes. What it is for such a thing to be the case remains a mystery.

What moral should be drawn from these reflections, and what should be done next? It would be a mistake to conclude that physicalism must be false. Nothing is proved by the inadequacy of physicalist hypotheses that assume a faulty objective analysis of mind. It would be truer to say that physicalism is a position we cannot understand because we do not at present have any conception of how it might be true. Perhaps it will be thought unreasonable to require such a conception as a condition of understanding. After all, it might be said, the meaning of physicalism is clear enough: mental states are states of the body; mental events are physical events. We do not know *which* physical states and events they are, but that should not prevent us from understanding the hypothesis. What could be clearer than the words "is" and "are"?

But I believe it is precisely this apparent clarity of the word "is" that is deceptive. Usually, when we are told that $X$ is $Y$ we know *how* it is supposed to be true, but that depends on a conceptual or theoretical background and is not conveyed by the "is" alone. We know how both "$X$" and "$Y$" refer, and the kinds of things to which they refer, and we have a rough idea how the two referential paths might converge on a single thing, be it an object, a person, a process, an event, or whatever. But when the two terms of the identification are very disparate it may not be so clear how it could be true. We may not have even a rough idea of how the two referential paths could converge, or what kind of things they might converge on, and a theoretical framework may have to be supplied to enable us to understand this. Without the framework, an air of mysticism surrounds the identification.

This explains the magical flavor of popular presentations of fundamental scientific discoveries, given out as propositions to which one must subscribe without really understanding them. For example, people are now told at an early age that all matter is really energy. But despite the fact that they know what "is" means, most of them never form a conception of what makes this claim true, because they lack the theoretical background.

At the present time the status of physicalism is similar to that which the hypothesis that matter is energy would have had if uttered by a pre-Socratic philosopher. We do not have the beginnings of a conception of how it might be true. In order to understand the hypothesis that a mental event is a physical event, we require more than an understanding of the word "is." The idea of how a mental and a physical term might refer to the same thing is lacking, and the usual analogies with theoretical identification

in other fields fail to supply it. They fail because if we construe the reference of mental terms to physical events on the usual model, we either get a reappearance of separate subjective events as the effects through which mental reference to physical events is secured, or else we get a false account of how mental terms refer (for example, a causal behaviorist one).

Strangely enough, we may have evidence for the truth of something we cannot really understand. Suppose a caterpillar is locked in a sterile safe by someone unfamiliar with insect metamorphosis, and weeks later the safe is reopened, revealing a butterfly. If the person knows that the safe has been shut the whole time, he has reason to believe that the butterfly is or was once the caterpillar, without having any idea in what sense this might be so. (One possibility is that the caterpillar contained a tiny winged parasite that devoured it and grew into the butterfly.)

It is conceivable that we are in such a position with regard to physicalism. Donald Davidson has argued that if mental events have physical causes and effects, they must have physical descriptions. He holds that we have reason to believe this even though we do not—and in fact *could* not—have a general psychophysical theory.[12] His argument applies to intentional mental events, but I think we also have some reason to believe that sensations are physical processes, without being in a position to understand how. Davidson's position is that certain physical events have irreducibly mental properties, and perhaps some view describable in this way is correct. But nothing of which we can now form a conception corresponds to it; nor have we any idea what a theory would be like that enabled us to conceive of it.[13]

Very little work has been done on the basic question (from which mention of the brain can be entirely omitted) whether any sense can be made of experiences' having an objective character at all. Does it make sense, in other words, to ask what my experiences are *really* like, as opposed to how they appear to me? We cannot genuinely understand the hypothesis that their nature is captured in a physical description unless we understand the more fundamental idea that they *have* an objective nature (or that objective processes can have a subjective nature).[14]

I should like to close with a speculative proposal. It may be possible to approach the gap between subjective and objective from another direction. Setting aside temporarily the relation between the mind and the brain, we can pursue a more objective understanding of the mental in its own right. At present we are completely unequipped to think about the subjective character of experience without relying on the imagination—without taking up the point of view of the experiential subject. This should be regarded as a challenge to form new concepts and devise a new method—an objective phenomenology not dependent on empathy or the imagination. Though presumably it would not capture everything, its goal would be to describe, at least in part, the subjective character of experiences in a form comprehensible to beings incapable of having those experiences.

We would have to develop such a phenomenology to describe the sonar experiences of bats; but it would also be possible to begin with humans. One might try, for example, to develop concepts that could be used to explain to a person blind from birth what it was like to see. One would reach a blank wall eventually, but it should be possible to devise a method of expressing in objective terms much more than we can at present, and with much greater precision. The loose intermodal analogies—for example, "Red is like the sound of a trumpet"—which crop up in discussions of this subject are of little use. That should be clear to anyone who has both heard a trumpet and seen red. But structural features of perception might be more accessible to objective description, even though something would be left out. And concepts alternative to those we learn in the first person may enable us to arrive at a kind of understanding even of our own experi-

ence which is denied us by the very ease of description and lack of distance that subjective concepts afford.

Apart from its own interest, a phenomenology that is in this sense objective may permit questions about the physical[15] basis of experience to assume a more intelligible form. Aspects of subjective experience that admitted this kind of objective description might be better candidates for objective explanations of a more familiar sort. But whether or not this guess is correct, it seems unlikely that any physical theory of mind can be contemplated until more thought has been given to the general problem of subjective and objective. Otherwise we cannot even pose the mind-body problem without sidestepping it.[16]

Thomas Nagel is professor of law and philosophy at the New York University School of Law. He is the author of several books including *Equality and Partiality* and *The Last Word*.

1    Examples are J. J. C. Smart, *Philosophy and Scientific Realism* (London, 1963); David K. Lewis, "An Argument for the Identity Theory," *Journal of Philosophy,* LXIII (1966), reprinted with addenda in David M. Rosenthal, *Materialism & the Mind-Body Problem* (Englewood Cliffs, N. J., 1971); Hilary Putnam, "Psychological Predicates" in Capitan and Merrill, *Art, Mind, & Religion* (Pittsburgh, 1967), reprinted in Rosenthal, *op. cit.,* as "The Nature of Mental States"; D. M. Armstrong, *A Materialist Theory of the Mind* (London, 1968); D. C. Dennett, *Content and Consciousness* (London, 1969). I have expressed earlier doubts in "Armstrong on the Mind," *Philosophical Review,* LXXIX (1970), 394-403; "Brain Bisection and the Unity of Consciousness," *Synthèse,* 22 (1971); and a review of Dennett, *Journal of Philosophy,* LXIX (1972). See also Saul Kripke, "Naming and Necessity" in Davidson and Harman, *Semantics of Natural Language* (Dordrecht, 1972), esp. pp. 334-342; and M. T. Thornton, "Ostensive Terms and Materialism," *The Monist,* 56 (1972).

2    Perhaps there could not actually be such robots. Perhaps anything complex enough to behave like a person would have experiences. But that, if true, is a fact which cannot be discovered merely by analyzing the concept of experience.

3    It is not equivalent to that about which we are incorrigible, both because we are not incorrigible about experience and because experience is present in animals lacking language and thought, who have no beliefs at all about their experiences.

4    Cf. Richard Rorty, "Mind-Body Identity, Privacy, and Categories," *The Review of Metaphysics,* XIX (1965), esp. 37-38.

5    By "our own case" I do not mean just "my own case," but rather the mentalistic ideas that we apply unproblematically to ourselves and other human beings.

6    Therefore the analogical form of the English expression "what it is *like*" is misleading. It does not mean "what (in our experience) it *resembles,*" but rather "how it is for the subject himself."

7    Any intelligent extraterrestrial beings totally different from us.

8    It may be easier than I suppose to transcend inter-species barriers with the aid of the imagination. For example, blind people are able to detect objects near them by a form of sonar, using vocal clicks or taps of a cane.

Perhaps if one knew what that was like, one could by extension imagine roughly what it was like to possess the much more refined sonar of a bat. The distance between oneself and other persons and other species can fall anywhere on a continuum. Even for other persons the understanding of what it is like to be them is only partial, and when one moves to species very different from oneself, a lesser degree of partial understanding may still be available. The imagination is remarkably flexible. My point, however, is not that we cannot *know* what it is like to be a bat. I am not raising that epistemological problem. My point is rather that even to form a *conception* of what it is like to be a bat (and a fortiori to know what it is like to be a bat) one must take up the bat's point of view. If one can take it up roughly, or partially, then one's conception will also be rough or partial. Or so it seems in our present state of understanding.

9    The problem I am going to raise can therefore be posed even if the distinction between more subjective and more objective descriptions or viewpoints can itself be made only within a larger human point of view. I do not accept this kind of conceptual relativism, but it need not be refuted to make the point that psychophysical reduction cannot be accommodated by the subjective-to-objective model familiar from other cases.

10    The problem is not just that when I look at the "Mona Lisa," my visual experience has a certain quality, no trace of which is to be found by someone looking into my brain. For even if he did observe there a tiny image of the "Mona Lisa," he would have no reason to identify it with the experience.

11    The relation would therefore not be a contingent one, like that of a cause and its distinct effect. It would be necessarily true that a certain physical state felt a certain way. Saul Kripke (*op. cit.*) argues that causal behaviorist and related analyses of the mental fail because they construe, e.g., "pain" as a merely contingent name of pains. The subjective character of an experience ("its immediate phenomenological quality" Kripke calls it) is the essential property left out by such analyses, and the one in virtue of which it is, necessarily, the experience it is. My view is closely related to his. Like Kripke, I find the hypothesis that a certain brain state should *necessarily* have a certain subjective character incomprehensible without further explanation. No such explanation emerges from theories which view the mind-brain relation as contingent, but perhaps there are other alternatives, not yet discovered.

A theory that explained how the mind-brain relation was necessary would still leave us with Kripke's problem of explaining why it nevertheless appears contingent. That difficulty seems to me surmountable, in the following way. We may imagine something by representing it to ourselves either perceptually, sympathetically, or symbolically. I shall not try to say how symbolic imagination works, but part of what happens in the other two cases is this. To imagine something perceptually, we put ourselves in a conscious state resembling the state we would be in if we perceived it. To imagine something sympathetically, we put ourselves in a conscious state resembling the thing itself. (This method can be used only to imagine mental events and states—our own or another's.) When we try to imagine a mental state occurring without its associated brain state, we first sympathetically imagine the occurrence of the mental state: that is, we put ourselves into a state that resembles it mentally. At the same time, we attempt to perceptually imagine the non-occurrence of the associated physical state, by putting ourselves into another state unconnected with the first: one resembling that which we would be in if we perceived the non-occurrence of the physical state. Where the imagination of physical features is perceptual and the imagination of mental features is sympathetic, it appears to us that we can imagine any experience occurring without its associated brain state, and vice versa. The relation between them will appear contingent even if it is necessary, because of the independence of the disparate types of imagination.

(Solipsism, incidentally, results if one misinterprets sympathetic imagination as if it worked like perceptual imagination: it then seems impossible to imagine any experience that is not one's own.)

12    See "Mental Events" in Foster and Swanson, *Experience and Theory* (Amherst, 1970); though I don't understand the argument against psychophysical laws.

13    Similar remarks apply to my paper "Physicalism," *Philosophical Review* LXXIV (1965), 339-356, reprinted with postscript in John O'Connor, *Modern Materialism* (New York, 1969).

14    This question also lies at the heart of the problem of other minds, whose close connection with the mind-body problem is often overlooked. If one understood how subjective experience could have an objective nature, one would understand the existence of subjects other than oneself.

15    I have not defined the term "physical." Obviously it does not apply just to what can be described by the concepts of contemporary physics, since we expect further developments. Some may think there is nothing to prevent mental phenomena from eventually being recognized as physical in their own right. But whatever else may be said of the physical, it has to be objective. So if our idea of the physical ever expands to include mental phenomena, it will have to assign them an objective character—whether or not this is done by analyzing them in terms of other phenomena already regarded as physical. It seems to me more likely, however, that mental-physical relations will eventually be expressed in a theory whose fundamental terms cannot be placed clearly in either category.

16    I have read versions of this paper to a number of audiences, and am indebted to many people for their comments.

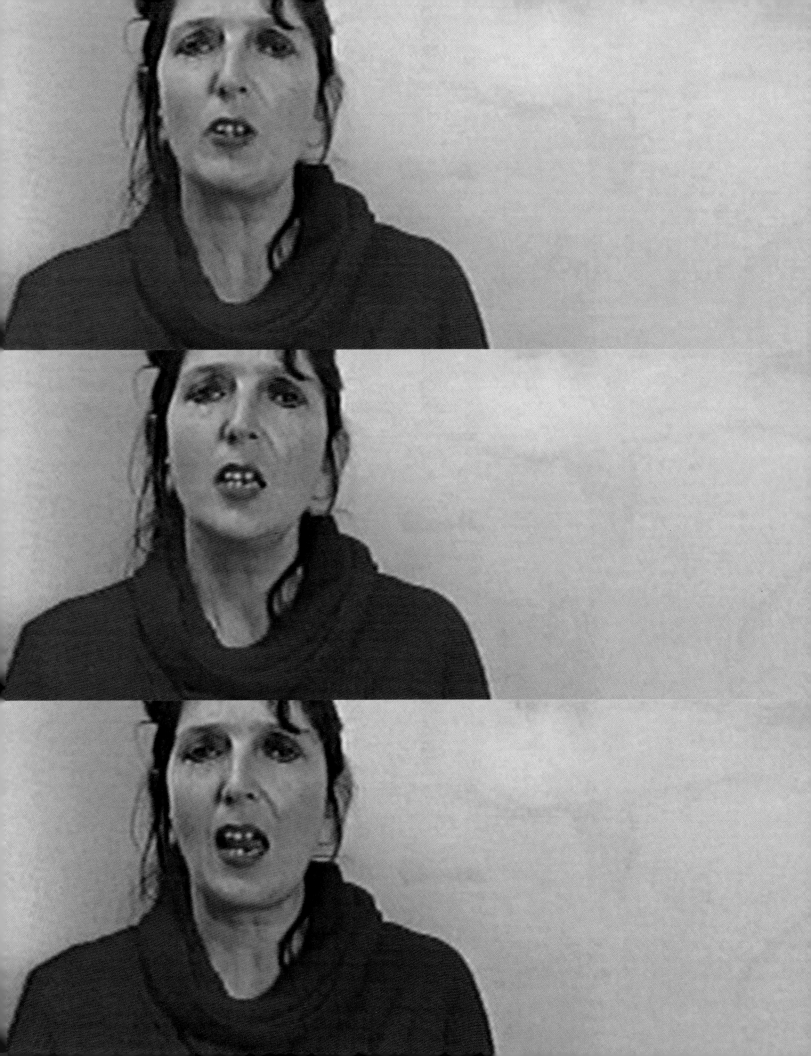

# the problem of consciousness

Francis Crick
Christof Koch

The overwhelming question in neurobiology **today is the relation between the mind and the brain. Everyone agrees that what we know as mind is closely related to certain aspects of the behavior of the brain, not to the heart, as Aristotle thought. Its most mysterious aspect is consciousness or awareness, which can take many forms, from the experience of pain to self-consciousness.** In the past the mind (or soul) was often regarded, as it was by Descartes, as something immaterial, separate from the brain but interacting with it in some way. A few neuroscientists, such as Sir John Eccles, still assert that the soul is distinct from the body. But most neuroscientists now believe that all aspects of mind, including its most puzzling attribute—consciousness or awareness—are likely to be explainable in a more materialistic way as the behavior of large sets of interacting neurons. As William James, the father of American psychology, said a century ago, consciousness is not a thing but a process.

Exactly what the process is, however, has yet to be discovered. For many years after James penned *The Principles of Psychology*, consciousness was a taboo concept in American psychology because of the dominance of the behaviorist movement. With the advent of cognitive science in the mid-1950s, it became possible once more for psychologists to consider mental processes as opposed to merely observing behavior. In spite of these changes, until recently most cognitive scientists ignored consciousness, as did almost all neuroscientists. The problem was felt to be either purely "philosophical" or too elusive to study experimentally. It would not have been easy for a neuroscientist to get a grant just to study consciousness.

In our opinion, such timidity is ridiculous, so a few years ago we began to think about how best to attack the problem scientifically. How to explain mental events as being caused by the firing of large sets of neurons? Although there are those who believe such an approach is hopeless, we feel it is not productive to worry too much over aspects of the problem that cannot be solved scientifically or, more precisely, cannot be solved solely by using existing scientific ideas. Radically new concepts may indeed be needed—recall the modifications of scientific thinking forced on us by quantum mechanics. The only sensible approach is to press the experimental attack until we are confronted with dilemmas that call for new ways of thinking.

There are many possible approaches to the problem of consciousness. Some psychologists feel that any satisfactory theory should try to explain as many aspects of consciousness as possible, including emotion, imagination, dreams, mystical experiences and so on. Although such an all-embracing theory will be necessary in the long run, we thought it wiser to begin with the particular aspect of consciousness that is likely to yield most easily. What this aspect may be is a matter of personal judgment. We selected the mammalian visual system because humans are very visual animals and because so much experimental and theoretical work has already been done on it (see "The Visual Image in Mind and Brain" by Semir Zeki').

It is not easy to grasp exactly what we need to explain, and it will take many careful experiments before visual consciousness can be described scientifically. We did not attempt to define consciousness itself because of the dangers of premature definition. (If this seems like a cop-out, try defining the word "gene"—you will not find it easy.) Yet the experimental evidence that already exists provides enough of a glimpse of the nature of visual consciousness to guide research. In this article, we will attempt to show how this evidence opens the way to attack this profound and intriguing problem.

Visual theorists agree that the problem of visual consciousness is ill posed. The mathematical term "ill posed" means that additional constraints are needed to solve the problem. Although the main function of the visual system is to perceive objects and events in the world around us, the information available to our eyes is not sufficient by itself to provide the brain with its unique interpretation of the visual world. The brain must use past experience (either its own or that of our distant ancestors, which is embedded in our genes) to help interpret the information coming into our eyes. An example would be the derivation of the three-dimensional representation of the world from the two-dimensional signals falling onto the retinas of our two eyes or even onto one of them.

Visual theorists also would agree that seeing is a constructive process, one in which the brain has to carry out complex

opposite and pages 138–139:
**Gillian Wearing**, *2 into 1*, 1997 (details)

activities (sometimes called computations) in order to decide which interpretation to adopt of the ambiguous visual input. "Computation" implies that the brain acts to form a symbolic representation of the visual world, with a mapping (in the mathematical sense) of certain aspects of that world onto elements in the brain.

Ray Jackendoff of Brandeis University postulates, as do most cognitive scientists, that the computations carried out by the brain are largely unconscious and that what we become aware of is the result of these computations. But while the customary view is that this awareness occurs at the highest levels of the computational system, Jackendoff has proposed an intermediate-level theory of consciousness.

What we see, Jackendoff suggests, relates to a representation of surfaces that are directly visible to us, together with their outline, orientation, color, texture and movement. (This idea has similarities to what the late David C. Marr of the Massachusetts Institute of Technology called a "2 1/2-dimensional sketch." It is more than a two-dimensional sketch because it conveys the orientation of the visible surfaces. It is less than three-dimensional because depth information is not explicitly represented.) In the next stage this sketch is processed by the brain to produce a three-dimensional representation. Jackendoff argues that we are not visually aware of this three-dimensional representation.

An example may make this process clearer. If you look at a person whose back is turned to you, you can see the back of the head but not the face. Nevertheless, your brain infers that the person has a face. We can deduce as much because if that person turned around and had no face, you would be very surprised.

The viewer-centered representation that corresponds to the visible back of the head is what you are vividly aware of. What your brain infers about the front would come from some kind of three-dimensional representation. This does not mean that information flows only from the surface representation to the three-dimensional one; it almost certainly flows in both directions. When you imagine the front of the face, what you are aware of is a surface representation generated by information from the three-dimensional model.

IT IS IMPORTANT to distinguish between an explicit and an implicit representation. An explicit representation is something that is symbolized without further processing. An implicit representation contains the same information but requires further processing to make it explicit. The pattern of colored dots on a television screen, for example, contains an implicit representation of objects (say, a person's face), but only the dots and their locations are explicit. When you see a face on the screen, there must be neurons in your brain whose firing, in some sense, symbolizes that face.

We call this pattern of firing neurons an active representation. A latent representation of a face must also be stored in the brain, probably as a special pattern of synaptic connections between neurons.[2] For example, you probably have a representation of the Statue of Liberty in your brain, a representation that usually is inactive. If you do think about the Statue, the representation becomes active, with the relevant neurons firing away.

An object, incidentally, may be represented in more than one way—as a visual image, as a set of words and their related sounds, or even as a touch or a smell. These different representations are likely to interact with one another. The representation is likely to be distributed over many neurons, both locally, as discussed in Geoffrey E. Hinton's article,[3] and more globally. Such a representation may not be as simple and straightforward as uncritical introspection might indicate. There is suggestive evidence, partly from studying how neurons fire in various parts of a monkey's brain and partly from examining the effects of certain types of brain damage in humans, that different aspects of a face—and of the implications of a face— may be represented in different parts of the brain.

First, there is the representation of a face as a face: two eyes, a nose, a mouth and so on. The neurons involved are usually not too fussy about the exact size or position of this face in the visual field, nor are they very sensitive to small changes in its orientation. In monkeys, there are neurons that respond best when the face is turning in a particular direction, while others seem to be more concerned with the direction in which the eyes are gazing.

Then there are representations of the parts of a face, as separate from those for the face as a whole. Further, the implications of seeing a face, such as that person's sex, the facial expression, the familiarity or unfamiliarity of the face, and in particular whose face it is, may each be correlated with neurons firing in other places.

What we are aware of at any moment, in one sense or another, is not a simple matter. We have suggested that there may be a very transient form of fleeting awareness that represents only rather simple features and does not require an attentional mechanism. From this brief awareness the brain constructs a viewer-centered representation—what we see vividly and clearly—that does require attention. This in turn probably leads to three-dimensional object representations and thence to more cognitive ones.

Representations corresponding to vivid consciousness are likely to have special properties. William James thought that consciousness involved both attention and short-term memory. Most psychologists today would agree with this view. Jackendoff writes that consciousness is "enriched" by attention, implying that while attention may not be essential for certain limited types of consciousness, it is necessary for full consciousness.

Yet it is not clear exactly which forms of memory are involved. Is long-term memory needed? Some forms of acquired knowledge are so embedded in the machinery of neural processing that they are almost certainly used in becoming aware of something. On the other hand, there is evidence from studies of brain-damaged patients (such as H. M., described in "The Biological Basis of Learning and Individuality," by Eric R. Kandel and Robert D. Hawkins) that the ability to lay down new long-term episodic memories is not essential for consciousness.

It is difficult to imagine that anyone could be conscious if he or she had no memory whatsoever of what had just happened, even an extremely short one. Visual psychologists talk of iconic memory, which lasts for a fraction of a second, and working memory (such as that used to remember a new telephone number) that lasts for only a few seconds unless it is rehearsed. It is not clear whether both of these are essential for consciousness. In any case, the division of short-term memory into these two categories may be too crude.

If these complex processes of visual awareness are localized in parts of the brain, which processes are likely to be where? Many regions of the brain may be involved, but it is almost certain that the cerebral neocortex plays a dominant role. Visual information from the retina reaches the neocortex mainly by way of a part of the thalamus (the lateral geniculate nucleus); another significant visual pathway from the retina is to the superior colliculus, at the top of the brain stem.

The cortex in humans consists of two intricately folded sheets of nerve tissue, one on each side of the head. These sheets are connected by a large tract of about half a billion axons called the corpus callosum. It is well known that if the corpus callosum is cut, as is done for certain cases of intractable epilepsy, one side of the brain is not aware of what the other side is seeing.

In particular, the left side of the brain (in a right-handed person) appears not to be aware of visual information received exclusively by the right side. This shows that none of the information required for visual awareness can reach the other side of the brain by traveling down to the brain stem and, from there, back up. In a normal person, such information can get to the other side only by using the axons in the corpus callosum.

A different part of the brain—the hippocampal system—is involved in one-shot, or episodic, memories that, over weeks and months, it passes on to the neocortex, as described in the article by Eric R. Kandel and Robert D. Hawkins.[4] This system is so placed that it receives inputs from, and projects to, many parts of the brain.

Thus, one might suspect that the hippocampal system is the essential seat of consciousness. This is not the case: evidence from studies of patients with damaged brains shows that this system is not essential for visual awareness, although naturally a patient lacking one, such as H. M., is severely handicapped in everyday life because he cannot remember anything that took place more than a minute or so in the past.

In broad terms, the neocortex of alert animals probably acts in two ways. By building on crude and somewhat redundant wiring, produced by our genes and by embryonic processes [see "The Developing Brain," by Carla J. Shatz],[5] the neocortex draws on visual and other experience to slowly "rewire" itself to create categories (or "features") it can respond to. A new category is not fully created in the neocortex after exposure to only one example of it, although some small modifications of the neural connections may be made.

The second function of the neocortex (at least of the visual part of it) is to respond extremely rapidly to incoming signals. To do so, it uses the categories it has learned and tries to find the combinations of active neurons that, on the basis of its past experience, are most likely to represent the relevant objects and events in the visual world at that moment. The formation of such coalitions of active neurons may also be influenced by biases coming from other parts of the brain: for example, signals telling it what best to attend to or high-level expectations about the nature of the stimulus.

Consciousness, as James noted, is always changing. These rapidly formed coalitions occur at different levels and interact to form even broader coalitions. They are transient, lasting usually for only a fraction of a second. Because coalitions in the visual system are the basis of what we see, evolution has seen to it that they form as fast as possible; otherwise, no animal could survive. The brain is handicapped in forming neuronal coalitions rapidly because, by computer standards, neurons act very slowly. The brain compensates for this relative slowness partly by using very many neurons, simultaneously and in parallel, and partly by arranging the system in a roughly hierarchical manner.

If visual awareness at any moment corresponds to sets of neurons firing, then the obvious question is: Where are these neurons located in the brain, and in what way are they firing? Visual awareness is highly unlikely to occupy all the neurons in the neocortex that happen to be firing above their background rate at a particular moment. We would expect that, theoretically, at least some of these neurons would be involved in doing computations—trying to arrive at the best coalitions—while others would express the results of these computations, in other words, what we see.

FORTUNATELY, some experimental evidence can be found to back up this theoretical conclusion. A phenomenon called binocular rivalry may help identify the neurons whose firing symbolizes awareness. This phenomenon can be seen in dramatic form in an exhibit prepared by Sally Duensing and Bob Miller at the Exploratorium in San Francisco.

Binocular rivalry occurs when each eye has a different visual input relating to the same part of the visual field. The early visual system on the left side of the brain receives an input from both eyes but sees only the part of the visual field to the right of the fixation point. The converse is true for the right side. If these two conflicting inputs are rivalrous, one sees not the two inputs superimposed but first one input, then the other, and so on in alternation.

In the exhibit, called "The Cheshire Cat," viewers put their heads in a fixed place and are told to keep the gaze fixed. By means of a suitably placed mirror, one of the eyes can look at another person's face, directly in front, while the other eye sees a blank white screen to the side. If the viewer waves a hand in front of this plain screen at the same location in his or her visual field occupied by the face, the face is wiped out. The movement of the hand, being visually very salient, has captured the brain's attention. Without attention the face cannot be seen. If the viewer moves the eyes, the face reappears.

In some cases, only part of the face disappears. Sometimes, for example, one eye, or both eyes, will remain. If the viewer looks at the smile on the person's face, the face may disappear, leaving only the smile. For this reason, the effect has been called the Cheshire Cat effect, after the cat in Lewis Carroll's *Alice's Adventures in Wonderland.*

ALTHOUGH it is very difficult to record activity in individual neurons in a human brain, such studies can be done in monkeys. A simple example of binocular rivalry has been studied in a monkey by Nikos K. Logothetis and Jeffrey D. Schall, both then at M.I.T. They trained a macaque to keep its eyes still and to signal whether it is seeing upward or downward movement of a horizontal grating. To produce rivalry, upward movement is projected into one

of the monkey's eyes and downward movement into the other, so that the two images overlap in the visual field. The monkey signals that it sees up and down movements alternatively, just as humans would. Even though the motion stimulus coming into the monkey's eyes is always the same, the monkey's percept changes every second or so.

Cortical area MT (which Semir Zeki calls in his article V5) is an area mainly concerned with movement. What do the neurons in MT do when the monkey's percept is sometimes up and sometimes down? (The researchers studied only the monkey's first response.) The simplified answer— the actual data are rather more messy— is that whereas the firing of some of the neurons correlates with the changes in the percept, for others the average firing rate is relatively unchanged and independent of which direction of movement the monkey is seeing at that moment. Thus, it is unlikely that the firing of all the neurons in the visual neocortex at one particular moment corresponds to the monkey's visual awareness. Exactly which neurons do correspond remains to be discovered.

We have postulated that when we clearly see something, there must be neurons actively firing that stand for what we see. This might be called the activity principle. Here, too, there is some experimental evidence. One example is the firing of neurons in cortical area V2 in response to illusory contours, as described by Zeki. Another and perhaps more striking case is the filling in of the blind spot. The blind spot in each eye is caused by the lack of photoreceptors in the area of the retina where the optic nerve leaves the retina and projects to the brain. Its location is about 15 degrees from the fovea (the visual center of the eye). Yet if you close one eye, you do not see a hole in your visual field.

Philosopher Daniel C. Dennett of Tufts University is unusual among philosophers in that he is interested both in psychology and in the brain. This interest is much to be welcomed. In a recent book, *Consciousness Explained,* he has argued that it is wrong to talk about filling in. He concludes, correctly, that "an absence of information is not the same as information about an absence." From this general principle he argues that the brain does not fill in the blind spot but rather ignores it.

Dennett's argument by itself, however, does not establish that filling in does not occur; it only suggests that it might not. Dennett also states that "your brain has no machinery for [filling in] at this location." This statement is incorrect. The primary visual cortex (V1) lacks a direct input from one eye, but normal "machinery" is there to deal with the input from the other eye. Ricardo Gattass and his colleagues at the Federal University of Rio de Janeiro have shown that in the macaque some of the neurons in the blind-spot area of V1 do respond to input from both eyes, probably assisted by inputs from other parts of the cortex. Moreover, in the case of simple filling in, some of the neurons in that region respond as if they were actively filling in.

Thus, Dennett's claim about blind spots is incorrect. In addition, psychological experiments by Vilayanur S. Ramachandran have shown that what is filled in can be quite complex depending on the overall context of the visual scene. How, he argues, can your brain be ignoring something that is in fact commanding attention?

Filling in, therefore, is not to be dismissed as nonexistent or unusual. It probably represents a basic interpolation process that can occur at many levels in the neocortex. It is, incidentally, a good example of what is meant by a constructive process.

How can we discover the neurons whose firing symbolizes a particular percept? William T. Newsome and his colleagues at Stanford University have done a series of brilliant experiments on neurons in cortical area MT of the macaque's brain. By studying a neuron in area MT, we may discover that it responds best to very specific visual features having to do with motion. A neu-ron, for instance, might fire strongly in response to the movement of a bar in a particular place in the visual field, but only when the bar is oriented at a certain angle, moving in one of the two directions perpendicular to its length within a certain range of speed.

It is technically difficult to excite just a single neuron, but it is known that neurons that respond to roughly the same position, orientation and direction of movement of a bar tend to be located near one another in the cortical sheet. The experimenters taught the monkey a simple task in movement discrimination using a mixture of dots, some moving randomly, the rest all in one direction. They showed that electrical stimulation of a small region in the right place in cortical area MT would bias the monkey's motion discrimination, almost always in the expected direction.

Thus, the stimulation of these neurons can influence the monkey's behavior and probably its visual percept. Such experiments do not, however, show decisively that the firing of such neurons is the exact neural correlate of the percept. The correlate could be only a subset of the neurons being activated. Or perhaps the real correlate is the firing of neurons in another part of the visual hierarchy that are strongly influenced by the neurons activated in area MT.

These same reservations apply also to cases of binocular rivalry. Clearly, the problem of finding the neurons whose firing symbolizes a particular percept is not going to be easy. It will take many careful experiments to track them down even for one kind of percept.

IT SEEMS OBVIOUS that the purpose of vivid visual awareness is to feed into the cortical areas concerned with the implications of what we see; from there the information shuttles on the one hand to the hippocampal system, to be encoded (temporarily) into long-term episodic memory, and on the other to the planning levels of the motor system. But is it possible to go from a visual input to a behavioral output without any relevant visual awareness?

That such a process can happen is demonstrated by the remarkable class of patients with "blindsight." These patients, all of whom have suffered damage to their visual cortex, can point with fair accuracy at visual targets or track them with their eyes while vigorously denying seeing anything. In fact, these patients are as surprised as their doctors by their abilities. The amount of information that "gets through," however, is limited: blindsight patients have some ability to respond to wavelength, orientation and motion, yet they cannot distinguish a triangle from a square.

It is naturally of great interest to know which neural pathways are being used in these patients. Investigators originally suspected that the pathway ran through the superior colliculus. Recent experiments suggest that a direct albeit weak connection may be involved between the lateral geniculate nucleus and other cortical areas, such as V4. It is unclear whether an intact V1 region is essential for immediate visual awareness. Conceivably the visual signal in blindsight is so weak that the neural activity cannot produce awareness, although it remains strong enough to get through to the motor system.

Normal-seeing people regularly respond to visual signals without being fully aware of them. In automatic actions, such as swimming or driving a car, complex but stereotypical actions occur with little, if any, associated visual awareness. In other cases, the information conveyed is either very limited or very attenuated. Thus, while we can function without visual awareness, our behavior without it is rather restricted.

Clearly, it takes a certain amount of time to experience a conscious percept. It is difficult to determine just how much time is needed for an episode of visual awareness, but one aspect of the problem that can be demonstrated experimentally is that signals received close together in time are treated by the brain as simultaneous.

A disk of red light is flashed for, say, 20 milliseconds, followed immediately by a 20-millisecond flash of green light in the same place. The subject reports that he did not see a red light followed by a green light. Instead he saw a yellow light, just as he would have if the red and the green light had been flashed simultaneously. Yet the subject could not have experienced yellow until after the information from the green flash had been processed and integrated with the preceding red one.

Experiments of this type led psychologist Robert Efron, now at the University of California at Davis, to conclude that the processing period for perception is about 60 to 70 milliseconds. Similar periods are found in experiments with tones in the auditory system. It is always possible, however, that the processing times may be different in higher parts of the visual hierarchy and in other parts of the brain. Processing is also more rapid in trained, compared with naive, observers.

Because it appears to be involved in some forms of visual awareness, it would help if we could discover the neural basis of attention. Eye movement is a form of attention, since the area of the visual field in which we see with high resolution is remarkably small, roughly the area of the thumbnail at arm's length. Thus, we move our eyes to gaze directly at an object in order to see it more clearly. Our eyes usually move three or four times a second. Psychologists have shown, however, that there appears to be a faster form of attention that moves around, in some sense, when our eyes are stationary.

The exact psychological nature of this faster attentional mechanism is at present controversial. Several neuroscientists, however, including Robert Desimone and his colleagues at the National Institute of Mental Health, have shown that the rate of firing of certain neurons in the macaque's visual system depends on what the monkey is attending to in the visual field. Thus, attention is not solely a psychological concept; it also has neural correlates that can be observed. Several researchers have found that the pulvinar, a region of the thalamus, appears to be involved in visual attention. We would like to believe that the thalamus deserves to be called "the organ of attention," but this status has yet to be established.

THE MAJOR PROBLEM is to find what activity in the brain corresponds directly to visual awareness. It has been speculated that each cortical area produces awareness of only those visual features that are "columnar," or arranged in the stack or column of neurons perpendicular to the cortical surface. Thus, area V1 could code for orientation and area MT for motion. So far, as Zeki has explained, experimentalists have not found one particular region in the brain where all the information needed for visual awareness appears to come together. Dennett has dubbed such a hypothetical place "The Cartesian Theater." He argues on theoretical grounds that it does not exist.

Awareness seems to be distributed not just on a local scale, as in some of the neural nets described by Hinton, but more widely over the neocortex. Vivid visual awareness is unlikely to be distributed over every cortical area because some areas show no response to visual signals. Awareness might, for example, be associated with only those areas that connect back directly to V1 or alternatively with those areas that project into each other's layer 4. (The latter areas are always at the same level in the visual hierarchy.)

The key issue, then, is how the brain forms its global representations from visual signals. If attention is indeed crucial for visual awareness, the brain could form representations by attending to just one object at a time, rapidly moving from one object to the next. For example, the neurons representing all the different aspects of the attended object could all fire together very rapidly for a short period, possibly in rapid bursts.

This fast, simultaneous firing might not only excite those neurons that symbolized the implications of that object but also temporarily strengthen the relevant synapses so that this particular pattern of firing could be quickly recalled—a form of short-term memory. (If only one representation needs to be held in short-term memory, as in remembering a single task, the neurons involved may continue to fire for a period, as described by Patricia S. Goldman-Rakic in "Working Memory and the Mind."[6])

A problem arises if it is necessary to be aware of more than one object at exactly the same time. If all the attributes of two or more objects were represented by neurons firing rapidly, their attributes might be confused. The color of one might become attached to the shape of another. This happens sometimes in very brief presentations.

Some time ago Christoph von der Malsburg, now at the Ruhr-Universität Bochum, suggested that this difficulty would be circumvented if the neurons associated with any one object all fired in synchrony (that is, if their times of firing were correlated) but out of synchrony with those representing other objects. More recently, two groups in Germany reported that there does appear to be correlated firing between neurons in the visual cortex of the cat, often in a rhythmic manner, with a frequency in the 35- to 75-hertz range, sometimes called 40-hertz, or γ, oscillation.

Von der Malsburg's proposal prompted us to suggest that this rhythmic and synchronized firing might be the neural correlate of awareness and that it might serve to bind together activity in different cortical areas concerning the same object. The matter is still undecided, but at present the fragmentary experimental evidence does rather little to support such an idea. Another possibility is that the 40-hertz oscillations may help distinguish figure from ground[7] or assist the mechanism of attention.

Are there some particular types of neurons, distributed over the visual neocortex, whose firing directly symbolizes the content of visual awareness? One very simplistic hypothesis is that the activities in the upper layers of the cortex are largely unconscious ones, whereas the activities in the lower layers (layers 5 and 6) mostly correlate with consciousness. We have wondered whether the pyramidal neurons in layer 5 of the neocortex, especially the larger ones, might play this latter role.

These are the only cortical neurons that project right out of the cortical system (that is, not to the neocortex, the thalamus or the claustrum). If visual awareness represents the results of neural computations in the cortex, one might expect that what the cortex sends elsewhere would symbolize those results. Moreover, the neurons in layer 5 show a rather unusual propensity to fire in bursts. The idea that the layer 5 neurons may directly symbolize visual awareness is attractive, but it still is too early to tell whether there is anything in it.

Visual awareness is clearly a difficult problem. More work is needed on the psychological and neural basis of both attention and very short term memory. Studying the neurons when a percept changes, even though the visual input is constant, should be a powerful experimental paradigm. We need to construct neurobiological theories of visual awareness and test them using a combination of molecular, neurobiological and clinical imaging studies.

We believe that once we have mastered the secret of this simple form of awareness, we may be close to understanding a central mystery of human life: how the physical events occurring in our brains while we think and act in the world relate to our subjective sensations—that is, how the brain relates to the mind.

1    Semir Zeki, "The Visual Image in Mind and Brain," *Scientific American,* September 1992, 68.

2    See Geoffrey E. Hinton, "How Neural Networks Learn from Experience," *Scientific American,* September 1992, 144.

3    Ibid.

4    Eric R. Kandel and Robert D. Hawkins, "The Biological Basis of Learning and Individuality," *Scientific American,* September 1992, 78.

5    Carla J. Shatz, "The Developing Brain," *Scientific American,* September 1992, 60.

6    Patricia S. Goldman-Rakic, "Working Memory and the Mind," *Scientific American,* September 1992, 110.

7    Irvin Rock and Stephen Palmer, "The Legacy of Gestalt Psychology," *Scientific American,* December 1990.

Francis Crick is the codiscoverer, with James Watson of the double helical structure of DNA, for which they received the Nobel Prize in Physiology or Medicine in 1962. Since 1976, he has been distinguished research professor at the Salk Institute for Biological Studies in San Diego. He is the author of *The Astonishing Hypothesis: The Scientific Search for the Soul.*

Christof Koch is associate professor of computation and neural systems at the California Institute of Technology. He is the author of *Biophysics of Computation: Information Processing in Single Neurons* and editor of *Large-Scale Neuronal Theories of the Brain* (coedited with Joel L. Davis).

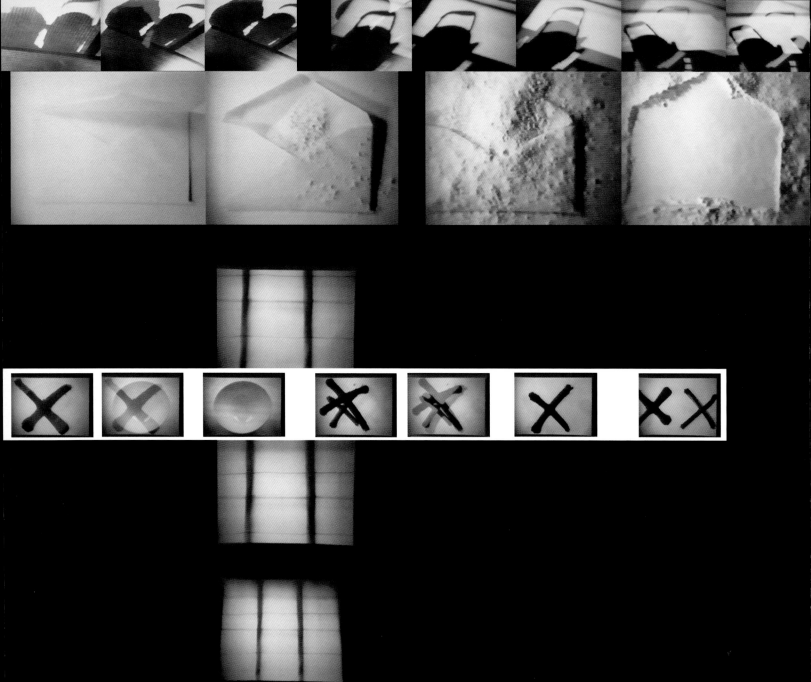

# the puzzle of conscious experience

David J. Chalmers

Conscious experience is at once **the most familiar thing in the world and the most mysterious. There is nothing we know about more directly than consciousness, but it is extraordinarily hard to reconcile it with everything else we know. Why does it exist? What does it do? How could it possibly arise from neural processes in the brain? These questions are among the most intriguing in all of science.**

From an objective viewpoint, the brain is relatively comprehensible. When you look at this page, there is a whir of processing: photons strike your retina, electrical signals are passed up your optic nerve and between different areas of your brain, and eventually you might respond with a smile, a perplexed frown or a remark. But there is also a subjective aspect. When you look at the page, you are conscious of it, directly experiencing the images and words as part of your private, mental life. You have vivid impressions of colored flowers and vibrant sky. At the same time, you may be feeling some emotions and forming some thoughts. Together such experiences make up consciousness: the subjective, inner life of the mind.

For many years, consciousness was shunned by researchers studying the brain and the mind. The prevailing view was that science, which depends on objectivity, could not accommodate something as subjective as consciousness. The behaviorist movement in psychology, dominant earlier in this century, concentrated on external behavior and disallowed any talk of internal mental processes. Later, the rise of cognitive science focused attention on processes inside the head. Still, consciousness remained off-limits, fit only for late-night discussion over drinks.

Over the past several years, however, an increasing number of neuroscientists, psychologists and philosophers have been rejecting the idea that consciousness cannot be studied and are attempting to delve into its secrets. As might be expected of a field so new, there is a tangle of diverse and conflicting theories, often using basic concepts in incompatible ways. To help unsnarl the tangle, philosophical reasoning is vital.

The myriad views within the field range from reductionist theories, according to which consciousness can be explained by the standard methods of neuroscience and psychology, to the position of the so-called mysterians, who say we will never understand consciousness at all. I believe that on close analysis both of these views can be seen to be mistaken and that the truth lies somewhere in the middle.

Against reductionism I will argue that the tools of neuroscience cannot provide a full account of conscious experience, although they have much to offer. Against mysterianism I will

hold that consciousness might be explained by a new kind of theory. The full details of such a theory are still out of reach, but careful reasoning and some educated inferences can reveal something of its general nature. For example, it will probably involve new fundamental laws, and the concept of information may play a central role. These faint glimmerings suggest that a theory of consciousness may have startling consequences for our view of the universe and of ourselves.

## The Hard Problem

RESEARCHERS USE the word "consciousness" in many different ways. To clarify the issues, we first have to separate the problems that are often clustered together under the name. For this purpose, I find it useful to distinguish between the "easy problems" and the "hard problem" of consciousness. The easy problems are by no means trivial—they are actually as challenging as most in psychology and biology—but it is with the hard problem that the central mystery lies.

The easy problems of consciousness include the following: How can a human subject discriminate sensory stimuli and react to them appropriately? How does the brain integrate information from many different sources and use this information to control behavior? How is it that subjects can verbalize their internal states? Although all these questions are associated with consciousness, they all concern the objective mechanisms of the cognitive system. Consequently, we have every reason to expect that continued work in cognitive psychology and neuroscience will answer them.

The hard problem, in contrast, is the question of how physical processes in the brain give rise to subjective experience. This puzzle involves the inner aspect of thought and perception: the way things feel for the subject. When we see, for example, we experience visual sensations, such as that of vivid blue. Or think of the ineffable sound of a distant oboe, the agony of an intense pain, the sparkle of happiness or the meditative quality of a moment lost in thought. All are part of what I am calling consciousness. It is these phenomena that pose the real mystery of the mind.

To illustrate the distinction, consider a thought experiment devised by the Australian philosopher Frank Jackson. Suppose that Mary, a neuroscientist in the 23rd century, is the world's leading expert on the brain processes responsible for color vision. But Mary has lived her whole life in a black-and-white room and has never seen any other colors. She knows everything there is to know about physical processes in the brain—its biology, structure and function. This understanding enables her to grasp everything there is to know about the easy problems: how the brain discriminates stimuli, integrates information and produces verbal reports. From her knowledge of color vision, she knows the way color names correspond with wavelengths on the light spectrum. But there is still something crucial about color vision that Mary does not know: what it is like to experience a color such as red. It follows that there are facts about conscious experience that cannot be deduced from physical facts about the functioning of the brain.

Indeed, nobody knows why these physical processes are accompanied by conscious experience at all. Why is it that when our brains process light of a certain wavelength, we have an experience of deep purple? Why do we have any experience at all? Could not an unconscious automaton have performed the same tasks just as well? These are questions that we would like a theory of consciousness to answer.

I am not denying that consciousness arises from the brain. We know, for example, that the subjective experience of vision is closely linked to processes in the visual cortex. It is the link itself that perplexes, however. Remarkably, subjective experience seems to emerge from a physical process. But we have no idea how or why this is.

### Is Neuroscience Enough?

GIVEN THE FLURRY of recent work on consciousness in neuroscience and psychology, one might think this mystery is starting to be cleared up. On closer examination, however, it turns out that almost all the current work addresses only the easy problems of consciousness. The confidence of the reductionist view comes from the progress on the easy problems, but none of this makes any difference where the hard problem is concerned.

Consider the hypothesis put forward by neurobiologists Francis Crick of the Salk Institute for Biological Studies in San Diego and Christof Koch of the California Institute of Technology. They suggest that consciousness may arise from certain oscillations in the cerebral cortex, which become synchronized as neurons fire 40 times per second. Crick and Koch believe the phenomenon might explain how different attributes of a single perceived object (its color and shape, for example), which are processed in different parts of the brain, are merged into a coherent whole. In this theory, two pieces of information become bound together precisely when they are represented by synchronized neural firings.

The hypothesis could conceivably elucidate one of the easy problems about how information is integrated in the brain. But why should synchronized oscillations give rise to a visual experience, no matter how much integration is taking place? This question involves the hard problem, about which the theory has nothing to offer. Indeed, Crick and Koch are agnostic about whether the hard problem can be solved by science at all.

The same kind of critique could be applied to almost all the recent work on consciousness. In his 1991 book *Consciousness Explained*, philosopher Daniel C. Dennett laid out a sophisticated theory of how numerous independent processes in the brain combine to produce a coherent response to a perceived event. The theory might do much to explain how we produce verbal reports on our internal states, but it tells us very little about why there should be a subjective experience behind these reports. Like other reductionist theories, Dennett's is a theory of the easy problems.

The critical common trait among these easy problems is that they all concern how a cognitive or behavioral function is performed. All are ultimately questions about how the brain carries out some task—how it discriminates stimuli, integrates information, produces reports and so on. Once neurobiology specifies appropriate neural mechanisms, showing how the functions are performed, the easy problems are solved.

The hard problem of consciousness, in contrast, goes beyond problems about how functions are performed. Even if every behavioral and cognitive function related to consciousness were explained, there would still remain a further mystery: Why is the performance of these functions accompanied by conscious experience? It is this additional conundrum that makes the hard problem hard.

## The Explanatory Gap

SOME HAVE suggested that to solve the hard problem, we need to bring in new tools of physical explanation: nonlinear dynamics, say, or new discoveries in neuroscience, or quantum mechanics. But these ideas suffer from exactly the same difficulty. Consider a proposal from Stuart R. Hameroff of the University of Arizona and Roger Penrose of the University of Oxford. They hold that consciousness arises from quantum-physical processes taking place in microtubules, which are protein structures inside neurons. It is possible (if not likely) that such a hypothesis will lead to an explanation of how the brain makes decisions or even how it proves mathematical theorems, as Hameroff and Penrose suggest. But even if it does, the theory is silent about how these processes might give rise to conscious experience. Indeed, the same problem arises with any theory of consciousness based only on physical processing.

The trouble is that physical theories are best suited to explaining why systems have a certain physical structure and how they perform various functions. Most problems in science have this form; to explain life, for example, we need to describe how a physical system can reproduce, adapt and metabolize. But consciousness is a different sort of problem entirely, as it goes beyond the explanation of structure and function.

Of course, neuroscience is not irrelevant to the study of consciousness. For one, it may be able to reveal the nature of the neural correlate of consciousness—the brain processes most directly associated with conscious experience. It may even give a detailed correspondence between specific processes in the brain and related components of experience. But until we know why these processes give rise to conscious experience at all, we will not have crossed what philosopher Joseph Levine has called the explanatory gap between physical processes and consciousness. Making that leap will demand a new kind of theory.

## A True Theory of Everything

IN SEARCHING for an alternative, a key observation is that not all entities in science are explained in terms of more basic entities. In physics, for example, space-time, mass and charge (among other things) are regarded as fundamental features of the world, as they are not reducible to anything simpler. Despite this irreducibility, detailed and useful theories relate these entities to one another in terms of fundamental laws. Together these features and laws explain a great variety of complex and subtle phenomena.

It is widely believed that physics provides a complete catalogue of the universe's fundamental features and laws. As physicist Steven Weinberg puts it in his 1992 book *Dreams of a Final Theory,* the goal of physics is a "theory of everything" from which all there is to know about the universe can be derived. But Weinberg con-cedes that there is a problem with consciousness. Despite the power of physical theory, the existence of consciousness does not seem to be derivable from physical laws. He defends physics by arguing that it might eventually explain what he calls the objective correlates of consciousness (that is, the neural correlates), but of course to do this is not to explain consciousness itself. If the existence of consciousness cannot be derived from physical laws, a theory of physics is not a true theory of everything. So a final theory must contain an additional fundamental component.

Toward this end, I propose that conscious experience be considered a fundamental feature, irreducible to anything more basic. The idea may seem strange at first, but consistency seems to demand it. In the 19th century it turned out that electromagnetic phenomena could not be explained in terms of previously known principles. As a consequence, scientists introduced electromagnetic charge as a new fundamental entity and studied the associated fundamental laws. Similar reasoning should apply to consciousness. If existing fundamental theories cannot encompass it, then something new is required.

Where there is a fundamental property, there are fundamental laws. In this case, the laws must relate experience to elements of physical theory. These laws will almost certainly not interfere with those of the physical world; it seems that the latter form a closed system in their own right. Rather the laws will serve as a bridge, specifying how experience depends on underlying physical processes. It is this bridge that will cross the explanatory gap.

Thus, a complete theory will have two components: physical laws, telling us about the behavior of physical systems from the infinitesimal to the cosmological, and what we might call psychophysical laws, telling us how some of those systems are associated with conscious experience. These two components will constitute a true theory of everything.

### Searching for a
### Theory

SUPPOSING for the moment that they exist, how might we uncover such psychophysical laws? The greatest hindrance in this pursuit will be a lack of data. As I have described it, consciousness is subjective, so there is no direct way to monitor it in others. But this difficulty is an obstacle, not a dead end. For a start, each one of us has access to our own experiences, a rich trove that can be used to formulate theories. We can also plausibly rely on indirect information, such as subjects' descriptions of their experiences. Philosophical arguments and thought experiments also have a role to play. Such methods have limitations, but they give us more than enough to get started.

These theories will not be conclusively testable, so they will inevitably be more speculative than those of more conventional scientific disciplines. Nevertheless, there is no reason they should not be strongly constrained to account accurately for our own first-person experiences, as well as the evidence from subjects' reports. If we find a theory that fits the data better than any other theory of equal simplicity, we will have good reason to accept it. Right now we do not have even a single theory that fits the data, so worries about testability are premature.

We might start by looking for high-level bridging laws, connecting physical processes to experience at an everyday level. The basic contour of such a law might be gleaned from the observation that when we are conscious of something, we are generally able to act on it and speak about it—which are objective, physical functions. Conversely, when some information is directly available for action and speech, it is generally conscious. Thus, consciousness correlates well with what we might call "awareness": the process by which information in the brain is made globally available to motor processes such as speech and bodily action.

The notion may seem trivial. But as defined here, awareness is objective and physical, whereas consciousness is not. Some refinements to the definition of awareness are needed, in order to extend the concept to animals and infants, which cannot speak. But at least in familiar cases, it is possible to see the rough outlines of a psychophysical law: where there is awareness, there is consciousness, and vice versa.

To take this line of reasoning a step further, consider the structure present in the conscious experience. The experience of a field of vision, for example, is a constantly changing mosaic of colors, shapes and patterns and as such has a detailed geometric structure. The fact that we can describe this structure, reach out in the direction of many of its components and perform other actions that depend on it suggests that the structure corresponds directly to that of the information made available in the brain through the neural processes of awareness.

Similarly, our experiences of color have an intrinsic three-dimensional structure that is mirrored in the structure of information processes in the brain's visual cortex. This structure is illustrated in the color wheels and charts used by artists. Colors are arranged in a systematic pattern—red to green on one axis, blue to yellow on another, and black to white on a third. Colors that are close to one another on a color wheel are experienced as similar. It is extremely likely that they also correspond to similar perceptual representations in the brain, as part of a system of complex three-dimensional coding among neurons that is not yet fully understood. We can recast the underlying concept as a principle of structural coherence: the structure of conscious experience is mirrored by the structure of information in awareness, and vice versa.

Another candidate for a psychophysical law is a principle of organizational invariance. It holds that physical systems with the same abstract organization will give rise to the same kind of conscious experience, no matter what they are made of. For example, if the precise interactions between our neurons could be duplicated with silicon chips, the same conscious experience would arise. The idea is somewhat controversial, but I believe it is strongly supported by thought experiments describing the gradual replacement of neurons by silicon chips. The remarkable implication is that consciousness might someday be achieved in machines.

### Information:
### Physical and
### Experiential

THE ULTIMATE GOAL of a theory of consciousness is a simple and elegant set of fundamental laws, analogous to the fundamental laws of physics. The principles described above are unlikely to be fundamental, however. Rather they seem to be high-level psychophysical laws, analogous to macroscopic principles in physics such as those of thermodynamics or kinematics. What might the underlying fundamental laws be? No one knows, but I don't mind speculating.

I suggest that the primary psychophysical laws may centrally involve the concept of information. The abstract notion of information, as put forward in the 1940s by Claude E. Shannon of the Massachusetts Institute of Technology, is that of a set of separate states with a basic structure of similarities and differences between them. We can think of a 10-bit binary code as an information state, for example. Such information states can be embodied in the physical world. This happens whenever they correspond to physical states (voltages, say); the differences between them can be transmitted along some pathway, such as a telephone line.

We can also find information embodied in conscious experience. The pattern of color patches in a visual field, for example, can be seen as analogous to that of the pixels covering a display screen. Intriguingly, it turns out that we find the same information states embedded in conscious experience and in underlying physical processes in the brain. The three-dimensional encoding of color spaces, for example, suggests that the information state in a color experience corresponds directly to an information state in the brain. We might even regard the two states as distinct aspects of a single information state, which is simultaneously embodied in both physical processing and conscious experience.

A natural hypothesis ensues. Perhaps information, or at least some information, has two basic aspects: a physical one and an experiential one. This hypothesis has the status of a fundamental principle that might underlie the relation between physical processes and experience. Wherever we find conscious experience, it exists as one aspect of an information state, the other aspect of which is embedded in a physical process in the brain. This proposal needs to be fleshed out to make a satisfying theory. But it fits nicely with the principles mentioned earlier—systems with the same organization will embody the same information, for example—and it could explain numerous features of our conscious experience.

The idea is at least compatible with several others, such as physicist John A. Wheeler's suggestion that information is fundamental to the physics of the universe. The laws of physics might ultimately be cast in informational terms, in which case we would have a satisfying congruence between the constructs in both physical and psychophysical laws. It may even be that a theory of physics and a theory of consciousness could eventually be consolidated into a single grander theory of information.

A potential problem is posed by the ubiquity of information. Even a thermostat embodies some information, for example, but is it conscious? There are at least two possible responses. First, we could constrain the fundamental laws so that only some information has an experiential aspect, perhaps depending on how it is physically processed. Second, we might bite the bullet and allow that all information has an experiential aspect—where there is complex information processing, there is complex experience, and where there is simple information processing, there is simple experience. If this is so, then even a thermostat might have experiences, although they would be much simpler than even a basic color experience, and there would certainly be no accompanying emotions or thoughts. This seems odd at first, but if experience is truly fundamental, we might expect it to be widespread. In any case, the choice between these alternatives should depend on which can be integrated into the most powerful theory.

Of course, such ideas may be all wrong. On the other hand, they might evolve into a more powerful proposal that predicts the precise structure of our conscious experience from physical processes in our brains. If this project succeeds, we will have good reason to accept the theory. If it fails, other avenues will be pursued, and alternative fundamental theories may be developed. In this way, we may one day resolve the greatest mystery of the mind.

Martin Creed, *a salt and pepper set,*
*Work No. 33,* 1990

## Dancing Qualia
## in a Synthetic Brain

WHETHER CONSCIOUSNESS could arise in a complex, synthetic system is a question many people find intrinsically fascinating. Although it may be decades or even centuries before such a system is built, a simple thought experiment offers strong evidence that an artificial brain, if organized appropriately, would indeed have precisely the same kind of conscious experiences as a human being.

Consider a silicon-based system in which the chips are organized and function in the same way as the neurons in your brain. That is, each chip in the silicon system does exactly what its natural analogue does and is interconnected to surrounding elements in precisely the same way. Thus, the behavior exhibited by the artificial system will be exactly the same as yours. The crucial question is: Will it be conscious in the same way that you are?

Let us assume, for the purpose of argument, that it would not be. (Here we use a reasoning technique known as reductio ad absurdum, in which the opposite hypothesis is assumed and then shown to lead to an untenable conclusion.) That is, it either has different experiences—an experience of blue, say, when you are seeing red—or no experience at all. We will consider the first case; the reasoning proceeds similarly in both cases.

Because chips and neurons have the same function, they are interchangeable, with the proper interfacing. Chips therefore can replace neurons, producing a continuum of cases in which a successively larger proportion of neurons are replaced by chips. Along this continuum, the conscious experience of the system will also change. For example, we might replace all the neurons in your visual cortex with an identically organized version

David J. Chalmers is professor of philosophy and associate director of the Center for Consciousness Studies at the University of Arizona. He is the author of *The Conscious Mind: In Search of a Fundamental Theory.*

made of silicon. The resulting brain, with an artificial visual cortex, will have a different conscious experience from the original: where you had previously seen red, you may now experience purple (or perhaps a faded pink, in the case where the wholly silicon system has no experience at all).

Both visual cortices are then attached to your brain, through a two-position switch. With the switch in one mode, you use the natural visual cortex; in the other, the artificial cortex is activated. When the switch is flipped, your experience changes from red to purple, or vice versa. When the switch is flipped repeatedly, your experiences "dance" between the two different conscious states (red and purple), known as qualia.

Because your brain's organization has not changed, however, there can be no behavioral change when the switch is thrown. Therefore, when asked about what you are seeing, you will say that nothing has changed. You will hold that you are seeing red and have seen

nothing but red—even though the two colors are dancing before your eyes. This conclusion is so unreasonable that it is best taken as a reductio ad absurdum of the original assumption—that an artificial system with identical organization and functioning has a different conscious experience from that of a neural brain. Retraction of the assumption establishes the opposite: that systems with the same organization have the same conscious experience.

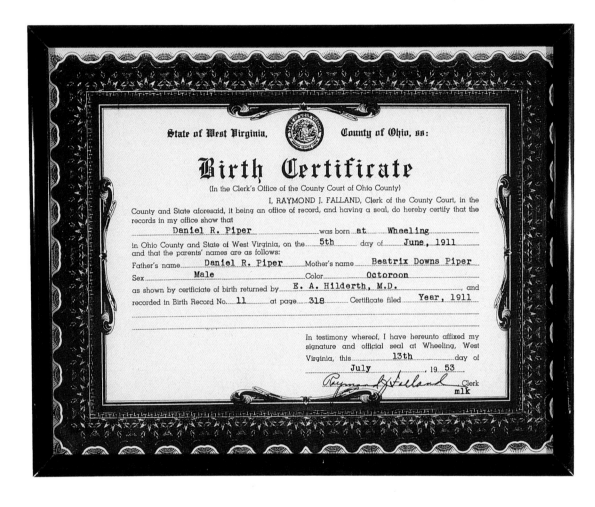

State of West Virginia.    County of Ohio, ss:

# Birth Certificate

(In the Clerk's Office of the County Court of Ohio County)

I, RAYMOND J. FALLAND, Clerk of the County Court, in the County and State aforesaid, it being an office of record, and having a seal, do hereby certify that the records in my office show that

Daniel R. Piper      was born at    Wheeling

in Ohio County and State of West Virginia, on the 5th day of June, 1911 and that the parents' names are as follows:

Father's name   Daniel R. Piper    Mother's name   Beatrix Downs Piper

Sex   Male     Color   Octoroon

as shown by certificate of birth returned by   E. A. Hilderth, M.D.  , and

recorded in Birth Record No. 11   at page 318   Certificate filed   Year, 1911

In testimony whereof, I have hereunto affixed my signature and official seal at Wheeling, West Virginia, this 13th day of July, 19 53

Raymond J Falland   Clerk

mlk

State of West Virginia,          County of Ohio, ss:

# Birth Certificate

### (In the Clerk's Office of the County Court of Ohio County)

I, RAYMOND J. FALLAND, Clerk of the County Court, in the County and State aforesaid, it being an office of record, and having a seal, do hereby certify that the records in my office show that

Daniel R. Piper _____ was born at ___ Wheeling ___

in Ohio County and State of West Virginia, on the __5th__ day of __June__ 19 11

Sex ___ Male ___          Color ___ White ___

and that the parents' names are as follows:

Father's name __Daniel R. Piper__          Mother's name __Beatrix Downs Piper__

Age of Father ___ 38 ___          Age of Mother ___ 22 ___

as shown by certificate of birth returned by __E. A. Hildreth, M. D.__ , and

recorded in Birth Record No. __11__ at page __318__ Certificate filed June, 1911

In testimony whereof, I have hereunto affixed my signature and official seal at Wheeling, West Virginia, this ___12th___ day of

__March__ , 19 65

_Raymond J. Falland_ , Clerk

mc

# is the brain's mind a computer program ?

John R. Searle

Can a machine think? **Can a machine have conscious thoughts in exactly the same sense that you and I have? If by "machine" one means a physical system capable of performing certain functions (and what else can one mean?), then humans are machines of a special biological kind, and humans can think, and so of course machines can think. And, for all we know, it might be possible to produce a thinking machine out of different materials altogether— say, out of silicon chips or vacuum tubes. Maybe it will turn out to be impossible, but we certainly do not know that yet.** In recent decades, however, the question of whether a machine can think has been given a different interpretation entirely. The question that has been posed in its place is, Could a machine think just by virtue of implementing a computer program? Is the program by itself constitutive of thinking? This is a completely different question because it is not about the physical, causal properties of actual or possible physical systems but rather about the abstract, computational properties of formal computer programs that can be implemented in any sort of substance at all, provided only that the substance is able to carry the program.

A fair number of researchers in artificial intelligence (AI) believe the answer to the second question is yes; that is, they believe that by designing the right programs with the right inputs and outputs, they are literally creating minds. They believe furthermore that they have a scientific test for determining success or failure: the Turing test devised by Alan M. Turing, the founding father of artificial intelligence. The Turing test, as currently understood, is simply this: if a computer can perform in such a way that an expert cannot distinguish its performance from that of a human who has a certain cognitive ability—say, the ability to do addition or to understand Chinese—then the computer also has that ability. So the goal is to design programs that will simulate human cognition in such a way as to pass the Turing test. What is more, such a program would not merely be a model of the mind; it would literally be a mind, in the same sense that a human mind is a mind.

By no means does every worker in artificial intelligence accept so extreme a view. A more cautious approach is to think of computer models as being useful in studying the mind in the same way that they are useful in studying the weather, economics or molecular biology. To distinguish these two approaches, I call the first strong AI and the second weak AI. It is important to see just how bold an approach strong AI is. Strong AI claims that thinking is merely the manipulation of formal symbols, and that is exactly what the computer does: manipulate formal symbols. This view is often summarized by saying, "The mind is to the brain as the program is to the hardware."

STRONG AI is unusual among theories of the mind in at least two respects: it can be stated clearly, and it admits of a simple and decisive refutation. The refutation is one that any person can try for himself or herself. Here is how it goes. Consider a language you don't understand. In my case, I do not understand Chinese. To me Chinese writing looks like so many meaningless squiggles. Now suppose I am placed in a room containing baskets full of Chinese symbols. Suppose also that I am given a rule book in English for matching Chinese symbols with other Chinese symbols. The rules identify the symbols entirely by their shapes and do not require that I understand any of them. The rules might say such things as, "Take a squiggle-squiggle sign from basket number one and put it next to a squoggle-squoggle sign from basket number two."

Imagine that people outside the room who understand Chinese hand in small bunches of symbols and that in response I manipulate the symbols according to the rule book and hand back more small bunches of symbols. Now, the rule book is the "computer program." The people who wrote it are "programmers," and I am the "computer." The baskets full of symbols are the "data base," the small bunches that are handed in to me are "questions" and the bunches I then hand out are "answers."

Now suppose that the rule book is written in such a way that my "answers" to the "questions" are indistinguishable from those of a native Chinese speaker. For example, the people outside might hand me some symbols that unknown to me mean, "What's your favorite color?" and I might after going through the rules give back symbols that, also unknown to me, mean, "My favorite is blue, but I also like green a lot." I satisfy the Turing test for understanding Chinese. All the

Markus Raetz, *Zeemansblik und Feldstechermann,* 1987–1988 (detail)

pages 158–159: **Adrian Piper,** *Cornered,* 1988 (details)

same, I am totally ignorant of Chinese. And there is no way I could come to understand Chinese in the system as described, since there is no way that I can learn the meanings of any of the symbols. Like a computer, I manipulate symbols, but I attach no meaning to the symbols.

The point of the thought experiment is this: if I do not understand Chinese solely on the basis of running a computer program for understanding Chinese, then neither does any other digital computer solely on that basis. Digital computers merely manipulate formal symbols according to rules in the program.

What goes for Chinese goes for other forms of cognition as well. Just manipulating the symbols is not by itself enough to guarantee cognition, perception, understanding, thinking and so forth. And since computers, qua computers, are symbol-manipulating devices, merely running the computer program is not enough to guarantee cognition.

This simple argument is decisive against the claims of strong AI. The first premise of the argument simply states the formal character of a computer program. Programs are defined in terms of symbol manipulations, and the symbols are purely formal, or "syntactic." The formal character of the program, by the way, is what makes computers so powerful. The same program can be run on an indefinite variety of hardwares, and one hardware system can run an indefinite range of computer programs. Let me abbreviate this "axiom" as

> Axiom 1
> Computer programs
> are formal (syntactic).

This point is so crucial that it is worth explaining in more detail. A digital computer processes information by first encoding it in the symbolism that the computer uses and then manipulating the symbols through a set of precisely stated rules. These rules constitute the program. For example, in Turing's early theory of computers, the symbols were simply 0's and 1's, and the rules of the program said such things as, "Print a 0 on the tape, move one square to the left and erase a 1." The astonishing thing about computers is that any information that can be stated in a language can be encoded in such a system, and any information-processing task that can be solved by explicit rules can be programmed.

TWO FURTHER POINTS are important. First, symbols and programs are purely abstract notions: they have no essential physical properties to define them and can be implemented in any physical medium whatsoever. The 0's and 1's, qua symbols, have no essential physical properties and a fortiori have no physical, causal properties. I emphasize this point because it is tempting to identify computers with some specific technology—say, silicon chips—and to think that the issues are about the physics of silicon chips or to think that syntax identifies some physical phenomenon that might have as yet unknown causal powers, in the way that actual physical phenomena such as electromagnetic radiation or hydrogen atoms have physical, causal properties. The second point is that symbols are manipulated without reference to any meanings. The symbols of the program can stand for anything the programmer or user wants. In this sense the program has syntax but no semantics.

The next axiom is just a reminder of the obvious fact that thoughts, perceptions, understandings and so forth have a mental content. By virtue of their content they can be about objects and states of affairs in the world. If the content involves language, there will be syntax in addition to semantics, but linguistic understanding requires at least a semantic framework. If, for example, I am thinking about the last presidential election, certain words will go through my mind, but the words are about the election only because I attach specific meanings to these words, in accordance with my knowledge of English. In this respect they are unlike Chinese symbols for me. Let me abbreviate this axiom as

> Axiom 2
> Human minds have
> mental contents
> (semantics).

Now let me add the point that the Chinese room demonstrated. Having the symbols by themselves—just having the syntax—is not sufficient for having the semantics. Merely manipulating symbols is not enough to guarantee knowledge of what they mean. I shall abbreviate this as

> Axiom 3
> Syntax by itself is
> neither constitutive of
> nor sufficient for
> semantics.

At one level this principle is true by definition. One might, of course, define the terms syntax and semantics differently. The point is that there is a distinction between formal elements, which have no intrinsic meaning or content, and those phenomena that have intrinsic content. From these premises it follows that

> Conclusion 1
> Programs are neither
> constitutive of nor
> sufficient for minds.

And that is just another way of saying that strong AI is false.

It is important to see what is proved and not proved by this argument.

First, I have not tried to prove that "a computer cannot think." Since anything that can be simulated computationally can be described as a computer, and since our brains can at some levels be simulated, it follows trivially that our brains are computers and they can certainly think. But from the fact that a system can be simulated by symbol manipulation and the fact that it is thinking, it does not follow that thinking is equivalent to formal symbol manipulation.

Second, I have not tried to show that only biologically based systems like our brains can think. Right now those are the only systems we know for a fact can think, but we might find other systems in the universe that can produce conscious thoughts, and we might even come to be able to create thinking systems artificially. I regard this issue as up for grabs.

Third, strong AI's thesis is not that, for all we know, computers with the right programs might be thinking, that they might have some as yet undetected psychological properties; rather it is that they must be thinking because that is all there is to thinking.

Fourth, I have tried to refute strong AI so defined. I have tried to demonstrate that the program by itself is not constitutive of thinking because the program is purely a matter of formal symbol manipulation—and we know independently that symbol manipulations by themselves are not sufficient to guarantee the presence of meanings. That is the principle on which the Chinese room argument works.

I emphasize these points here partly because it seems to me the Churchlands [see "Could a Machine Think?" by Paul M. Churchland and Patricia Smith Churchland, page 171] have not quite understood the issues. They think that strong AI is claiming that computers might turn out to think and that I am denying this possibility on commonsense grounds. But that is not the claim of strong AI, and my argument against it has nothing to do with common sense.

I will have more to say about their objections later. Meanwhile I should point out that, contrary to what the Churchlands suggest, the Chinese room argument also refutes any strong-AI claims made for the new parallel technologies that are inspired by and modeled on neural networks. Unlike the traditional von Neumann computer, which proceeds in a step-by-step fashion, these systems have many computational elements that operate in parallel and interact with one another according to rules inspired by neurobiology. Although the results are still modest, these "parallel distributed processing," or "connectionist," models raise useful questions about how complex, parallel network systems like those in brains might actually function in the production of intelligent behavior.

The parallel, "brainlike" character of the processing, however, is irrelevant to the purely computational aspects of the process. Any function that can be computed on a parallel machine can also be computed on a serial machine. Indeed, because parallel machines are still rare, connectionist programs are usually run on traditional serial machines. Parallel processing, then, does not afford a way around the Chinese room argument.

What is more, the connectionist system is subject even on its own terms to a variant of the objection presented by the original Chinese room argument. Imagine that instead of a Chinese room, I have a Chinese gym: a hall containing many monolingual, English-speaking men. These men would carry out the same operations as the nodes and synapses in a connectionist architecture as described by the Churchlands, and the outcome would be the same as having one man manipulate symbols according to a rule book. No one in the gym speaks a word of Chinese, and there is no way for the system as a whole to learn the meanings of any Chinese words. Yet with appropriate adjustments, the system could give the correct answers to Chinese questions.

There are, as I suggested earlier, interesting properties of connectionist nets that enable them to simulate brain processes more accurately than traditional serial architecture does. But the advantages of parallel architecture for weak AI are quite irrelevant to the issues between the Chinese room argument and strong AI.

The Churchlands miss this point when they say that a big enough Chinese gym might have higher-level mental features that emerge from the size and complexity of the system, just as whole brains have mental features that are not had by individual neurons. That is, of course, a possibility, but it has nothing to do with computation. Computationally, serial and parallel systems are equivalent: any computation that can be done in parallel can be done in serial. If the man in the Chinese room is computationally equivalent to both, then if he does not understand Chinese solely by virtue of doing the computations, neither do they. The Churchlands are correct in saying that the original Chinese room argument was designed with traditional AI in mind but wrong in thinking that connectionism is immune to the argument. It applies to any computational system. You can't get semantically loaded thought contents from formal computations alone, whether they are done in serial or in parallel; that is why the Chinese room argument refutes strong AI in any form.

MANY PEOPLE who are impressed by this argument are nonetheless puzzled about the differences between people and computers. If humans are, at least in a trivial sense, computers, and if humans have a semantics, then why couldn't we give semantics to other computers? Why couldn't we program a Vax or a Cray so that it too would have thoughts and feelings? Or why couldn't some new computer technology overcome the gulf between form and content, between syntax and semantics? What, in fact, are the differences between animal brains and computer systems that enable the Chinese room argument to work against computers but not against brains?

The most obvious difference is that the processes that define something as a computer—computational processes—are completely independent of any reference to a specific type of hardware implementation. One could in principle make a computer out of old beer cans strung together with wires and powered by windmills.

But when it comes to brains, although science is largely ignorant of how brains function to produce mental states, one is struck by the extreme specificity of the anatomy and the physiology. Where some understanding exists of how brain processes produce mental phenomena—for example, pain, thirst, vision, smell—it is clear that specific neurobiological processes are involved. Thirst, at least of certain kinds, is caused by certain types of neuron firings in the hypothalamus, which in turn are caused by the action of a specific peptide, angiotensin II. The causation is from the "bottom up" in the sense that lower-level neuronal processes cause higher-level mental phenomena. Indeed, as far as we know, every "mental" event, ranging from feelings of thirst to thoughts of mathematical theorems and memories of childhood, is caused by specific neurons firing in specific neural architectures.

But why should this specificity matter? After all, neuron firings could be simulated on computers that had a completely different physics and chemistry from that of the brain. The answer is that the brain does not merely instantiate a formal pattern or program (it does that, too), but it also *causes* mental events by virtue of specific neurobiological processes. Brains are specific biological organs, and their specific biochemical properties enable them to cause consciousness and other sorts of mental phenomena. Computer simulations of brain processes provide models of the formal aspects of these processes. But the simulation should not be confused with duplication. The computational model of mental processes is no more real than the computational model of any other natural phenomenon.

One can imagine a computer simulation of the action of peptides in the hypothalamus that is accurate down to the last synapse. But equally one can imagine a computer simulation of the oxidation of hydrocarbons in a car engine or the action of digestive processes in a stomach when it is digesting pizza. And the simulation is no more the real thing in the case of the brain than it is in the case of the car or the stomach. Barring miracles, you could not run your car by doing a computer simulation of the oxidation of gasoline, and you could not digest pizza by running the program that simulates such digestion. It seems obvious that a simulation of cognition will similarly not produce the effects of the neurobiology of cognition.

All mental phenomena, then, are caused by neurophysiological processes in the brain. Hence,

Axiom 4
Brains cause minds.

In conjunction with my earlier derivation, I immediately derive, trivially,

Conclusion 2
Any other system
capable of causing
minds would have to
have causal powers
(at least) equivalent
to those of brains.

This is like saying that if an electrical engine is to be able to run a car as fast as a gas engine, it must have (at least) an equivalent power output. This conclusion says nothing about the mechanisms. As a matter of fact, cognition is a biological phenomenon: mental states and processes are caused by brain processes. This does not imply that only a biological system could think, but it does imply that any alternative system, whether made of silicon, beer cans or whatever, would have to have the relevant causal capacities equivalent to those of brains. So now I can derive

Conclusion 3
Any artifact that
produced mental
phenomena, any
artificial brain, would
have to be able to
duplicate the specific
causal powers of
brains, and it could
not do that just by
running a formal
program.

Furthermore, I can derive an important conclusion about human brains:

Conclusion 4
The way that
human brains
actually produce
mental phenomena cannot
be solely by virtue
of running a
computer program.

I FIRST PRESENTED the Chinese room parable in the pages of *Behavioral and Brain Sciences* in 1980, where it appeared, as is the practice of the journal, along with peer commentary, in this case, 26 commentaries. Frankly, I think the point it makes is rather obvious, but to my surprise the publication was followed by a further flood of objections that—more surprisingly—continues to the present day. The Chinese room argument clearly touched some sensitive nerve.

The thesis of strong AI is that any system whatsoever—whether it is made of beer cans, silicon chips or toilet paper—not only might have thoughts and feelings but *must* have thoughts and feelings, provided only that it implements the right program, with the right inputs and outputs. Now, that is a profoundly antibiological view, and one would think that people in AI would be glad to abandon it. Many of them, especially the younger generation, agree with me, but I am amazed at the number and vehemence of the defenders. Here are some of the common objections.

A    In the Chinese room you really do understand Chinese, even though you don't know it. It is, after all, possible to understand something without knowing that one understands it.

B    You don't understand Chinese, but there is an (unconscious) subsystem in you that does. It is, after all, possible to have unconscious mental states, and there is no reason why your understanding of Chinese should not be wholly unconscious.

C    You don't understand Chinese, but the whole room does. You are like a single neuron in the brain, and just as such a single neuron by itself cannot understand but only contributes to the understanding of the whole system, you don't understand, but the whole system does.

D    Semantics doesn't exist anyway; there is only syntax. It is a kind of prescientific illusion to suppose that there exist in the brain some mysterious "mental contents," "thought processes" or "semantics." All that exists in the brain is the same sort of syntactic symbol manipulation that goes on in computers. Nothing more.

E    You are not really running the computer program—you only think you are. Once you have a conscious agent going through the steps of the program, it ceases to be a case of implementing a program at all.

F    Computers would have semantics and not just syntax if their inputs and outputs were put in appropriate causal relation to the rest of the world. Imagine that we put the computer into a robot, attached television cameras to the robot's head, installed transducers connecting the television messages to the computer and had the computer output operate the robot's arms and legs. Then the whole system would have a semantics.

G    If the program simulated the operation of the brain of a Chinese speaker, then it would understand Chinese. Suppose that we simulated the brain of a Chinese person at the level of neurons. Then surely such a system would understand Chinese as well as any Chinese person's brain.

And so on.

All of these arguments share a common feature: they are all inadequate because they fail to come to grips with the actual Chinese room argument. That argument rests on the distinction between the formal symbol manipulation that is done by the computer and the mental contents biologically produced by the brain, a distinction I have abbreviated—I hope not misleadingly—as the distinction between syntax and semantics. I will not repeat my answers to all of these objections, but it will help to clarify the issues if I explain the weaknesses of the most widely held objection, argument c—what I call the systems reply. (The brain simulator reply, argument g, is another popular one, but I have already addressed that one in the previous section.)

THE SYSTEMS REPLY asserts that of course *you* don't understand Chinese but the whole system—you, the room, the rule book, the bushel baskets full of symbols—does. When I first heard this explanation, I asked one of its proponents, "Do you mean the room understands Chinese?" His answer was yes. It is a daring move, but aside from its implausibility, it will not work on purely logical grounds. The point of the original argument was that symbol shuffling by itself does not give any access to the meanings of the symbols. But this is as much true of the whole room as it is of the person inside. One can see this point by extending the thought experiment. Imagine that I memorize the contents of the baskets and the rule book, and I do all the calculations in my head. You can even imagine that I work out in the open. There is nothing in the "system" that is not in me, and since I don't understand Chinese, neither does the system.

The Churchlands in their companion piece produce a variant of the systems reply by imagining an amusing analogy. Suppose that someone said that light could not be electromagnetic because if you shake a bar magnet in a dark room, the system still will not give off visible light. Now, the Churchlands ask, is not the Chinese room argument just like that? Does it not merely say that if you shake Chinese symbols in a semantically dark room, they will not give off the light of Chinese understanding? But just as later investigation showed that light was entirely constituted by electromagnetic radiation, could not later investigation also show that semantics are entirely constituted of syntax? Is this not a question for further scientific investigation?

Arguments from analogy are notoriously weak, because before one can make the argument work, one has to establish that the two cases are truly analogous. And here I think they are not. The account of light in terms of electromagnetic radiation is a causal story right down to the ground. It is a causal account of the physics of electromagnetic radiation. But the analogy with formal symbols fails because formal symbols have no physical, causal powers. The only power that symbols have, qua symbols, is the power to cause the next step in the program when the machine is running. And there is no question of waiting on further research to reveal the physical, causal properties of 0's and 1's. The only relevant properties of 0's and 1's are abstract computational properties, and they are already well known.

The Churchlands complain that I am "begging the question" when I say that uninterpreted formal symbols are not identical to mental contents. Well, I certainly did not spend much time arguing for it, because I take it as a logical truth. As with any logical truth, one can quickly see that it is true, because one gets inconsistencies if one tries to imagine the converse. So let us try it. Suppose that in the Chinese room some undetectable Chinese thinking really is going on. What exactly is supposed to make the manipulation of the syntactic elements into specifically Chinese thought contents? Well, after all, I am assuming that the programmers were Chinese speakers, programming the system to process Chinese information.

Fine. But now imagine that as I am sitting in the Chinese room shuffling the Chinese symbols, I get bored with just shuffling the—to me—meaningless symbols. So, suppose that I decide to interpret the symbols as standing for moves in a chess game. Which semantics is the system giving off now? Is it giving off a Chinese semantics or a chess semantics, or both simultaneously? Suppose there is a third person looking in through the window, and she decides that the symbol manipulations can all be interpreted as stock-market predictions. And so on. There is no limit to the number of semantic interpretations that can be assigned to the symbols because, to repeat, the symbols are purely formal. They have no intrinsic semantics.

Is there any way to rescue the Churchlands' analogy from incoherence? I said above that formal symbols do not have causal properties. But of course the program will always be implemented in some hardware or another, and the hardware will have specific physical, causal powers. And any real computer will give off various phenomena. My computers, for example, give off heat, and they make a humming noise and sometimes crunching sounds. So is there some logically compelling reason why they could not also give off consciousness? No. Scientifically, the idea is out of the question, but it is not something the Chinese room argument is supposed to refute, and it is not something that an adherent of strong AI would wish to defend, because any such giving off would have to derive from the physical features of the implementing medium. But the basic premise of strong AI is that the physical features of the implementing medium are totally irrelevant. What matters are programs, and programs are purely formal.

The Churchlands' analogy between syntax and electromagnetism, then, is confronted with a dilemma; either the syntax is construed purely formally in terms of its abstract mathematical properties, or it is not. If it is, then the analogy breaks down, because syntax so construed has no physical powers and hence no physical, causal powers. If, on the other hand, one is supposed to think in terms of the physics of the implementing medium, then there is indeed an analogy, but it is not one that is relevant to strong AI.

BECAUSE THE POINTS I have been making are rather obvious— syntax is not the same as semantics, brain processes cause mental phenomena—the question arises, How did we get into this mess? How could anyone have supposed that a computer simulation of a mental process must be the real thing? After all, the whole point of models is that they contain only certain features of the modeled domain and leave out the rest. No one expects to get wet in a pool filled with Ping-Pong-ball models of water

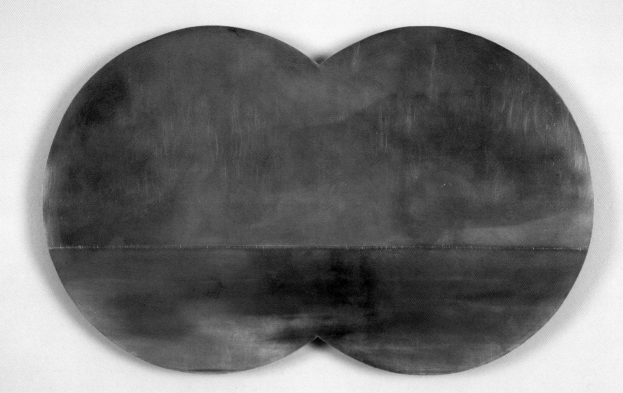

John R. Searle is Mills professor of philosophy at the University of California, Berkeley. He is the author of numerous works on the philosophy of language and the philosophy of mind, including *The Rediscovery of the Mind; Speech Acts; The Mystery of Consciousness;* and *Mind, Language, and Society: Philosophy in the Real World.*

molecules. So why would anyone think a computer model of thought processes would actually think?

Part of the answer is that people have inherited a residue of behaviorist psychological theories of the past generation. The Turing test enshrines the temptation to think that if something behaves as if it had certain mental processes, then it must actually have those mental processes. And this is part of the behaviorists' mistaken assumption that in order to be scientific, psychology must confine its study to externally observable behavior. Paradoxically, this residual behaviorism is tied to a residual dualism. Nobody thinks that a computer simulation of digestion would actually digest anything, but where cognition is concerned, people are willing to believe in such a miracle because they fail to recognize that the mind is just as much a biological phenomenon as digestion. The mind, they suppose, is something formal and abstract, not a part of the wet and slimy stuff in our heads. The polemical literature in AI usually contains attacks on something the authors call dualism, but what they fail to see is that they themselves display dualism in a strong form, for unless one accepts the idea that the mind is completely independent of the brain or of any other physically specific system, one could not possibly hope to create minds just by designing programs.

Historically, scientific developments in the West that have treated humans as just a part of the ordinary physical, biological order have often been opposed by various rearguard actions. Copernicus and Galileo were opposed because they denied that the earth was the center of the universe; Darwin was opposed because he claimed that humans had descended from the lower animals. It is best to see strong AI as one of the last gasps of this antiscientific tradition, for it denies that there is anything essentially physical and biological about the human mind. The mind according to strong AI is independent of the brain. It is a computer program and as such has no essential connection to any specific hardware.

Many people who have doubts about the psychological significance of AI think that computers might be able to understand Chinese and think about numbers but cannot do the crucially human things, namely—and then follows their favorite human specialty—falling in love, having a sense of humor, feeling the angst of postindustrial society under late capitalism, or whatever. But workers in AI complain—correctly—that this is a case of moving the goalposts. As soon as an AI simulation succeeds, it ceases to be of psychological importance. In this debate both sides fail to see the distinction between simulation and duplication. As far as simulation is concerned, there is no difficulty in programming my computer so that it prints out, "I love you, Suzy"; "Ha ha"; or "I am suffering the angst of postindustrial society under late capitalism." The important point is that simulation is not the same as duplication, and that fact holds as much import for thinking about arithmetic as it does for feeling angst. The point is not that the computer gets only to the 40-yard line and not all the way to the goal line. The computer doesn't even get started. It is not playing that game.

Markus Raetz, *Zeemansblik und Feldstechermann,* 1987–1988 (detail)

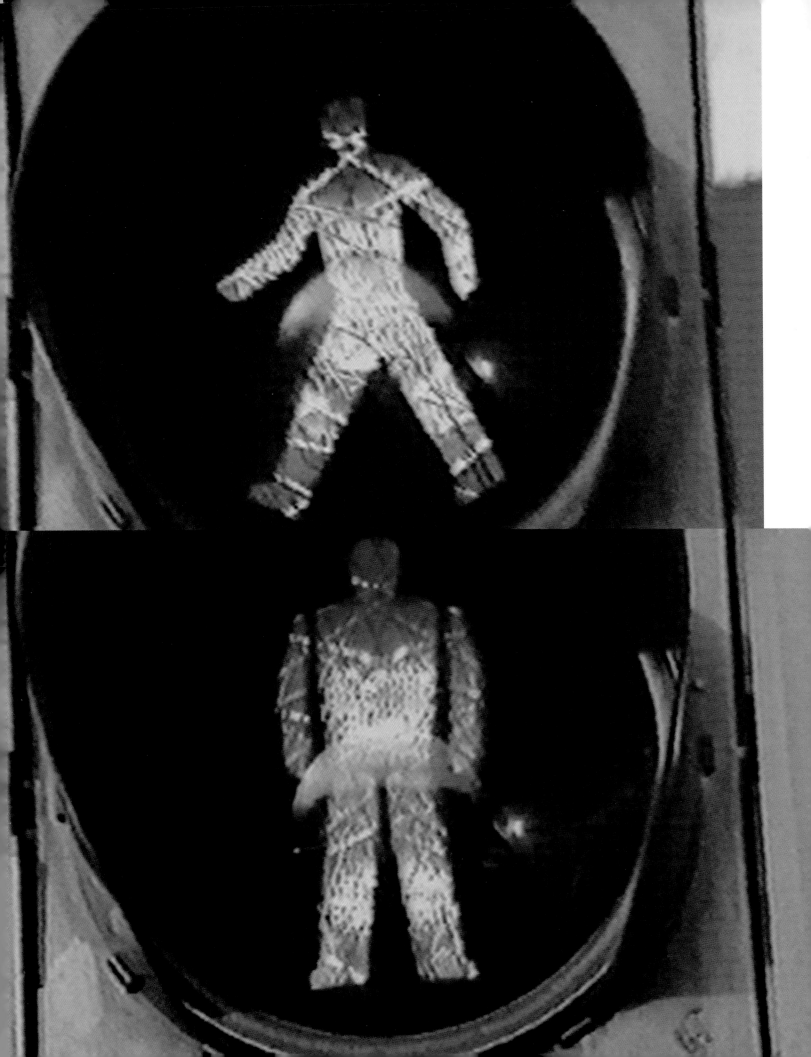

# could a machine think ?

Paul M. Churchland
Patricia Smith Churchland

Artificial-intelligence research is undergoing **a revolution. To explain how and why, and to put John R. Searle's argument [see "Is the Brain's Mind a Computer Program?" page 161] in perspective, we first need a flashback.**

**By the early 1950's the old, vague question, Could a machine think? had been replaced by the more approachable question, Could a machine that manipulated physical symbols according to structure-sensitive rules think? This question was an improvement because formal logic and computational theory had seen major developments in the preceding half-century. Theorists had come to appreciate the enormous power of abstract systems of symbols that undergo rule-governed transformations. If those systems could just be automated, then their abstract computational power, it seemed, would be displayed in a real physical system. This insight spawned a well-defined research program with deep theoretical underpinnings.**

Could a machine think? There were many reasons for saying yes. One of the earliest and deepest reasons lay in two important results in computational theory. The first was Church's thesis, which states that every effectively computable function is recursively computable. Effectively computable means that there is a "rote" procedure for determining, in finite time, the output of the function for a given input. Recursively computable means more specifically that there is a finite set of operations that can be applied to a given input, and then applied again and again to the successive results of such applications, to yield the function's output in finite time. The notion of a rote procedure is nonformal and intuitive; thus, Church's thesis does not admit of a formal proof. But it does go to the heart of what it is to compute, and many lines of evidence converge in supporting it.

The second important result was Alan M. Turing's demonstration that any recursively computable function can be computed in finite time by a maximally simple sort of symbol-manipulating machine that has come to be called a universal Turing machine. This machine is guided by a set of recursively applicable rules that are sensitive to the identity, order and arrangement of the elementary symbols it encounters as input.

THESE TWO RESULTS entail something remarkable, namely that a standard digital computer, given only the right program, a large enough memory and sufficient time, can compute *any* rule-governed input-output function. That is, it can display any systematic pattern of responses to the environment whatsoever.

More specifically, these results imply that a suitably programmed symbol-manipulating machine (hereafter, SM machine) should be able to pass the Turing test for conscious intelligence. The Turing test is a purely behavioral test for conscious intelligence, but it is a very demanding test even so. (Whether it is a fair test will be addressed below, where we shall also encounter a second and quite different "test" for conscious intelligence.) In the original version of the Turing test, the inputs to the SM machine are conversational questions and remarks typed into a console by you or me, and the outputs are typewritten responses from the SM machine. The machine passes this test for conscious intelligence if its responses cannot be discriminated from the typewritten responses of a real, intelligent person. Of course, at present no one knows the function that would produce the output behavior of a conscious person. But the Church and Turing results assure us that, whatever that (presumably effective) function might be, a suitable SM machine could compute it.

This is a significant conclusion, especially since Turing's portrayal of a purely teletyped interaction is an unnecessary restriction. The same conclusion follows even if the SM machine interacts with the world in more complex ways: by direct vision, real speech and so forth. After all, a more complex recursive function is still Turing-computable. The only remaining problem is to identify the undoubtedly complex function that governs the human pattern of response to the environment and then write the program (the set of recursively applicable rules) by which the SM machine will compute it. These goals form the fundamental research program of classical AI.

Initial results were positive. SM machines with clever programs performed a variety of ostensibly cognitive activities. They responded to complex instructions, solved complex arithmetic, algebraic and tactical problems, played checkers and chess, proved theorems and engaged in simple dialogue. Performance continued to improve with the

opposite and pages 168–169:
**Stuart Sherman,** *Berlin (West)/Andere Richtungen,* 1986 (details)

appearance of larger memories and faster machines and with the use of longer and more cunning programs. Classical, or "program-writing," AI was a vigorous and successful research effort from almost every perspective. The occasional denial that an SM machine might eventually think appeared uninformed and ill motivated. The case for a positive answer to our title question was overwhelming.

There were a few puzzles, of course. For one thing, SM machines were admittedly not very brain-like. Even here, however, the classical approach had a convincing answer. First, the physical material of any SM machine has nothing essential to do with what function it computes. That is fixed by its program. Second, the engineering details of any machine's functional architecture are also irrelevant, since different architectures running quite different programs can still be computing the same input-output function.

Accordingly, AI sought to find the input-output *function* characteristic of intelligence and the most efficient of the many possible programs for computing it. The idiosyncratic way in which the brain computes the function just doesn't matter, it was said. This completes the rationale for classical AI and for a positive answer to our title question.

COULD   A   MACHINE think? There were also some arguments for saying no. Through the 1960's interesting negative arguments were relatively rare. The objection was occasionally made that thinking was a nonphysical process in an immaterial soul. But such dualistic resistance was neither evolutionarily nor explanatorily plausible. It had a negligible impact on AI research.

A quite different line of objection was more successful in gaining the AI community's attention. In 1972 Hubert L. Dreyfus published a book that was highly critical of the parade-case simulations of cognitive activity. He argued for their inadequacy as simulations of genuine cognition, and he pointed to a pattern of failure in these attempts. What they were missing, he suggested, was the vast store of inarticulate background knowledge every person possesses and the commonsense capacity for drawing on relevant aspects of that knowledge as changing circumstance demands. Dreyfus did not deny the possibility that an artificial physical system of some kind might think, but he was highly critical of the idea that this could be achieved solely by symbol manipulation at the hands of recursively applicable rules.

Dreyfus's complaints were broadly perceived within the AI community, and within the discipline of philosophy as well, as shortsighted and unsympathetic, as harping on the inevitable simplifications of a research effort still in its youth. These deficits might be real, but surely they were temporary. Bigger machines and better programs should repair them in due course. Time, it was felt, was on AI's side. Here again the impact on research was negligible.

Time was on Dreyfus's side as well: the rate of cognitive return on increasing speed and memory began to slacken in the late 1970's and early 1980's. The simulation of object recognition in the visual system, for example, proved computationally intensive to an unexpected degree. Realistic results required longer and longer periods of computer time, periods far in excess of what a real visual system requires. This relative slowness of the simulations was darkly curious; signal propagation in a computer is roughly a million times faster than in the brain, and the clock frequency of a computer's central processor is greater than any frequency found in the brain by a similarly dramatic margin. And yet, on realistic problems, the tortoise easily outran the hare.

Furthermore, realistic performance required that the computer program have access to an extremely large knowledge base. Constructing the relevant knowledge base was problem enough, and it was compounded by the problem of how to access just the contextually relevant parts of that knowledge base in real time. As the knowledge base got bigger and better, the access problem got worse. Exhaustive search took too much time, and heuristics for relevance did poorly. Worries of the sort Dreyfus had raised finally began to take hold here and there even among AI researchers.

At about this time (1980) John Searle authored a new and quite different criticism aimed at the most basic assumption of the classical research program: the idea that the appropriate manipulation of structured symbols by the recursive application of structure-sensitive rules could constitute conscious intelligence.

Searle's argument is based on a thought experiment that displays two crucial features. First, he describes a SM machine that realizes, we are to suppose, an input-output function adequate to sustain a successful Turing test conversation conducted entirely in Chinese. Second, the internal structure of the machine is such that, however it behaves, an observer remains certain that neither the machine nor any part of it understands Chinese. All it contains is a monolingual English speaker following a written set of instructions for manipulating the Chinese symbols that arrive and leave through a mail slot. In short, the system is supposed to pass the Turing test, while the system itself lacks any genuine understanding of Chinese or real Chinese semantic content [see "Is the Brain's Mind a Computer Program?" by John R. Searle, page 161].

The general lesson drawn is that any system that merely manipulates physical symbols in accordance with structure-sensitive rules will be at best a hollow mock-up of real conscious intelligence, because it is impossible to generate "real semantics" merely by cranking away on "empty syntax." Here, we should point out, Searle is imposing a nonbehavioral test for consciousness: the elements of conscious intelligence must possess real semantic content.

One is tempted to complain that Searle's thought experiment is unfair because his Rube Goldberg system will compute with absurd slowness. Searle insists, however, that speed is strictly irrelevant here. A slow thinker should still be a real thinker. Everything essential to the duplication of thought, as per classical AI, is said to be present in the Chinese room.

Searle's paper provoked a lively reaction from AI researchers, psychologists and philosophers alike. On the whole, however, he was met with an even more hostile reception than Dreyfus had experienced. In his companion piece in this issue, Searle forthrightly lists a number of these critical responses. We think many of them are reasonable, especially those that "bite the bullet" by insisting that, although it is appallingly slow, the overall system of the room-plus-contents does understand Chinese.

We think those are good responses, but not because we think that the room understands Chinese. We agree with Searle that it does not. Rather they are good responses because they reflect a refusal to accept the crucial third axiom of Searle's argument: *"Syntax by itself is neither constitutive of nor sufficient for semantics."* Perhaps this axiom is true, but Searle cannot rightly pretend to know that it is. Moreover, to assume its truth is tantamount to begging the question against the research program of classical AI, for that program is predicated on the very interesting assumption that if one can just set in motion an appropriately structured internal dance of syntactic elements, appropriately connected to inputs and outputs, it can produce the same cognitive states and achievements found in human beings.

The question-begging character of Searle's axiom 3 becomes clear when it is compared directly with his conclusion 1: *"Programs are neither constitutive of nor sufficient for minds."* Plainly, his third axiom is already carrying 90 percent of the weight of this almost identical conclusion. That is why Searle's thought experiment is devoted to shoring up axiom 3 specifically. That is the point of the Chinese room.

Although the story of the Chinese room makes axiom 3 tempting to the unwary, we do not think it succeeds in establishing axiom 3, and we offer a parallel argument below in illustration of its failure. A single transparently fallacious instance of a disputed argument often provides far more insight than a book full of logic chopping.

Searle's style of skepticism has ample precedent in the history of science. The 18th-century Irish bishop George Berkeley found it unintelligible that compression waves in the air, by themselves, could constitute or be sufficient for objective sound. The English poet-artist William Blake and the German poet-naturalist Johann W. von Goethe found it inconceivable that small particles by

themselves could constitute or be sufficient for the objective phenomenon of light. Even in this century, there have been people who found it beyond imagining that inanimate matter by itself, and however organized, could ever constitute or be sufficient for life. Plainly, what people can or cannot imagine often has nothing to do with what is or is not the case, even where the people involved are highly intelligent.

To see how this lesson applies to Searle's case, consider a deliberately manufactured parallel to his argument and its supporting thought experiment.

Axiom 1
Electricity and magnetism are forces.

Axiom 2
The essential property of light is luminance.

Axiom 3
Forces by themselves are neither constitutive of nor sufficient for luminance.

Conclusion 1
Electricity and magnetism are neither constitutive of nor sufficient for light.

Imagine this argument raised shortly after James Clerk Maxwell's 1864 suggestion that light and electromagnetic waves are identical but before the world's full appreciation of the systematic parallels between the properties of light and the properties of electromagnetic waves. This argument could have served as a compelling objection to Maxwell's imaginative hypothesis, especially if it were accompanied by the following commentary in support of axiom 3.

"Consider a dark room containing a man holding a bar magnet or charged object. If the man pumps the magnet up and down, then, according to Maxwell's theory of artificial luminance (AL), it will initiate a spreading circle of electromagnetic waves and will thus be luminous. But as all of us who have toyed with magnets or charged balls well know, their forces (or any other forces for that matter), even when set in motion, produce no luminance at all. It is inconceivable that you might constitute real luminance just by moving forces around!"

How should Maxwell respond to this challenge? He might begin by insisting that the "luminous room" experiment is a misleading display of the phenomenon of luminance because the frequency of oscillation of the magnet is absurdly low, too low by a factor of $10^{15}$. This might well elicit the impatient response that frequency has nothing to do with it, that the room with the bobbing magnet already contains everything essential to light, according to Maxwell's own theory.

In response Maxwell might bite the bullet and claim, quite correctly, that the room really is bathed in luminance, albeit a grade or quality too feeble to appreciate. (Given the low frequency with which the man can oscillate the magnet, the wavelength of the electromagnetic waves produced is far too long and their intensity is much too weak for human retinas to respond to them.) But in the climate of understanding here contemplated —the 1860's—this tactic is likely to elicit laughter and hoots of derision. "Luminous room, my foot, Mr. Maxwell. It's pitch-black in there!"

Alas, poor Maxwell has no easy route out of this predicament. All he can do is insist on the following three points. First, axiom 3 of the above argument is false. Indeed, it begs the question despite its intuitive plausibility. Second, the luminous room experiment demonstrates nothing of interest one way or the other about the nature of light. And third, what is needed to settle the problem of light and the possibility of artificial luminance is an ongoing research program to determine whether under the appropriate conditions the behavior of electromagnetic waves does indeed mirror perfectly the behavior of light.

This is also the response that classical AI should give to Searle's argument. Even though Searle's Chinese room may appear to be "semantically dark," he is in no position to insist, on the strength of this appearance, that rule-governed symbol manipulation can never constitute semantic phenomena, especially when people have only an uninformed commonsense understanding of the semantic and cognitive phenomena that need to be explained. Rather than exploit one's understanding of these things, Searle's argument freely exploits one's ignorance of them.

With these criticisms of Searle's argument in place, we return to the question of whether the research program of classical AI has a realistic chance of solving the problem of conscious intelligence and of producing a machine that thinks. We believe that the prospects are poor, but we rest this opinion on reasons very different from Searle's. Our reasons derive from the specific performance failures of the classical research program in AI and from a variety of lessons learned from the biological brain and a new class of computational models inspired by its structure. We have already indicated some of the failures of classical AI regarding tasks that the brain performs swiftly and efficiently. The emerging consensus on these failures is that the functional architecture of classical SM machines is simply the wrong architecture for the very demanding jobs required.

WHAT WE NEED TO KNOW IS THIS: How does the brain achieve cognition? Reverse engineering is a common practice in industry. When a new piece of technology comes on the market, competitors find out how it works by taking it apart and divining its structural rationale. In the case of the brain, this strategy presents an unusually stiff challenge, for the brain is the most complicated and sophisticated thing on the planet. Even so, the neurosciences have revealed much about the brain on a wide variety of structural levels. Three anatomic points will provide a basic contrast with the architecture of conventional electronic computers.

First, nervous systems are parallel machines, in the sense that signals are processed in millions of different pathways simultaneously. The retina, for example, presents its complex input to the brain not in chunks of eight, 16 or 32 elements, as in a desktop computer, but rather in the form of almost a million distinct signal elements arriving simultaneously at the target of the optic nerve (the lateral geniculate nucleus), there to be processed collectively, simultaneously and in one fell swoop. Second, the brain's basic processing unit, the neuron, is comparatively simple. Furthermore, its response to incoming signals is analog, not digital, inasmuch as its output spiking frequency varies continuously with its input signals. Third, in the brain, axons projecting from one neuronal population to another are often matched by axons returning from their target population. These descending or recurrent projections allow the brain to modulate the character of its sensory processing. More important still, their existence makes the brain a genuine dynamical system whose continuing behavior is both highly complex and to some degree independent of its peripheral stimuli.

Highly simplified model networks have been useful in suggesting how real neural networks might work and in revealing the computational properties of parallel architectures. For example, consider a three-layer model consisting of neuronlike units fully connected by axonlike connections to the units at the next layer. An input stimulus produces some activation level in a given input unit, which conveys a signal of proportional strength along its "axon" to its many "synaptic" connections to the hidden units. The global effect is that a pattern of activations across the set of input units produces a distinct pattern of activations across the set of hidden units.

The same story applies to the output units. As before, an activation pattern across the hidden units produces a distinct activation pattern across the output units. All told, this network is a device for transforming any one of a great many possible input vectors (activation patterns) into a uniquely corresponding output vector. It is a device for computing a specific function. Exactly which function it computes is fixed by the global configuration of its synaptic weights.

There are various procedures for adjusting the weights so as to yield a network that computes almost any function—that is, any vector-to-vector transformation—that one might desire. In fact, one can even impose on it a function one is unable to specify, so long as one can supply a set of examples of the desired input-output pairs. This process, called "training up the network," proceeds by successive adjustment of the network's weights until it performs the input-output transformations desired.

Although this model network vastly oversimplifies the structure of the brain, it does illustrate several important ideas. First, a parallel architecture provides a dramatic speed advantage over a conventional computer, for the many synapses at each level perform many small computations simultaneously instead of in laborious sequence. This advantage gets larger as the number of neurons increases at each layer. Strikingly, the speed of processing is entirely independent of both the number of units involved in each layer and the complexity of the function they are computing. Each layer could have four units or a hundred million; its configuration of synaptic weights could be computing simple one-digit sums or second-order differential equations. It would make no difference. The computation time would be exactly the same.

Second, massive parallelism means that the system if fault-tolerant and functionally persistent; the loss of a few connections, even quite a few, has a negligible effect on the character of the overall transformation performed by the surviving network.

Third, a parallel system stores large amounts of information in a distributed fashion, any part of which can be accessed in milliseconds. That information is stored in the specific configuration of synaptic connection strengths, as shaped by past learning. Relevant information is "released" as the input vector passes through— and is transformed by—that configuration of connections.

Parallel processing is not ideal for all types of computation. On tasks that require only a small input vector, but many millions of swiftly iterated recursive computations, the brain performs very badly, whereas classical SM machines excel. This class of computations is very large and important, so classical machines will always be useful, indeed, vital. There is, however, an equally large class of computations for which the brain's architecture is the superior technology. These are the computations that typically confront living creatures: recognizing a predator's outline in a noisy environment; recalling instantly how to avoid its gaze, flee its approach or fend off its attack; distinguishing food from nonfood and mates from nonmates; navigating through a complex and ever-changing physical/social environment; and so on.

Finally, it is important to note that the parallel system described is not manipulating symbols according to structure-sensitive rules. Rather symbol manipulation appears to be just one of many cognitive skills that a network may or may not learn to display. Rule-governed symbol manipulation is not its basic mode of operation. Searle's argument is directed against rule-governed SM machines; vector transformers of the kind we describe are therefore not threatened by his Chinese room argument even if it were sound, which we have found independent reason to doubt.

Searle is aware of parallel processors but thinks they too will be devoid of real semantic content. To illustrate their inevitable failure, he outlines a second thought experiment, the Chinese gym, which has a gymnasium full of people organized into a parallel network. From there his argument proceeds as in the Chinese room.

We find this second story far less responsive or compelling than his first. For one, it is irrelevant that no unit in his system understands Chinese, since the same is true of nervous systems: no neuron in my brain understands English, although my whole brain does. For another, Searle neglects to mention that his simulation (using one person per neuron, plus a fleet-footed child for each synaptic connection) will require at least $10^{14}$ people, since the human brain has $10^{11}$ neurons,

each of which averages over $10^3$ connections. His system will require the entire human populations of over 10,000 earths. One gymnasium will not begin to hold a fair simulation.

On the other hand, if such a system were to be assembled on a suitably cosmic scale, with all its pathways faithfully modeled on the human case, we might then have a large, slow, oddly made but still functional brain on our hands. In that case the default assumption is surely that, given proper inputs, it would think, not that it couldn't. There is no guarantee that its activity would constitute real thought, because the vector-processing theory sketched above may not be the correct theory of how brains work. But neither is there any a priori guarantee that it could not be thinking. Searle is once more mistaking the limits on his (or the reader's) current imagination for the limits on objective reality.

THE BRAIN is a kind of computer, although most of its properties remain to be discovered. Characterizing the brain as a kind of computer is neither trivial nor frivolous. The brain does compute functions, functions of great complexity, but not in the classical AI fashion. When brains are said to be computers, it should not be implied that they are serial, digital computers, that they are programmed, that they exhibit the distinction between hardware and software or that they must be symbol manipulators or rule followers. Brains are computers in a radically different style.

How the brain manages meaning is still unknown, but it is clear that the problem reaches beyond language use and beyond humans. A small mound of fresh dirt signifies to a person, and also to coyotes, that a gopher is around; an echo with a certain spectral character signifies to a bat the presence of a moth. To develop a theory of meaning, more must be known about how neurons code and transform sensory signals, about the neural basis of memory, learning and emotion and about the interaction of these capacities and the motor system. A neurally grounded theory of meaning may require revision of the very intuitions that now seem so secure and that are so freely exploited in Searle's arguments. Such revisions are common in the history of science.

Could science construct an artificial intelligence by exploiting what is known about the nervous system? We see no principled reason why not. Searle appears to agree, although he qualifies his claim by saying that "any other system capable of causing minds would have to have causal powers (at least) equivalent to those of brains." We close by addressing this claim. We presume that Searle is not claiming that a successful artificial mind must have *all* the causal powers of the brain, such as the power to smell bad when rotting, to harbor slow viruses such as kuru, to stain yellow with horseradish peroxidase and so forth. Requiring perfect parity would be like requiring that an artificial flying device lay eggs.

Presumably he means only to require of an artificial mind all of the causal powers relevant, as he says, to conscious intelligence. But which exactly are they? We are back to

Diana Thater, *Perspective is an energy,* 1995 (details)

Paul M. Churchland and Patricia Smith Churchland are professors of philosophy, and members of the cognitive science faculty and the Institute for Neural Computation at the University of California, San Diego. They are the authors of *Contrary: Critical Essays, 1987–1997.* Paul M. Churchland is the author of *The Engine of Reason, The Seat of the Soul: A Philosophical Journey into the Brain,* and *A Neurocomputational Perspective: The Nature of Mind and the Structure of Science.* Patricia Smith Churchland is the author of *The Computational Brain* (coauthored with Terrence J. Sejnowski) and *Neurophilosophy: Toward a Unified Science of Mind-Brain.*

quarreling about what is and is not relevant. This is an entirely reasonable place for a disagreement, but it is an empirical matter, to be tried and tested. Because so little is known about what goes into the process of cognition and semantics, it is premature to be very confident about what features are essential. Searle hints at various points that every level, including the biochemical, must be represented in any machine that is a candidate for artificial intelligence. This claim is almost surely too strong. An artificial brain might use something other than biochemicals to achieve the same ends.

This possibility is illustrated by Carver A. Mead's research at the California Institute of Technology. Mead and his colleagues have used analog VLSI techniques to build an artificial retina and an artificial cochlea. (In animals the retina and cochlea are not mere transducers: both systems embody a complex processing network.) These are not mere simulations in a minicomputer of the kind that Searle derides; they are real information-processing units responding in real time to real light, in the case of the artificial retina, and to real sound, in the case of the artificial cochlea. Their circuitry is based on the known anatomy and physiology of the cat retina and the barn owl cochlea, and their output is dramatically similar to the known output of the organs at issue.

These chips do not use any neurochemicals, so neurochemicals are clearly not necessary to achieve the evident results. Of course, the artificial retina cannot be said to see anything, because its output does not have an artificial thalamus or cortex to go to. Whether Mead's program could be sustained to build an entire artificial brain remains to be seen, but there is no evidence now that the absence of biochemicals renders it quixotic.

WE, AND SEARLE, reject the Turing test as a sufficient condition for conscious intelligence. At one level our reasons for doing so are similar: we agree that it is also very important how the input-output function is achieved; it is important that the right sorts of things be going on inside the artificial machine. At another level, our reasons are quite different. Searle bases his position on commonsense intuitions about the presence or absence of semantic content. We base ours on the specific behavioral failures of the classical SM machines and on the specific virtues of machines with a more brainlike architecture. These contrasts show that certain computational strategies have vast and decisive advantages over others where typical cognitive tasks are concerned, advantages that are empirically inescapable. Clearly, the brain is making systematic use of these computational advantages. But it need not be the only physical system capable of doing so. Artificial intelligence, in a nonbiological but massively parallel machine, remains a compelling and discernible prospect.

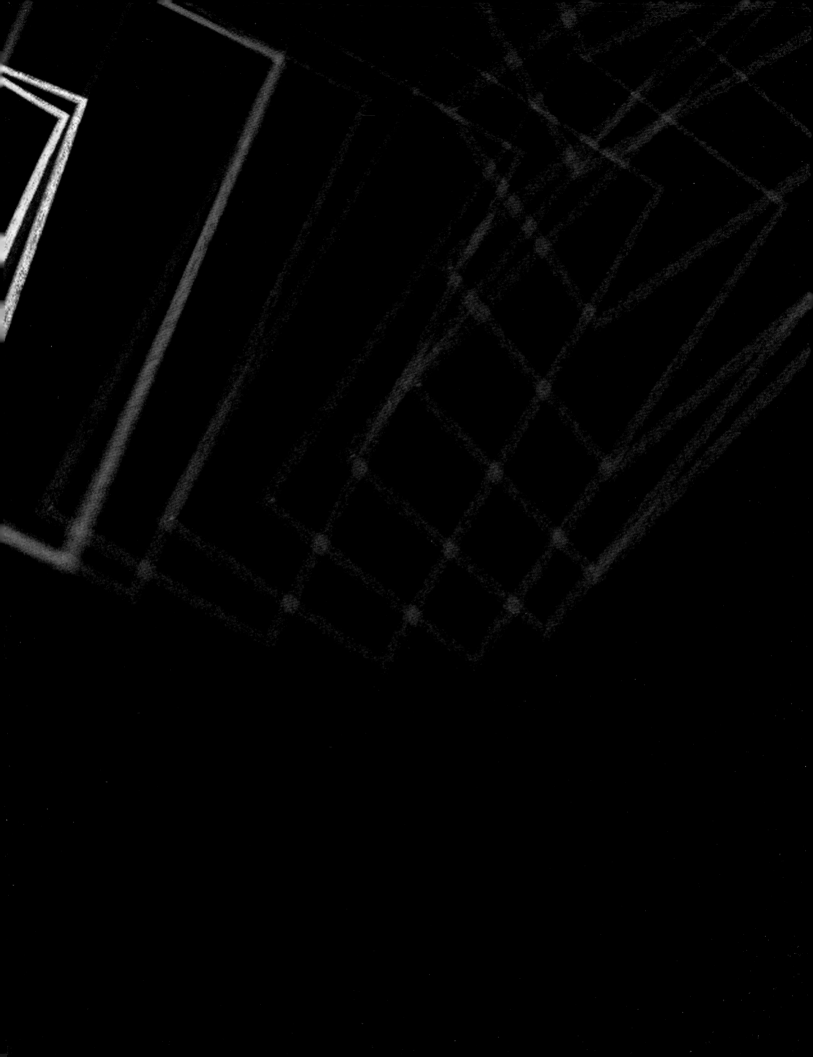

# perception
# and consciousness :     a     conversation

Edited by
Jeremy W. Hayward and
Francisco J. Varela

### From
### Sensory to
### Conceptual
### Consciousness

DALAI LAMA     In ancient India many Hindu philosophers maintained that the mode of conceptual thoughts engaging with objects was direct and nonselective. It's a matter of engagement through affirmation. It's a matter of the mind engaging with the object—"Ah, this is this"—by a process of pure affirmation rather than a process of "not this, not this, not this." The Buddhist logicians, on the other hand, maintain that the relation of conceptual thought and the object develops through exclusion. You perceive what something is by excluding what it is not.

JEREMY W. HAYWARD     If I look through the window and say, "I see a tree," in the first moment what happens is that I see something, then I name it tree. Is it correct from the Buddhists' point of view that there is a sequence, a small time interval, during which that something becomes "tree" in my mind?

DALAI LAMA     When you see something and you think it's a tree, there are two levels of discrimination, one being sensory and the other operating in the realm of the conceptual. When you first see an object like a tree, the first moment of awareness is sensory. In English you would say there is no consciousness; you're not conscious of it. But after that, perhaps a split-second later, you're conscious of it. Then you know it's a tree, and the mental consciousness is working. This mental consciousness can be active while you're looking at the tree, and also, even when you're not looking at the tree, you might be conscious of the tree. You can have an image of it. Between the two, there is a difference. The mental consciousness that you have of tree when you're actually looking at a tree is much more vivid than the one you have when you're not looking at it.

HAYWARD     The sensory level is not yet conscious, but how does it go from sensory to conscious? From the scientific point of view, there is a time between the beginning of treeness arising and the final tree. Even if I see the tree as continuous—treeeeeeeeeeeeeee—actually, in my perceptual system, what is taking place is tree, tree, tree, tree, tree, very fast. When light from that external reality impinges on the retina, some vague form occurs due to the operation of the retina itself. This vague form is then acted on, although it's still not conscious, and is either accepted or rejected by the brain. This is then further operated on, and some name occurs, at which point the experience becomes conscious. At that point it becomes the tree, while at the beginning it was that vague nameless formless object.

This is why I was asking about the time sequence. This vague whatever-it-is that hits the eye seems to go through several stages, until suddenly I see a tree. That process takes time.

FRANCISCO J. VARELA     From the point of view of neuroscientists, this is a matter of the emerging patterns in the human brain. It takes a little while for a pattern to emerge, and this little while is something like that [Varela snaps his fingers]. I think this is a question that has been of great interest to scientists; and also, this point connects with the meditative practitioner's discovery of the intermittency of the self in meditation. My self is not one solid thing but is composed of moments of experience. I see that and I see that and I see that. Perhaps there is a correspondence between the intermittency of self and the fact that, for the brain to construct a perception, it takes a little while, on the order of one-tenth of a second. I think Jeremy's point is that from the Western standpoint this process actually takes time, at least a fraction of a second. The question is, Between the moment my eye encounters a sensory moment and I can see patches up to the point where I discriminate an object, what is the process? Is that a unitary duration or can it be divided? Is there observation of that in meditation? What would be the shortest duration that we are capable of perceiving as "now"?

GESHE PALDEN DRAKPA     We can answer with certainty that there is a sequence that does occur in perception. Let's take the example of the visual perception of the color blue. The visual perception of the color blue occurs, but the perceiver has not yet ascertained it, so a mental ascertainment does follow that visual perception. It would be very rapid, a matter of two or three moments (moments in the Buddhist sense of extremely brief durations). But exactly what fraction of a second, this tradition does not say.

From
*Gentle Bridges:
Conversations with
the Dalai Lama
on the Sciences
of Mind,* edited by
Jeremy W. Hayward
and Francisco J.
Varela, ©1992.
Reprinted by
arrangement with
Shambhala
Publications, Inc.,
Boston.

Paul Kaiser and Shelley Eshkar,
*If by Chance,* 1999 (detail)

pages 178–179: **Cristabel Davé,** Untitled,
ca. 1995

## Ascertaining and Nonascertaining Consciousness

DALAI LAMA    There are two types of perceptions. One happens when you are distracted to a second object at the moment when you are already looking at something. At that time there is a perception of the first object, which is one type of perception. There is another type where you are actually paying attention to the object. Both are perceptions, but the second one is ascertaining and the other one is not ascertaining.

HAYWARD    In the nonascertaining one, there can nevertheless be action. The organism can act on the basis of that nonascertaining cognition even though it doesn't become conscious.

VARELA    This is factually true. For example, you do something, and only afterward there is a second moment in which you become conscious of your action, but the action is already done. For example, in driving my car, I often brake before I am conscious of doing so.

B. ALAN WALLACE [interpreter]    His Holiness points out that this comes from past conditioning. If you have never driven a car before and you see someone coming toward you, you don't have the response of hitting the brake immediately. Likewise with something coming toward your eye, you don't have to have a whole conceptual process to think to close the eye. This does seem to depend on previous conditioning.

THUBTEN JINPA [interpreter]    I think we have to make clear what we mean by consciousness, because in English it seems that when you say "conscious," there is some kind of mental conceptual ascertainment. When we use consciousness in the Buddhist context, the term is wider. Anything that is the subject of experience is consciousness, including nonascertaining awareness.

HAYWARD    Say I am sitting here and you are translating something His Holiness just said, so I'm very interested and paying attention. Now from the corner of my eye I see this glass and I take a drink, because my throat is dry. Then I put the glass down, all the while continuing to listen. Later on, I think I would like a drink, but I discover the glass is empty! As I was listening I never knew that I took a drink. Now, do you call that action conscious?

DALAI LAMA    It is conscious. But if you didn't know the glass was there in the first place, how would you do that?

WALLACE    His Holiness, Thubten Jinpa and I have tried to understand what you mean by conscious, and what we've come up with is *conceptual mental ascertainment*. Now this is very, very important.

DALAI LAMA    In Buddhist philosophy, when you speak of something being ascertained, you consider it to be identified; you know, you are sure, it is there. And that ascertaining awareness would seem to be necessarily mental and necessarily conceptual. Thus a conceptual ascertainment would seem to be equivalent to what you are speaking of as consciousness. Buddhists also speak of visual perception apprehending an object. But what determines whether visual perception knows the object or not is whether it's able to lead to or yield a mental ascertainment. With this criterion, you can have something that appears to visual perception without its knowing it, because this was nonascertaining awareness. Although it appeared to visual perception, later on you don't know whether you've seen it or not, because it did not yield the mental ascertainment. Therefore you would say that visual perception did not know its object even though the object appeared to it. The criterion is whether or not the visual perception yields an ascertainment.

## A Buddhist Definition of Consciousness

ELEANOR ROSCH    I think it might be important to elaborate on the Buddhist meaning of consciousness, because it is not the same as what we mean.

DALAI LAMA        Yes, that's right. The Buddhist definition of consciousness, from one point of view, is a subjective agent that has the potential to arise correspondent to an object that appears to it. Through the force of the stimulus of the object, consciousness has the ability to arise in an aspect corresponding to the object.

ROSCH            But I thought the object and the consciousness were codependent? How can the object of cognition come before the cognition?

DALAI LAMA        The object's being dependent on the subject doesn't mean that the object is dependent on a subject that *precedes* it. It is important to make discriminations between two types of analysis—relative and ultimate analysis. The fact is that the object cannot withstand ultimate analysis and is ultimately unfindable.

The only mode of existence the object has left is that it exists by the force of designation, by the force of imputation, of consciousness. For example, when you see this as a cup and you use it for drinking tea, you do this by relying on the conventional experience; you don't question the validity of that convention. But this cup doesn't exist when you analyze it with the ultimate analysis. The only mode of existence it has is the existence it has by the force of conceptual designation.

Now, we could further analyze this as follows: Which conceptual mind designated it, mine or yours, in an earlier moment, in the next moment? Which cognition does it depend on? If you search whether that cognition was in an earlier moment or a subsequent moment or whether it's something that was coexistent with it, or whether it is my consciousness or your consciousness, again you are falling into the extreme of ultimate analysis, and then again you won't find anything.

ROSCH            Are you saying that in relative analysis, where there is a cup, this requires that the object precede consciousness?

DALAI LAMA        According to the Prasangika, it is sequential.

VARELA           Is it required to have a *thing* there already preceding the perception, a thing that later, in the second or third moments, we will call the cup? Because in terms of neuroscience, that is factually wrong. You cannot say that I will perceive yellow because yellow first arrives and then it's picked up by my brain. So I think we are trying to track to what extent in the Buddhists' [relative] description is the object already constituted? Or is it acceptable to say, as a neuroscientist would, that the object is an *emergence* of this interaction and is not in itself already constituted.

JINPA            But according to your presentation it sounds as though neuroscientists would say that you don't actually see the object. What you see is the picture of it!

VARELA           That is precisely correct.

ROBERT B. LIVINGSTON        It occurs in your head. Assuming that it occurs outside is called the "phenomenal fallacy."

DALAI LAMA        There is a lot of debate between Sautrantikas and Yogacharins about this question. Whether the appearance of the object is one with the object or whether it is something different; whether the appearance of the object is simultaneous with perception or is sequential.

VARELA           But then it is not considered a fundamental tenet that the object has to be already there preceding its cognition? Would it be acceptable, as it would be for a neuroscientist, to say that the object arises in the cognition, that it is not separable?

DALAI LAMA        Here our Buddhist schools have different views. One view that is common to all of the Buddhist schools (leaving aside the view of Vaibhashikas, which is very different, more realist) is that the appearance or image of the object has to be simultaneous with the actual cognition. And also it is of the same nature as the actual cognition. The difference is that when the Yogacharins identify what the image is, they say it is a product of one's own imprints, the imprints of earlier moments of consciousness. They refute an external reality, the external world, as independent of mind. Therefore, they say the perceptual image is a product of one's own past imprints. Other schools say the image is a projection of the object.

Although Prasangika Madhyamikas and Sautrantikas accept external objects or external reality, there is a big difference. When Sautrantikas explain external reality, they base their theory on the fundamental belief that there are partless particles. Theirs is something like the reductionist philosophy with assorted elementary particles, some elementary basis that the entire world or universe can be reduced to. The Prasangika school speaks of external reality, but they say when you analyze it, there is no such thing as fundamental entities. They break down under analysis.

VARELA    Most neuroscientists would feel very comfortable with the idea that there is one level that you could call an inviolate essential level of physical reality. There is a world out there; then, in come living beings with different brains, and each one makes a different construction of this world, all of them slightly different pictures of the same thing. But we neuroscientists want to have a foundation. We want to be able to rely on the idea that all of those different constructions refer to the same ultimately inviolate level. That is the dogma, and it *is* a dogma; there is no absolute proof for it.

DALAI LAMA    I think there is a similarity between the Buddhist outlook and your point of view; even the Prasangikas speak of relating to an object through an image. This image is simultaneous with cognition, so that what you actually see is the image.

VARELA    That is the similarity. The difference I'm trying to point out, which I think is equally important, is that for the Prasangikas there is no external existence as such. By contrast, though the neuroscientists, too, would accept the simultaneous arising of the object and the perceiver, they would nevertheless hold to the reductionist analysis of external reality.

### Is Perception of a World "Out There"?

WALLACE    There are people with amputated limbs, say, a hand, and where the hand would be they can experience pain? His Holiness finds this very unbelievable.

LIVINGSTON    That's right! They may not feel pain, but they may also feel pain. In other words, they can feel normal sensibility and even motion, or they may have no sense of motion. Any of these conditions is possible.

DALAI LAMA    Does the sense of pain or motion decrease over the years?

LIVINGSTON    It may, it may not. I've had people who have had a phantom limb for forty years or more. For instance, there was a man with his right arm missing. If you asked him where he felt the sensation of the missing arm, he could localize it in space. It was so real to him that if you asked him to make a motion that would make the missing arm, in his sensation of it, pass through the table, he would do it but it felt very strange to him, very bizarre, as if he were violating some law of physics, or something like that. It gave him gooseflesh or he would shudder and get frightened. It's very real.

DALAI LAMA    It's like during meditation, when you feel yourself going out of your body, sometimes you are surprised because you don't get obstructed by the door. It is quite similar to that.

VARELA    I would like to suggest an experiment we can do right now to show Your Holiness that you can have a phantom nose! Cross your middle and index fingers and then touch the tip of your nose. Do you feel two noses or just one?

DALAI LAMA    I was already prepared for that, so I was already thinking there wouldn't be one nose! Yes.

VARELA    You always find two noses. That's just an example of how one undoes the natural sensory situation. Perception changes and you can have something that seems very real because you feel it directly, but from the ordinary point of view, these perceptions do not correspond to the actual situation.

LIVINGSTON    Then there is another kind of phenomenon. If you tie a monkey's fingers together with a little bandage and then explore the motor cortex in the opposite hemisphere, you find that there is a change in activity of the neurons corresponding to the limitation of movement imposed by the bandages. If you amputate fingers, there is a migration of neurons to compensate for the gap in motor capability, and the monkey's brain has a different map of the changed hand. So the brain rebuilds itself in close correspondence to what happens on the periphery.

I'll give you another example of brain development in correspondence with the environment: The cerebellum in the newborn is much smaller relative to the rest of the brain in proportion to adult size, and it is my supposition that the cerebellum doesn't develop until the child emerges into the world because in the uterus there is flotation. There is very little inertial mass in the movement of the limbs, but when the baby comes out into the world, its limbs become wired to its growing cerebellum and this wiring becomes an accurate neurological map of the body and the gravitational field and the environment that the child is in. There's something else interesting here—that the brain undergoes this major growth, doubling in size in six months, and doubling again by the fourth year. We know from some experiments with animals that the environment, or the things the individual learns from it, do have an effect on the mapping or the organization of the growing brain. So it is my belief, though I don't have any evidence for humans, that this enlargement and organization is bound to the environment. If the environment changes radically later, there can be some readjustment, but in early life this binding is very close.

DALAI LAMA          Wouldn't there be some difference, then, in the brains of aborigines who lived a very, very simple life as opposed to those of, let's say, Westerners in a very, very complex society, very sophisticated? Would that have a strong effect on the brain?

LIVINGSTON          But the aborigines don't lead a very simple life, because they have to know the specific names, not the type names, of all the trees and bushes within about a hundred-mile range. They have to know them as individuals. They have to have a proper name for any persistent foliage, tree, bush or whatever, so they have a tremendous memory challenge. They have a very difficult life! Now this is very practical. They have to learn the names of things so that if they're told to go someplace, they can find their way by the proper names of these trees and plants and bushes and so forth.

VARELA          Here's an example to illustrate further the point that perception is bound up with motor interaction with the environment. This is an absolutely fundamental point about how neuroscientists understand perception that is not often brought out. The experiment was done some time ago and in it two small newborn kittens were taken and kept in the dark. When a cat is born, its eyes are closed—it has no vision. These two kittens were only taken out into the light in an empty round room painted with stripes. This was their whole world. One kitten was allowed to walk around normally. The other one was strapped into a little cart where it could not use its feet. The one who could walk would pull the confined one around in the cart so that it, too, experienced passive motion around this round striped universe. So as their eyes began to open both kittens were exposed to an identical environment. The only difference is that one was walking around on its own four feet and the other was moving around passively, pulled around by the first. Every day they were taken out for a period of activity in this container and afterward were returned to the dark. This was continued for several weeks while their eyes opened and they learned to see. The question is, What happens when after a few weeks you take these two cats out of this controlled situation and let them out in the world? The animal that was allowed to walk in the striped room could walk around normally in a regular environment, even though it had first begun to see in such a restricted environment. It did not bump into things and did not fall off the edges. It behaved like a normal cat. The other one, although its eyes, nervous system, and legs were absolutely intact, behaved like a blind cat. It bumped into things and fell off edges. The common saying, that cats see with their feet, is not just a joke from the neuroscientists' point of view!

We can conclude from this that, clearly, perception is not merely a matter of having an object outside and getting an image of it inside. The brain is an active configuration that participates in the organism's interaction with its environment. It's as if the brain actually makes the world come through in perception. It responds to all the integrated processes involved in interacting with the world.

LIVINGSTON          I would like to tell you about an experiment that can be done with humans. This is an experiment in which there are three small rooms. They are like a dollhouse. These rooms are accessible from a chair, which can be moved from one position to another to enable a subject to see the three rooms through a peephole. These rooms are set up in relation to the peephole and they appear correct. One is correct. It is an ordinary little room. Another is distorted with the left wall twice as high as the right wall, the roof sloping down, and the floor sloping up. Still, from the peephole it looks correct and ordinary. The third one has a top-down distortion. The walls lean out. All the rooms are decorated with furniture, curtains, windows, and so forth, all correspondingly distorted. All three rooms look normal because they project to the point where the peephole is as if they were rectilinear with one eye. When people who don't know the experiment sit in a chair and look with one eye into rooms A, B, and C, they say that the rooms look the same.

Now the experiment is this: We put subjects in a position where they are viewing the left-right-distorted room. We give them a stick and tell them to touch the butterfly on the left wall. They reach out and don't get close to it. They reach further and further without reaching it, and finally they start to giggle, because things are countering their expectation. They finally reach the butterfly, and then we tell them to touch the fly on the opposite wall. They try and hit the back wall, then they hit the side wall far from the fly, and so on. They miss again and again and laugh, because that's unexpected. After about ten inaccurate attempts, they finally begin to see the room as left-right distorted.

Once they have learned to do this correctly, you ask them to look at room A, which is the ordinary room. They look at room A and see it, too, as left-right distorted. At this point, they are just as inept at touching the fly and the butterfly in this room as they were earlier in the distorted room. They must readjust again to the normal conditions. The point is that you cannot know the room without behavior. Purely on the basis of passive perception, you can be fooled, and this is something that can be generalized.

VARELA         This is interesting from the point of view of epistemology. From this point of view, it's impossible to say that something, this pen, for example, is "out there" with any kind of substantial quality, in spite of the fact that, as we have been discussing, that is the belief in the West. Conventionally, you would say about your perception of room A, "Oh, that was a mistake; that was an error." But in fact what we discover by looking at

the brain this way is that it is not an error; rather, it is something that is normally the case. We learn that the world is shaped according to expectations, to history, to the way we are wired, to development, so that the picture of the world is inseparable from that particular brain or, I should say, person. This raises for Westerners, too, the question of what I mean when I say that there is something objectively "out there." What is "objectively"? The usual answer Westerners give is that there is some kind of physical quality at least. But even that becomes suspect, because the physicist says that this physical quality is in itself not very easy to find and specify.

DALAI LAMA         The Yogacharins find in their analysis that external reality is not substantial. When you search beyond the conventional level, you can't find it. However, they conclude there is a subjective kind of reality that is truly existent. They assert substantial existence of the subject of experience, because one can feel it. In neuroscience, when you analyze along the lines you spoke of through the examination of the brain and how it perceives, you find there isn't any substantial entity "out there." When you apply this analysis to the neurons, the subjective side, do you feel the same way?

WALLACE         His Holiness' question is simply: When you're looking out, you find that there's nothing substantial out there. Now, leaving outside a non-physical cognition, if the subject is actually the brain, do you say that the brain that is doing the perceiving is also as nonsubstantial as anything out there, in which case you have nothing substantial out there and nothing substantial on the subject side? Is that the conclusion for you as a neuroscientist?

VARELA         I will speak only for myself, because at this point you have to realize that we're dealing with an area that lies outside any prevailing consensus. The prevailing view, even in neuroscience, is that there *is* a pen out there, and in spite of the fact that there are little things going on inside my brain, basically there is an image of the pen inside. What I am saying in fact is that this view can be questioned on the basis of science itself. That one can re-understand neuroscience and show that there is no basis for this belief that there is a stable solid substantial reality that we can rely upon, so in fact cognition is not a representation in any way. Now let me see if I can follow your question well.

WALLACE    Let's forget the whole issue of whether there is consciousness apart from matter. We're taking the neuroscientists' viewpoint that it is the brain that sees and the neurons that are doing all the cognizing. Let's assume that this is the context we're speaking in. Forget Buddhist doctrines for the time being. On the objective side, when we use this kind of very perceptive approach that you're dealing with now (although you say most neuroscientists don't penetrate that far), you say the evidence that there are these substantially existent external entities out there really seems to start falling apart. Well, similarly, wouldn't you also have to conclude that the neurons, the stuff inside the subject that are presumably making these perceptions, lack that substantiality in the same way as anything out there? In which case, what are you left with?

VARELA    That's right. There are two steps there. I think that, mostly, the first reaction you get in discussing this with colleagues is, "Oh, if you don't think there's anything out there, then you must believe in some internal reality that is projecting what appears to be the outer world. You must believe in some solid, some kind of innate categories that are real." That is, they would assume that we must hold some kind of a subjectivist or idealist position. This is, in fact, not at all the case, because we can show that you can influence what you perceive as the world, by manipulating it. So you can manipulate your perception from outside, but you can also manipulate it from inside. The only real conclusion is that you cannot find substantiality either inside or outside. So I would say that on purely scientific grounds, you can defend the position that the perception of this

world is in fact a codependence, a strict codependence of what we call the world and what we call the brain. These two things meet together and merge, making this reality. So purely on scientific grounds, we do come closer to a more Buddhist, Prasangika, point of view. But it must be said that while some of us would hold this view, it would not be a majority view. On the other hand, I think it is scientifically a perfectly reasonable point of view, and I think Dr. Livingston or I could stand up and argue this point of view with our colleagues without being thrown out of the building! They might think we were a little crazy, but still they wouldn't think we had completely gone off the deep end.

LIVINGSTON    Yes, I agree.

### When Is a Perception Valid?

DALAI LAMA    In the neuroscientists' approach, identification of everything that is cognitive, like perception and so forth, is made on the basis of something that is physical matter, like neurons, and so forth. On such a basis, how do we discriminate between a wrong perception and a valid perception? We assume that individual neurons or the whole system, the whole circuitry of the neurons, cognizes. This occurs whether there is a valid perception going on or an invalid perception going on. Since they're all working either way, how do you make any distinction from a neurophysiological point of view?

VARELA    My nervous system will function and identify something, such as food. All the programs say "food," but then if I try to eat it, I may find I cannot. There is feedback from the environment saying "misrepresentation, wrong take, correct your approach." So it is like that: back and forth, trial and error. If you make too many mistakes, you die. So evolution carries on by making many attempts until something is arrived at that is appropriate or adequate. That is how you discriminate between correct and incorrect, by the consequences of that perception. A perception would be established as valid if it allowed a life form to do what it needed to do—to eat, to reproduce, to plan behavior, and so forth. The consequences decide.

DALAI LAMA    There is no way of making the distinction at the time of the actual experience?

VARELA    Neuroscientists can find many ways to cause the nervous system to make an error. Because the system works the way it does, you can trick it into perceiving things that only another action can convince you is not so. This is what is called perceptual or sensory illusion. As an example, close one eye and look at your thumb with your arm outstretched, and then bring it back half the distance toward your eye. Do you see your thumb doubling in size? It becomes a little larger but it doesn't become double the size, does it? Although the image of the thumb on the retina has doubled in size, you don't see it as double. Check it as follows: Put your other thumb close to your eye as a reference point and do the same experiment with the first thumb. You will see that the thumb now looks bigger. Doesn't it? So there you are. Which is the valid perception of the thumb?

DALAI LAMA        In this case I think that a lot of environmental factors have to be taken into account. For example, let's shift now to conceptual cognition. Let's imagine a continuum of conceptual cognition in which a prior moment of awareness of conceptual cognition is in fact a false cognition. It was mistaken, but now you come to a new cognition, a conceptual cognition that is valid. Being valid, it damages or refutes the preceding conceptual cognition that was wrong. Now in that case, from the neurophysiological point of view, how would you describe the refutation of the prior cognition?

VARELA        We could call it "learning," I suppose, that is, the process I described before. You have a hypothesis that something is food and you try it out. You then have a perception that doesn't match your expectations. The nervous system rearranges itself by making synaptic changes so that the next time you see that something, the association with food won't be there. This is a perfectly good example of an emergent property: before, the notion of food came up; but the next time, the notion of food will not come up. The system rearranges itself; it learns.

But I didn't feel that we were finished with the less conceptual example of the thumb's size. If you ask yourself, What is the real size of the thumb? which one do you choose? Surely putting one thumb next to the other doesn't affect the size of the first one. Nevertheless your perception at the moment of having the experience is that it does.

DALAI LAMA        All these terms for measurement are based on human convention. Now, for example, for a cat or dog, would the whole concept of size and things like that be different?

VARELA        Surely these same things would happen for them. In fact, you can trick dogs and other animals into believing that there are things where there are none. For example, you can take a frog's eye and cut the retina and rotate it and sew it back into place after the rotation. Normally the frog sees a fly and snaps it up very precisely. After rotation of the eye, you show the fly and the frog behaves as if the fly were behind it. Never in its life will the frog learn again to catch the fly with its tongue. That is an invalid perception in the sense that the frog won't eat.

DALAI LAMA        In Buddhist terminology you would say that the source of the deception is actually within the eye organ, because you have changed it. In the case of my thumb, the source of deception is within the object.

VARELA        Why is it in the object? You haven't changed the object! What you have done from a scientific point of view, I think, is change the context of perception. The rotated eye creates another context of perception, and it is not possible to say that this is more real than that. If I see my thumb in the context of another nearby object, then I use one evaluation. If the context changes, the evaluation will be different. This is again the problem of trying to say what is the real valid cognition of the size of a thumb. From this point of view, there is no such thing as the true perception of the thumb. It's only in reference to a previous action; it's not valid in itself.

LIVINGSTON        I have two more experiments I would like to present. If you show a picture very briefly, people may not be able to perceive the picture exactly or accurately. These experiments, done at Harvard, were the following. There was a classroom full of students and a big screen and a big projector that could make a very abrupt flash of an image on the screen. The students were to look at the screen. At first maybe they just saw a flash. Then the image was exposed just a little bit longer. As soon as they got some impression of what this image was about, they were to write it down in their note-books. Then these notebooks were collected. It was found that even after considerable exposure of the image, the students would maintain an incorrect interpretation of it and would continue to do so even to the point where the expo-sure was so long that somebody coming in from outside could easily perceive that it was mistaken. The students started perceiving something and they got locked, anchored, into a certain percep-tion. They stayed with that, clung to that, until it was absurd. They had a very long exposure of the image, and they still saw it in the original inaccurate way.

I'll give you an example: They had some very simple pictures, such as a bicycle leaning up against a fire hydrant some-where on the campus, with some steps of a building in the background—something that these students should have seen at one time or another. When the picture was exposed to some students, they said: "I see a ship. It's a full rig ship, it has a wave under it, and it's coming full blast toward me." They wrote this down in their notebooks and kept seeing that ship and the waves and so on until they had seen the image exposed to four times the length of time it would take a new person to see it's a bicycle against a hydrant in front of some steps! I'm trying to illus-trate the problem that once you form an image about somebody or some room or some thing or some event, you may be unable to let it go.

A second experiment that is relevant, I think, is the following: It was found early on in the experiment described above that if an image was disagreeable to the per-son who was being tested, it would take a long time, with a lot of exposure being built up, before the person finally saw what it was. Now, it could be said that this result was due to the quality of the picture, or the way it was being present-ed, or some other variable. So they set up an experiment with four images at once. The experimentalists showed the subjects sets of four pictures in sample tests, so that they became familiar with looking at four figures with a brief expo-sure. Then the experimentalists took the picture that was disagree-able to somebody and put it once in one corner and another time in another corner. They randomly sorted those disagreeable pic-tures among the others. In this way they were able to find out what a person was sensitive to, didn't like, was fearful of, or what a person found immoral or had a censorship impediment about. For example, you could have four pictures of animals in a zoo. You'd have monkeys in one quarter, elephants in another and dogs in a third. Then you would have dogs fornicating in the fourth quarter. The pictures were equivalent for light and dark and so on, so irrelevant factors like those were ruled out. Now, the subjects would go on trying to identify what is in the pictures until they get them all correct. When the unpleasant picture was put in along with the other animal pictures, people would guess the three other pictures correctly very quickly and would then have to get ten times more exposure to see the picture that they were censoring.

The reason I bring this up is that it suggests very powerfully, I think, that before we see anything, we already have exercised a certain censorship in respect to that image. Before we perceive, the image has already gone through some filters that say, we like this, or we don't like it, or we must avoid it, and so on. The point is that the visual cortex or some other part of the brain is already exercising before you get to a conceptual confirmation.

WALLACE          Maybe on some subconscious or semicon-scious level there is already identification, suggesting that the sub-conscious is a bit faster than the conscious mind?

LIVINGSTON          That's the conclusion that Western scientists came to. I must say something a little conservative about this, because what is known is that the subjects do not give testimony that they perceive the image correctly. They tell us, and we expe-rience ourselves, that we do not see the picture clearly. But that doesn't tell you exactly what's going on. It may be that the brain is protecting the individual from being exposed as a person who would talk about something as bad as dogs fornicating, and that protection is sufficiently strong to maybe wipe out or blur or oth-erwise modify the image. It doesn't tell us exactly where these processes take place or exactly what is taking place.

WALLACE          Concerning how you translate "subconscious" in Tibetan, I must mention that Tibetans do not speak in terms of subconscious and conscious, but in terms of the grossness and subtlety of mind. The subconscious is a subtle level of mind, and what we consider identification or ascertainment is a grosser level. So when I translated the experiment to His Holiness, he respond-ed, "Doesn't this imply that the more subtle mind is faster?"

VARELA          This is confusing for me. Previous discussions had led me to think that the occurrence or nonoccurrence of men-tal ascertainment had nothing to do with levels of subtlety.

WALLACE          I think we are working with the temporary hypothesis that during the waking state there are two levels of mental ascertainment, the gross one that you can talk about, but possibly also a preceding one that is more subtle and is already conditioning how long it takes for the grosser, expressible mental ascertainment to occur. Both ascertainments have to be there for you to know whether you like something or not. If you're seeing fornicating dogs and you don't like to see that, both kinds of ascertainment have to be there. Whether or not both kinds of ascertainment belong to the gross level of consciousness still or have been shifted down to subtle consciousness is a point of discussion. His Holiness was open to the possibility that there is some degree of subtlety.

He now raises a further point. Imagine a single event, on the one hand, that is actually experienced while in the waking state, and then on the other hand, an identical event experienced in the dream state. To each of these events we have an emotional response. When you wake up from the dream, if it was a bad experience, you kind of feel lousy even though you've awakened. So the question is, Given these two states of mind, waking consciousness and dream consciousness, and given a similar event to which you're responding, is there a different strength to the emotional response? The reason for the question is that, from the Buddhist point of view, the dream consciousness is a more subtle one, more akin to a subconscious level of mind. That it is more subtle than waking consciousness suggests that it would be more powerful.

ROSCH     When the original experiment of this type was done with words, it was found that people took much longer to say that they had seen "dirty" words than regular words. So the criticism was that they saw them just as fast, but they didn't want to say them because they were taught not to. So whether it was on the level of perception or expression was never resolved completely. This is a very controversial area of research in psychology, and the controversy comes from the fact that in the psychoanalytic tradition that Freud and Jung began, there is a very intelligent

unconscious. This is a major point, and it's so major that it has become a cultural belief among educated Americans that they have a thing called the unconscious. They feel that this unconscious is implicated if they ever notice some kind of impermanence or discontinuity in their consciousness in daily life, or when they notice some change in themselves from one situation to another or from childhood to adulthood. All of the things that Buddhists point to as evidence of impermanence—all these discontinuities—can be denied or discounted by referring back to a presumably continuous unconscious. Such a personified, functioning unconscious is also a great challenge to scientific method, since by definition it cannot be observed directly. So there has been a huge amount of research to try to see whether people actually perceive things and think and defend themselves perceptually on the unconscious level, without conscious awareness.

## How Does Buddhism Validate Perception?

VARELA     I would really like to hear His Holiness' comments on how, from a Buddhist standpoint, one can establish what a valid perception of my thumb is?

DALAI LAMA     One criterion for proving a valid cognition is by its consequences. You have three criteria for existence in the Prasangika system: first, being in accordance with convention; second, not being damaged or refuted by a valid or conventional cognition. Then there's a third one, which is similar to the second one but invokes another experience, the Yogacharins' viewpoint. According to this third criterion, what certifies the existence of an object is a valid cognition, therefore it is the subjective mind that certifies whether or not something exists. If the validation of the cognition in turn depends on the object, then the subjective experience wouldn't have much authority. Therefore, according to the Yogachara school, the validation of this cognition depends on some other factor called apperception, or one could also call it self-cognizing aware- ness. So this self-cognizing conscious- ness is a factor of the subjective mind that validates cognition.

Now the Prasangikas' view is that the Yogacharins have to go through such a complicated process because they have this basic theory of something inherently existent, the *alaya,* consciousness. Because of this they have to search for some kind of objective essence, some final authority that really confirms cogni- tion. And since you can't get it from the object side (which, from their point of view, doesn't exist), you must get it from the subject side. But it can't be the ini- tial perception, because it has to be something that confirms this initial per- ception. Therefore, they had to posit this self-cognizing awareness. Because the Prasangikas negate the inherent exis- tence of both the objective and subjec- tive, they say that just as the validation of the object depends on the subjective condition, in the same manner the sub- jective condition depends for its valida- tion on the object. This corresponds closely to how we validate cognition in our everyday life. If you perceive some- thing in a certain way, then you relate with the object to check that perception. When you find the object to be in accor- dance with your perception, then you know that your cognition is valid. So, for the Prasangikas there is no such thing as inherently valid cognition. Even a direct experience of shunyata, emptiness, is not intrinsically valid.

HAYWARD          Then how is the cognition of shunyata validated?

DALAI LAMA          When you have the experience of emptiness, the Prasangika view is that the actual existence of empti- ness is not perceived by that conscious- ness, only the total absence of inherent existence. Emptiness is approached by the negation of inherent existence. The wisdom that directly realizes shunyata does not realize the *existence* of shunya- ta. We make a distinction between shuny- ata and the existence of shunyata. It's

only in a subsequent recollection that you say, "Oh, I'm now aware of shunyata." At this point, the existence of shunyata is once again a conventional reality. Shunyata itself, simply shunyata, is ultimate reality. An awareness that perceives the existence of shunyata is already a recollection and not the direct perception. Shunyata itself is a concealed entity in the threefold classification we mentioned before. The three categories were: evident, slightly concealed, and extremely concealed. Shunyata is slightly con- cealed. The existence of shunyata is evident in that it is a conven- tional designation that doesn't require inference. The reasoning processes through which you reach the conclusion that things lack inherent existence also prove that the experience you have of it is valid. The very reasoning process that proves the emptiness of phenomena also proves the validity of that cognition, because it tallies with reality.

Another way to verify it is to look at what the consequences are of a direct cognition or direct perception of shunyata, and this is also a strongly validating factor. That is, what effect does it have on the mind in terms of how your kleshas, your mental distortions, are doing? A direct perception of shunyata would drastically reduce the level of mental distortion and also give rise to tremendous powers that are opened up by the sheer force of that realization. If you have a fraudulent realization, that is, you think this is direct realization but it's actually fraudulent or far more superficial than you think, it will not have that impact on the mind, neither in puri- fying the mind nor in enhancing its power.

Another point in the Prasangika view is the intimate relationship between phenomena existing as dependently related events and their having an empty nature or lacking intrinsic existence.* And so another effect of the direct realization of shunyata is that, fol- lowing that experience, even seeing a slight interaction of causal- ity or conditioning of one entity by another, we get a very, very penetrating ascertainment or certainty. The force of your medita- tive experience very strongly enhances your insight into everyday phenomena. When the Prasangikas explain emptiness, they include emptiness with dependent arising. They're not isolated from each other. Actually the meaning of emptiness is something like the absence of independent existence. The absence of inde- pendent existence is actually the basis of all the things that can move. This great certainty, that even the slightest cause can bring about a great impact on the effects, is a result of this experience. And this certainty also validates the authenticity of your realization of emptiness.

---

* A fundamental doctrine of Buddhism is dependent arising (Skt., *pratityasamutpada*), according to which phenomena arise in interdependence on each other, that is, as part of a web of causation through which phenomena mutually condition each other. In virtue of this interdependence, no phenome- non can be said to have an inherent existence of its own.

Jeremy W. Hayward is the author of *Shifting Worlds, Changing Minds: Where the Sciences and Buddhism Meet.*

Francisco J. Varela is professor of cognitive science at the Ecole Polytechnique and director of epistemological research at Naropa Institute in Boulder, Colorado. He is the author of *The Tree of Knowledge* and *The Embodied Spirit: Cognitive Science and Human Experience* (coauthored with Eleanor Rosch).

# works in the exhibition

**Anonymous**

Eighteen untitled tantric drawings,
ca. 1995

Gouache on paper, various dimensions

Collection of Franck André Jamme

**Lutz Bacher**

*A Normal Life,* 1995–96

Video projection, color with sound, 13 minutes

Collection of the artist; courtesy of Pat Hearn
Gallery, New York

**Robert Barry**

*All the Things I Know But of Which I
Am Not at the Moment Thinking—
1:36 pm; June 15, 1969,* 1969

Text on wall, dimensions variable

Collection of the artist

**Samuel Beckett**

*Film,* 1963–65

16mm film in video format, directed by Alan
Schneider and Samuel Beckett, with Buster
Keaton, Nell Harrison, James Karen, and Susan
Reed; director of photography Boris Kaufman,
camera operator Joe Coffey; produced by the
Evergreen Theater, New York

Collection of Barney Rosset, New York

**Louise Bourgeois**

*Culprit Number Two,* 1998

Steel, wood, mirror, 150" x 114" x 132"

Collection of the artist; courtesy of Cheim &
Reid Gallery, New York

**Theresa Hak Kyung Cha**

*Exilée,* 1980

Film-video installation, 50 minutes

Collection of the University of California,
Berkeley Art Museum; gift of the Theresa
Hak Kyung Cha Memorial Foundation

**Martin Creed**

*a salt and pepper set, Work No. 33,* 1990

Brass, chrome; two parts, each part 2" diameter

Collection of the artist: courtesy of Cabinet, London

*chrome and brass, Work No. 42,* 1990

Single-channel video, color with sound, 18 minutes

Collection of the artist: courtesy of Cabinet, London

**Cristabel Davé**

Untitled, ca. 1995

Natural dye on bark cloth, approximately 34" x 72"

Collection of Lafcadio Cortesi

Untitled, ca. 1995

Natural dye on bark cloth, approximately 37" x 72"

Collection of Lafcadio Cortesi

**Stan Douglas**

*Overture,* 1986

Film-loop installation: one black-and-white 16mm film with mono-optical soundtrack, one 16mm tungsten film projector, one 16mm film, one amplifier, two
speakers, one loop device, 7 minutes each rotation, 13' x 10' projection area,
edition of two

Collection of the Art Gallery of Ontario, Toronto, and private collection;
courtesy of David Zwirner, New York

**Douglas Gordon**

*30 Seconds Text,* 1996

Text on wall, light bulb, timing device, dimensions variable

Private collection; courtesy of Lisson Gallery, London, and Bloom
Gallery, Amsterdam

**Rodney Graham**

*Vexation Island,* 1997

Cinemascope film installation

Collection of the artist: courtesy of Angles Gallery, Santa Monica, and
303 Gallery, New York

**David Hannah**

*heidegger.3,* 1997

Ink, Mylar, silicone, 72 1/2" x 58 1/2"

Collection of the artist; courtesy of Gallery Paule Anglim, San Francisco

**Jörg Herold**

*Körper im Körper,* 1989

Film installation

Collection of the artist; courtesy of
EIGEN+ART, Berlin

**Gary Hill**

*Searchlight,* 1986–94

Single-channel video-sound installation

Collection of the artist; courtesy of Donald
Young Gallery, Chicago

*Why Do Things Get in a Muddle?
(Come on Petunia),* 1984

Single-channel video, 32 minutes

Collection of the artist; courtesy of Donald
Young Gallery, Chicago

**Robert Irwin**

Untitled, 1969

Acrylic lacquer on shaped acrylic plastic disc,
53 1/4" diameter

Collection of the University of California,
Berkeley Art Museum

**Paul Kaiser and Shelley Eshkar**

*If by Chance,* 1999

Computer projection

Collection of the artists; courtesy of Riverbed,
New York

**Agnes Martin**

*Untitled #3,* 1993

Acrylic and graphite on linen, 60" x 60"

Collection of Byron R. Meyer

**The Museum of Jurassic Technology**

*The Voice of the American Gray Fox,*
1984

Mixed media, 19 1/2" x 66" x 24"

Collection of The Museum of Jurassic Technology, Culver City, California

**Yoko Ono**

*Closet Piece II,* 1964
Instruction piece, dimensions variable
Collection of the artist

*Collecting Piece,* 1963
Instruction piece, dimensions variable
Collection of the artist

*Falling Piece,* 1964
Instruction piece, dimensions variable
Collection of the artist

*Map Piece,* 1962
Instruction piece, dimensions variable
Collection of the artist

*Tunafish Sandwich Piece,* 1964
Instruction piece, dimensions variable
Collection of the artist

**Kristin Oppenheim**

*Hey Joe,* 1996
Light-sound installation
Collection of the artist; courtesy of 303
Gallery, New York

**Adrian Piper**

*Cornered,* 1988
Video installation with birth certificates,
videotape, monitor, table, chairs, dimensions
variable
Collection of Museum of Contemporary Art,
Chicago: Bernice and Kenneth Newberger
Fund

**Markus Raetz**

*Kopf II,* 1992
Cast iron, 11" x 8" x 7 7/8"
Collection of Donald L. Bryant, Jr. Family

*Zeemansblik und Feldstechermann,* 1987–88
Sheet zinc on wooden frame, pinewood, cardboard, plywood, overall dimensions variable: zinc panel 28 3/4" x 46 1/2"; sculpture with pedestal
75 1/2" x 19 5/8"
Collection of Museum of Contemporary Art, San Diego

**Ad Reinhardt**

*Abstract Painting, no. 3,* 1960–63
Oil on canvas, 60 1/4" x 60"
Collection of the University of California, Berkeley Art Museum

**Stuart Sherman**

*Berlin (West)/Andere Richtungen,* 1986
Single-channel video, color with sound, 6 minutes
Collection of the artist

**Imogen Stidworthy**

*To,* 1996–97
Video installation
Collection of the artist

**Diana Thater**

*Perspective is an energy,* 1995
Four laser discs, four laser-disc players, four video monitors, table, dimensions variable
Collection of Hauser & Wirth, Zurich; courtesy of David Zwirner,
New York

**Rosie Lee Tompkins**

Untitled (quilted by Willia Ette Graham), 1986
Velvet and velveteen, 85" x 77"
Collection of Eli Leon

**Bill Viola**

*Pneuma,* 1994
Video-sound installation
Collection of the artist; courtesy of 242, New York

**Gillian Wearing**

*2 into 1,* 1997
Single-channel video
Collection of Eileen and Peter Norton, Santa Monica

**Pascale Wiedemann**

*Heimlich,* 1996
Single-channel video with sound, acrylic (hand-knitted), 23 2/5" x 31 1/5" x 331 1/2"
Collection of the artist

**La Monte Young and Marian Zazeela**

*Music and Light Box,* 1967–68
Electronic circuitry, ultraviolet lighting system,
litho film, painted acetate, audio speakers, and
plexiglass on wooden base, 24" x 16" x 16"
Collection of the artists

opposite: **Jörg Herold,** *Körper im Körper,* 1989 (details)

page 196: **Yoko Ono,** *Tunafish Sandwich Piece,* 1964

*Tunafish Sandwich Piece*

Imagine one thousand suns in the
sky at the same time.
Let them shine for one hour.
Then, let them gradually melt
into the sky.
Make one tunafish sandwich and eat.


1964 spring